RELIGION IN PHILANTHROPIC ORGANIZATIONS

PHILANTHROPIC AND NONPROFIT STUDIES

Dwight F. Burlingame and David C. Hammack, *editors*

RELIGION IN PHILANTHROPIC ORGANIZATIONS

Family, Friend, Foe?

Edited by Thomas J. Davis

Indiana University Press

Bloomington and Indianapolis

This book is a publication of

Indiana University Press
Herman B Wells Library 350
1320 East 10th Street
Bloomington, Indiana 47405 USA

iupress.indiana.edu

Telephone orders   800-842-6796
Fax orders   812-855-7931

Library of Congress Cataloging-in-Publication Data

Religion in philanthropic organizations : family, friend, foe? / edited
by Thomas J. Davis. — 1st [edition].
    pages cm. — (Philanthropic and nonprofit studies)
  Includes bibliographical references and index.
  ISBN 978-0-253-00992-0 (cloth : alk. paper) — ISBN 978-0-253-
00995-1 (pbk : alk. paper) — ISBN 978-0-253-00997-5 (eb)
  1. Faith-based human services—United States.   2. Church
charities—United States.   3. Social service—United States—Religious
aspects.   4. Humanitarianism—Religious aspects.   I. Davis,
Thomas J. (Thomas Jeffery), 1958– editor of compilation.
  HV530.R247 2013
  361.7′50973—dc23   2013011147

1 2 3 4 5   17 16 15 14 13

*This book is dedicated to the memory of Karen Lake Buttrey,
whose vision and generosity were instrumental in the
establishment of the Lake Institute on Faith and Giving.*

Contents

Acknowledgments

T HIS VOLUME EVOLVED from a public symposium entitled "Family, Friend, Foe? The Relationship of Religion and Philanthropy in Religious Philanthropic Organizations," held on the campus of Indiana University–Purdue University Indianapolis (IUPUI) on October 7–9, 2010, and from a public lecture held at the auditorium of the Indiana Historical Society the next week. I gratefully acknowledge here the following for their generous support and funding for these two events: the IUPUI Arts and Humanities Internal (IAHI) Grant Program; the Indiana University School of Liberal Arts at IUPUI and its dean, Dr. William Blomquist; the Center for the Study of Religion and American Culture, housed at IUPUI, and its director, Dr. Philip Goff; the IUPUI Department of Religious Studies and its chair, Dr. Peter Thuesen; and the Lake Institute on Faith and Giving, with its home at IUPUI in the Center on Philanthropy, and its director, Dr. William Enright. In addition to funding from the Lake Institute, I was privileged to hold, for a three-year period, the Lake Chair in Religion and Philanthropy, from which came funds to help underwrite the symposium and this book. To learn more about the Lake Institute's work and history, please visit http://www.philanthropy.iupui.edu/lake-about-us.

Two doctoral students in philanthropic studies at IUPUI provided assistance with this project. Thanks go to Peter Weber for his work compiling bibliography related to religion and philanthropy and to William Cleveland for logistical support during the symposium and public lecture.

Introduction

Thomas J. Davis

PHILANTHROPY, AS A descriptive term, has evolved over time, and its particular meaning is often subject to the perspective from which it is studied. From the ancient Greeks, from whom the word came, to contemporary America, the word has meant many things. In the context of its usage in the United States, it has designated a literal and general "love of humanity," indicated a rational and systematic approach to the elimination of social ills, gained currency as a label for the process of distribution of money and goods by the wealthy, and, most recently, been redefined in a variety of ways to indicate voluntary action (gifts of money, time, commitment, etc.) for the public good. Other definitions can also be found, especially ones that seek to distinguish philanthropy from religious notions of charity and obligation, emphasizing philanthropy's nonsectarian, scientific, and professional nature. This last impulse became a very popular way of looking at philanthropy, especially in the first three-fourths of the twentieth century (and, in fact, persists widely today).[1]

Yet much of the emerging scholarly literature on philanthropy (a field of study that has emerged just over the past thirty to forty years, with much of the historical analyses of philanthropy quite recent) notes the close connections between charity and philanthropic work. So, while the two can certainly be distinguished, there is good reason not to separate them because, together, they tell the story of giving, especially in the United States.[2] Thus, many of the motivations that move one toward religious charity can also encourage philanthropic activity. The most common distinction between the two has to do with the ultimate purpose of each: for charity, it is a matter of helping an individual; for philanthropy, it is about changing society for the better (which, of course, in the long run and averaged out, should carry good consequences for individuals).

One can speak, then, of religious philanthropy. By this, one would mean religiously motivated actions (giving, volunteering, etc.) that aim to alleviate ills at a societal level. Though individuals would be helped in the course of the execution of such philanthropic activity, the goal is a betterment of society as a whole. Oftentimes, especially in religious philanthropy (as opposed to foundation-type philanthropy, where the institutional mechanisms are often funded by a wealthy individual), the work is corporate in nature, one that is organized on a scale that exists beyond the individual or small group of individuals.

Of course, giving is a complicated matter, whether undertaken as the charity of an individual, for religious or nonreligious reasons; whether through the mechanisms of an institutionalized philanthropy; or whether it is a gift of time, money, or talent.

Especially because many who are engaged in religious philanthropy value giving specifically as a religious responsibility, it is wise to keep in mind just how complicated giving can be. Even when done on a large and seemingly impersonal scale, philanthropy of all kinds is still talked about in terms of giving *something* that addresses social problems with the intent of making a better world. Certainly, it is helpful to keep in mind the dynamics of the gift economy; someone like Lewis Hyde (relying in part on Marcel Mauss) can help untangle the complexity of a gift, even outside the structure of a strictly gift economy.[3]

This complexity is captured, in part, in the argument that "philanthropy inevitably has a two-sided character in which kindness and privilege experience an uncomfortable marriage to one another. . . . Philanthropy's forms are inextricably wedded to the particular forms of dominance and privilege in each historical time and each historical place."[4] What is more, if philanthropy is a means by which individuals realize their values, as has been suggested, there will be some level of conflict inherent in the functioning of any philanthropic activity because different individuals and different groups within a society hold substantially different values.[5] Certainly, one would expect this insight to be true in religious philanthropies, wherein those who hold religious worldviews understand philanthropic activity to be an expression of obedience to divine mandate—and not just obedience but also an expression of devotion. Thus, a host of issues—complexities, if you like, or tensions—arises about philanthropic work and its relationship to religion when a religious organization uses such work as a means to realize religious goals.

One could point to a number of salient issues. Donor–donee dynamics certainly come into play in a variety of ways, for example, as one considers that a religious philanthropic organization often serves those of another faith or no faith at all yet still needs to maintain and highlight, for itself and its religious supporters, the essentially spiritual quality of the philanthropic work. An analysis that adopts a stance of solidarity with the donee can call into question the real motives involved in philanthropic work, especially that which is religiously inspired. One might refer to a particular sharp portion of a poem by John Boyle O'Reilly, a nineteenth-century poet, novelist, and newspaper editor, who sought, from his own perspective as an advocate for the dispossessed (especially the Irish who came stateside to escape the terrible Irish potato famine), to capture and expose the dark side of dynamics that relate to tensions inherent in both religion and philanthropy:

> But the thirsty of soul soon learn to know
> The moistureless froth of the social show;
> The vulgar sham of the pompous feast
> Where the heaviest purse is the highest priest;
> The organized charity, scrimped and iced,
> In the name of a cautious, statistical Christ;
> The smile restrained, the respectable cant,

When a friend in need is a friend in want;
Where the only aim is to keep afloat,
And a brother may drown with a cry in his throat.[6]

At the time of O'Reilly's writing, charitable balls had become long established in both religious and nonreligious settings as a way to raise money for worthy causes, often poor relief. He found the practice, however, to be wanting in human soul, and he thought the events too disconnected from those suffering the effects of extreme poverty—the root, it was thought, of most urban ills. He lamented the lack of real community in such events, and he thought they primarily glamorized the givers at the expense of those who would receive. The poem implies that the organized charity contributed to the shriveling of the soul ("cautious, statistical Christ"). There was, O'Reilly recognized, a power dynamic at work in the relation of giver and receiver in the charity balls that he thought at odds with the true community of humanity he found "in Bohemia."

Though the mechanisms of giving changed over time—the charitable ball gave way after the turn of the century to the so-called professional philanthropy advocated by the extremely wealthy—new types of problems arose to stand beside the older ones. The rising philanthropic class advocated giving that was professional, scientific, and nonsectarian (all three terms, to some extent, were used to set the new philanthropy apart from the older mode of religious charity). This new development, however, did not eliminate the reality of power dynamics; indeed, it may well have heightened them.[7] Furthermore, as the monied philanthropic class engaged the emerging social sciences to evaluate and resolve social ills, many within religious establishments sought to follow suit. Indeed, one sees in the early twentieth century such things as the development of departments of "Christian sociology"; the establishment of the first school of social work at the University of Chicago with the help of a Christian minister, Graham Taylor, who also sought to apply sociology to the problems of urban existence; and the work of some early sociologists who sought to fulfill their religious calling through the application of sociological principles to the needs of others.[8] Yet the marriage of sociology and Christian philanthropic work oftentimes was a strained union and, as we shall see in chapter 6, it was a union that did not, at least in one case, serve either party well because of fundamental differences in outlook and worldview. That case highlights what happened when a religious group, in its desire to follow the trajectory of professional philanthropy and rely upon the social sciences, found that such a scientific and professional outlook actually conflicted, to some extent, with that group's self-understanding.

Church–state issues loom large when considering religion in philanthropic activity. One question that arises is the role of governmental rules and regulations. During the twentieth century and into the twenty-first, various legislative acts set the framework for philanthropic giving. There are laws that deal with the tax-deductible status of certain types of gifts—most often, gifts that are given for religious, educational, research (especially medical), or society-enhancing reasons. The government's role in determining which gifts receive this preferred status cannot be underestimated in terms of the power it gives the government in choosing those things that it thinks benefits society. There is also the issue of which organizations can receive not-for-profit status, thus becoming exempt from a variety of taxes. Finally, there is the government's role in actually funding the work of certain organizations on behalf of the common good. Philanthropic organizations with concomitant religious outlooks can and do receive government aid, oftentimes serving as a point of distribution for disaster relief, humanitarian aid, and development projects.

So how does a religious philanthropic organization navigate the demands of governmental regulations when that organization is the recipient of federal dollars—regulations that, some would suggest, compromise the essentially religious outlook of that organization? Or, even more starkly, how does a religious organization deal with a government that is suspicious of its philanthropic endeavors? And how does one keep a bright line of distinction between church and state in the religiously inspired delivery of aid provided from government funds? Even if government funds are not involved, other questions arise about the relationship between government and religiously motivated philanthropic work when religious groups take (quite visibly and explicitly religiously) to the public square, using religious ritual to raise awareness of and combat human rights abuses. Such activity certainly meets Robert Payton's view of philanthropy as "voluntary action for the public good,"[9] even though it is a good that is politically charged. These complications of religious philanthropy are addressed in the chapters that follow.

In many of the chapters, the issues are discussed in such a way that there emerges an important theme—religious identity. Though we noted above that tensions arise between donor and donee, sometimes because of the inherent play of power dynamics in philanthropic work, it would be too simple to suggest that all of the power and all of the privilege reside entirely on the side of the religious philanthropic organization. Some certainly does. But in exploring the ways religious philanthropies try to embody their vision of the good society (or the good world) through their philanthropic work, one quickly bumps into another reality: Other social structures, interests, and powers, including government but not confined to just that sector, work toward different visions of the good. Thus, in a number of the case studies here presented, philanthropic work seems to be a double-edged sword; that is, religious groups undertake philanthropic endeavors as an expression of their religious outlook, but a number of pressures related to how philanthropic work is undertaken and how it is understood more broadly by the larger society can be seen to modify, reshape, or challenge religious identity in the process.

It has been argued that, in terms of size of program or program activities, religious identity makes only a small difference, at best, for those religious groups that maintain relief and development organizations.[10] While that may be true, in terms of an organization's self-understanding, however, or in terms of how religious partners around the world understand the work of an organization, there is a difference, and it comes down to the religious motivations that push the work forward for those involved. The religious aspect of philanthropic work matters for those who engage in that work as an expression of their religious identity. It is, moreover, a source of tension when the philanthropic work itself somehow replaces the religious component as *the* identifying core for the religious organization engaged in philanthropic work.[11]

The organizations examined in this volume have been chosen because they illustrate the complexities of the issues outlined above. An exploration of some of the tensions within these religious philanthropic organizations shows how the study of such groups can illuminate religion, philanthropy, and culture in particular times and place. After all, philanthropy and religion, especially with government thrown into the mix, exemplify struggles by various parties to define and create "the common good."

In chapter 1, "New Wineskins or New Wine? The Evolution of Ecumenical Humanitarian Assistance," Elizabeth G. Ferris examines the humanitarian-aid activities of the World Council of Churches (WCC) over a sixty-year period. Since its inception in 1948, service to people and churches in need has been central to the work and identity of the WCC. For decades, churches supported one another through the multilateral instrument of the WCC. When an emergency occurred, the WCC would contact the churches in the affected area and issue an appeal that churches around the world would support. The WCC would monitor the expenditure of funds and, by working multilaterally, would prevent duplication of effort and ensure that small churches as well as large ones were supported. This system began to change in the 1980s as large church-related agencies emerged in the global North; those agencies saw themselves as development or humanitarian agencies and aspired to both a professional level of engagement and access to government funding. The agencies developed significant expertise in their fields, they worked closely with their secular counterparts, and they chafed at turning over funds to the somewhat antiquated WCC system of interchurch aid. Ferris explores the reasons behind the transition from interchurch aid to professional development agency, with a particular focus on the power dynamics of North–South ecumenical relationships, the role of government funding, the tensions between solidarity and professionalism, and the implications these developments have on relationships among churches.

In chapter 2, "Religious Ambivalence in Jewish American Philanthropy," Shaul Kelner examines the ambivalence over the place of religion in American Jewish philanthropy. Since the early 1900s, a national network of community chests has served not only as the Jewish community's primary apparatus of charitable fund-raising and distribution but also as its central agent of communal governance. From its inception, the Jewish federation system proffered a notion of an American Jewish public square that maintained separation between matters of religion (left to the synagogues) and matters of "state" (represented by the philanthropic federations). So long as Judaism remained institutionalized within synagogues, this arrangement worked. In the 1960s, however, a religiously framed American Jewish campaign to alleviate the plight of Soviet Jews brought Judaism out of the synagogues and into the streets. This movement into the public square included the celebration of politically themed Passover seders in such places as in front of the Russian embassy in New York City. Through this case study, Kelner explores (1) the challenges posed to the federation's legitimizing ideology by this public display of religious ritual, (2) the federation system's ambivalent embrace of a role in religious affairs, and (3) the implications of the erosion of religion–"state" separation for the Jewish philanthropic system.

In chapter 3, "The Price of Success: The Impact of News on Religious Identity and Philanthropy," Diane Winston charts the fortunes of the Salvation Army as portrayed in the print media. The Salvation Army is one of the best known and most trusted philanthropic organizations in the United States. Yet it was not always so. Considered outsiders by the religious establishment in the late nineteenth century, the Army's activities were looked upon with suspicion and, at times, hostility. One of the turning points for the American Salvation Army came during the course of relief efforts in World War I, when the Army's image was reshaped through its relief work. For several decades, the media downplayed the Army's religious commitments, focusing almost entirely upon the positive aspects of its philanthropic endeavors. A new phase in coverage began, however, in the 1960s, when the Army's conservative religious values clashed with the spirit of the 1960s. Conflicts arose, in addition, because of new government regulations the Army was obliged to uphold because of its receipt of public dollars for use in its delivery of social services. The final thirty years of the twentieth century, which saw increasing conflict over the role of religion in public life, brought the glare of media attention to the Army's evangelical commitments. How to maintain its religious identity, work within government regulations because of the federal funds it receives, deliver its religiously motivated social services, and do so while in the media spotlight is the task of the twenty-first-century American Salvation Army.

David P. King provides a look into the work of a religious man who founded two philanthropic organizations. In chapter 4, "Heartbroken for God's World: The Story of Bob Pierce, Founder of World Vision and Samaritan's Purse," King provides the book's only biographical chapter. Bob Pierce started World Vision in 1950 with a mission of evangelism and child care in Korea. The organization's success was due entirely to Pierce's charisma. He traveled the world to discover the needs of missionaries and orphans, and he promised them immediate support. While an insider to an American evangelical audience, he was an outsider to mainstream development discourse. The 1960s brought transition. Acceptance of governmental funding and increased public prominence required greater board oversight that Pierce felt handcuffed his simple faith in God's provision. Professionalization eclipsed charisma. By 1967, Pierce resigned in frustration. By the late 1970s, World Vision transitioned into a major player in global relief and development. They marketed to a wider public, engaged mainline and secular nongovernmental organizations (NGOs), and raised enormous private and public financial support. In contrast, Pierce founded Samaritan's Purse in 1970 to recreate the World Vision of the 1950s. Again globetrotting for God, Pierce was in his element, personally promising support to individual causes and relying on God to provide the funds.

Both organizations still bear the marks of their relationships to their founder. How each has dealt with issues of religious identity while engaging the broader philanthropic community continues to define each organization.

Fred Kammer examines "Catholic Charities, Religion, and Philanthropy" in chapter 5, wherein he provides an overview of Catholic Charities USA, looking at its organizational structure, its clientele, its variety of services, its employees and volunteers, and its funding apparatus. He then moves to a history of the relationship between government and Catholic-sponsored philanthropic work, exploring especially the faith-based initiatives of the Clinton/Bush/Obama years. In the wake of the confusing history and dubious state of the faith-based initiative of the past decade or two, he charts the complex and nuanced position of Catholic Charities on pluralism—as articulated and practiced in various ways across the country and in conversation with what makes Catholic Charities *Catholic*. Pluralism brings a number of "stresses" on the structure of Catholic Charities from the various stakeholders in the system of American social services; for example, some argue that Catholic Charities is too Catholic, while others argue that it is not Catholic enough. He concludes that the opportunities for weaving together so many stakeholders—the Catholic Church, the government, social service providers, and those who receive services, among others—should not be taken lightly, nor should they be easily dismissed by those unfamiliar with the realities and complexities of contemporary social welfare in this country.

In chapter 6, "'Intelligent Leadership in the Cause of Racial Brotherhood': Quakers, Social Science, and the American Friends Service Committee's Interwar Racial Activism," Allan W. Austin portrays a slice of history that illustrates the tensions that arose as a religious service organization engaged current social scientific thinking to help direct its philanthropic work. (Certainly, if one accepts Payton's definition of philanthropy—voluntary action for the public good—the AFSC's engagement with race issues qualifies as philanthropy, in that it sought to embody values and a vision that would lead to a better society.) After pursuing racial justice in the latter half of the 1920s, the AFSC took a step back from concerted interracial action for much of the 1930s, instead exploring the intellectual scaffolding that underlay their earlier efforts and that might support future activism. Austin examines this introspective turn via the Institute of Race Relations, an annual conference held from 1933 to1941 that drew many of the best-known scholars of race and ethnicity in the United States. He details how the AFSC came into contact with "scientific" ideas about race, responded to them, and ultimately made academic thought meaningful for itself in a religious context, though struggling to balance the social structure emphases of the emerging social sciences with the "inner-light" theology of the Friends' religious tradition that guided its motivations. Indeed, especially in the early years of the institute, there was attention given almost exclusively to social science, with Quaker thought and practice ignored; more than that, the early curriculum expressed the doubts of the social scientists that religious organizations could, in fact, function in such a way as to contribute to an improvement in racial attitudes.

In chapter 7, "Religious Philanthropies and Government Social Programs," Sheila S. Kennedy analyzes the types of tensions involved in contracts between religious philanthropies and agencies of government. The concerns raised by "faith-based" contracting are both constitutional and religious. Government agencies must ensure that services comply with the Establishment Clause of the U.S. Constitution, which prohibits government endorsement or sponsorship of religion; religious organizations worry about being co-opted—about losing their distinctive religious approach to service, or losing their prophetic voice. In other words, they worry about losing their religious identity and distinctiveness. Kennedy reminds readers that, whatever the merits of the Bush administration's faith-based initiative, it generated significant research into the issues implicated by partnerships between religious organizations and government. These issues are not new; faith-based contracting preceded George W. Bush by many decades (as the chapters by Winston, King, and Kammer make clear), and religious organizations will continue to work with government agencies to deliver services to those in need. Kennedy concludes that religious organizations contemplating a partnership with government should consult the scholarly literature for advice on how best to structure such relationships.

The book returns to World Vision in chapter 8, Susan McDonic's "Juggling the Religious and the Secular: World Visions." Whereas chapter 5 by King is biographical and historical in nature, McDonic's work is contemporary and more social scientific. World Vision, though engaged in faith-based development, is forced to grapple with a world of professional development that is wedded to the secular. McDonic argues that World Vision is successful as a global organization due, in large part, to the fact that the various World Vision branches share idioms of both Christianity and development. On one level, these discourses lend themselves to each other in ways that are mutually reinforcing; both are based on an ethic of care and compassion, and both are marked by the dream of a more equitable and just world. On another level, however, these discourses are incompatible. At this level, McDonic argues, the secular and the religious diverge because they hold two very different understandings of the world. Through her comparative study of World Vision Canada and World Vision Ghana, she finds that the inherent tensions between the secular and the religious are minimized as each of the two World Vision branches emphasizes one worldview over the other. In World Vision Canada, development practice is stressed at the expense of its institutional Christian message; World Vision Ghana foregrounds faith and the Christian underpinnings of its development efforts.

In chapter 9, "Philanthropic Decisions of American Jews: The Influence of Religious Identity on Charitable Choices," the starting point for Arnold Dashefsky and Bernard Lazerwitz is the substantial research in the social sciences that has approached charitable giving from a variety of perspectives, such as the economic, psychological, sociological, and anthropological. Dashefsky and Lazerwitz, however, present an alternative social-psychological perspective to explain both the motivations of individuals who make charitable gifts and the barriers that constrain them. To explore this issue, they examine several datasets of studies in the Jewish community, including data from the National Jewish Population Survey (NJPS), nonprobability samples of donors and non-donors, and professional directors of fund-raising. Dashefsky and Lazerwitz find that age, family income, Jewish education, denominational preference, synagogue member-ship and attendance, involvement in Jewish primary groups, home religious practices, and a positive orientation toward Israel were positively related to Jewish philanthropy. For many Jews, activity in Jewish fund-raising, in its turn, led to activity in non-Jewish (general community) fund-raising. The authors conclude that participation in the orga-nized Jewish community is the key to giving. Therefore, in order to expand the ability of the private sector to augment the role of government in relieving social problems, it is necessary to improve the involvement of people in their local community networks.

Finally, in chapter 10, Shariq A. Siddiqui presents "Myth vs. Reality: Muslim Ameri-can Philanthropy since 9/11." Many might assume that, since September 11, 2001, Muslim American philanthropy has decreased. As Siddiqui argues, however, formalized philan-thropic activity among Muslim Americans has actually increased since September 11, 2001. A survey of fifteen of the largest Muslim American charities suggests that Mus-lim American philanthropy has grown by over 230 percent. Furthermore, the number of Muslim American philanthropic organizations at the grassroots level is also on the rise. As Siddiqui points out, however, the heightened scrutiny experienced by Muslim Americans and their charities has had a chilling effect on the means of philanthropic activity and how certain types of philanthropy are pursued. Regarding the former, some Muslim Americans are forgoing the benefits that accrue to most Americans in the exer-cise of philanthropic giving because many have changed how they give—eschewing, for example, certain credit card transactions that would actually benefit the giver if he or she were to use a card. Regarding the latter, Siddiqui argues that private remittances to the developing world (immigrants sending money home to families, for example) can be viewed as important philanthropic acts, and he points to how the post-9/11 frame-work has led to greater concerns about how such contributions by immigrants may be subject to especially intense oversight by the government. Muslim Americans must go through tougher and more formalized forms of philanthropic activity in order to feel safe from government's scrutiny.

These chapters, separately and taken together as a book, underscore the need to understand the very real complexities of the relationship between religion and phi-lanthropy in religious philanthropic work. Religion has played and continues to play a large part in America's philanthropic activities, and it has been intimately involved in the public arena, putting forth various visions of the good society and pursuing the means necessary to produce results. There are a large number of religiously inspired and motivated agencies that devote themselves to the eradication of social ills. The power of religion to motivate will continue to make an impact on the varieties of philanthropic activities undertaken by many Americans, and so it is important to understand fully the complex social interactions, competitions, conflicts, motivations, and cultural influences involved in channeling sizable resources that have the effect of not only doing good but also of ordering, to some extent, how we think of the public good.

Notes

1. See Robert H. Bremner, *Giving: Charity and Philanthropy in History* (New Brunswick, N.J.: Transaction, 1996); and Lawrence J. Friedman, "Philanthropy in America: Historicism and Its Discontents," in *Charity, Philanthropy, and Civility in American History,* ed. Lawrence J. Friedman and Mark D. McGarvie (New York: Cambridge University Press, 2003), esp. 6–8, but also *passim*. In terms of definition, Friedman states, "We postulate that charity and philanthropy themselves can sometimes have multiple and shifting meanings. In definition as well as in practice, it is sometimes rather challenging to determine what charity and philanthropy are not" (6).
2. Following Robert A. Gross, "Together, [charity and philanthropy] form the story of giving in America. They belong together, both in our scholarship and in everyday life." Robert A. Gross, "Giving in America: From Charity to Philanthropy," in *Charity, Philanthropy, and Civility in American History,* 31. Gross goes on to explain:

> Charity expresses an impulse to personal service; it engages individuals in concrete, direct acts of compassion and connection to other people. . . . [Philanthropy] aspires not so much to aid individuals as to reform society. Its object is the promotion of progress through the advance of knowledge. . . . Such are the two traditions of American humanitarianism. . . . Charity and philanthropy stand at opposite poles: the one concrete and individual, the other abstract and institutional. But they need not be at odds.

3. Though writing in quite different contexts, both Hyde and Mauss are good starting places when one begins an analysis of philanthropy and its many expressions. See Lewis Hyde, *The Gift: Creativity and the Artist in the Modern World,* 25th anniversary ed. (New York: Vintage, 2007); and Marcel Mauss, *The Gift: Forms and Functions in Archaic Societies,* trans. Ian Cunnison (New York: Norton, 1967).
4. Steven Feierman, "Reciprocity and Assistance in Precolonial Africa," in *Philanthropy in the World's Traditions,* ed. Warren F. Ilchman, Stanley N. Katz, and Edward L. Queen II (Bloomington: Indiana University Press, 1998), 20, 21.
5. Warren F. Ilchman, Stanley N. Katz, and Edward L. Queen II, "Introduction," in *Philanthropy in the World's Traditions,* xiv.
6. John Boyle O'Reilly, "In Bohemia," in *In Bohemia* (Boston: Pilot, 1886), 15.
7. To give one small example, Andrew Carnegie thought it important to help college professors—generally ill paid—with retirement so as to prevent a slide into genteel poverty. This program led to the creation of Teachers Insurance and Annuity (part of TIAA-CREF, the backbone of professorial retirement in the United States). In order to participate, however, colleges had to be nonsectarian, a principle held dear by Carnegie. Thus, a number of historically religious colleges changed their charters to reflect a nonsectarian stance. See William C. Greenough and Francis P. King, *Retirement and Insurance Plans in American Colleges* (New York: Columbia University Press, 1959), 15. Whether one finally deems the change to nonsectarian status a good, bad, or neutral thing in and of itself, the point is that the philanthropic vision of a single individual—Carnegie—engineered a result that reestablished many institutions of higher education on a basis in line with that individual's view of what made for a good society. Later philanthropic acts from wealthy philanthropists and the foundations they established would duplicate this exercise of power in a variety of ways (such as the Rockefeller and Ford foundations underwriting efforts to fight the Cold War; see Gary R. Hess, "Waging the Cold War in the Third

World: The Foundations and the Challenges of Development," in *Charity, Philanthropy, and Civility in American History*, 319–39).

8. For one analysis of this interesting history, see Susan E. Henking, "Sociological Christianity and Christian Sociology: The Paradox of Early American Sociology," *Religion and American Culture: A Journal of Interpretation* 3, no. 1 (Winter 1993): 49–67.

9. Robert G. Payton, *Philanthropy: Voluntary Action for the Public Good* (New York: American Council on Education/Macmillan, 1988). It should be noted that several of the chapters in this present book suggest different understandings of "philanthropy," or they at least seek to expand beyond the definition that Payton provides. See especially chapters 1 (where Ferris reminds readers that the term of choice in the historic Christian ecumenical movement is *diakonia*), 2 (where Kelner complicates the term by suggesting that more is going on in Jewish philanthropy than simply private action meant to serve the public good), and 10 (where Siddiqui suggests that the classic Islamic definitions of philanthropy are more expansive than modern definitions).

10. Fred Kniss and David Todd Campbell, "The Effect of Religious Orientation on International Relief and Development Organizations," *Journal for the Scientific Study of Religion* 36, no. 1 (1997): 102.

11. The issue of core identity is highlighted in David P. King's chapter on Bob Pierce and World Vision. There are other facets of the identity question, however, that go beyond the clear-cut case of Pierce. For example, what happens when philanthropic work becomes an alternative identity marker, accepted by some but not by others, so that there is a sense that there is possibly a competition between philanthropic work and religion as an expression of peoplehood? This concern has received extensive attention in regard to Jewish religious identity and philanthropic work. The issue is addressed by essays in this collection, but it is a discussion that stretches back several decades. See, for example, Harold D. Hahn, "Synagogue-Federation Relations," in *Understanding American Jewish Philanthropy*, ed. Marc Lee Raphael (New York: Ktav, 1979). Shaul Kelner, in chapter 2 of this book, with his expansion of the meaning of philanthropy complicates the simple dichotomies of synagogue/federation and sacred/secular. Another facet of this issue of religion, philanthropy, and identity appears when others outside the religion reduce that religion's identity to its philanthropic work. As noted in Diane Winston's essay (chapter 3), the Salvation Army is better known by many as a charity than as a religion (as highlighted in a 2000 *Washington Post* holiday headline, "A Church Better Known as a Charity"). Winston points tellingly to a young Salvationist woman who, in the *Post* story, sums up the problem when she states that her friends think she worships in a thrift store.

RELIGION IN PHILANTHROPIC ORGANIZATIONS

1 New Wineskins or New Wine?

The Evolution of Ecumenical Humanitarian Assistance

Elizabeth G. Ferris

This is the story of the global ecumenical movement and the way it has structured its philanthropic action in response to the needs of the world—and the needs of its members. In particular, it is the story of six decades of the World Council of Churches (WCC) and its many related organizations as they have grappled with the question of Christian responsibility to the poor and needy, to refugees, and to victims of floods, tsunamis, and earthquakes. The focus of this essay is on ecumenical humanitarian response—a term that perhaps needs some unpacking. An "ecumenical response" is one in which churches work together in their humanitarian action and see themselves as part of the global movement toward Christian unity. "Humanitarian response" refers to those actions toward people in immediate need or for people who are victims of conflicts, natural disasters, or oppressive governments. In its ideal form, humanitarian work is shaped by the basic principles of humanity, independence, impartiality, and neutrality.

The essay looks at this story in three phases: the era of interchurch aid, 1948–1961; the time of solidarity with the world, 1961–1994; and the transition to new ecumenical instruments, 1994–present. Furthermore, it looks at these three periods through three lenses: the relationship between ecumenism and Christian service (diakonia), the power dynamics within the ecumenical movement over questions of assistance, and the relationship between diakonia and the professional secular world.

The model of interchurch aid as practiced in its first four decades strengthened ecumenism and the ecumenical movement. The decline of interchurch aid in the 1980s and its eventual demise by 2010 weakened ecumenical structures, although it was far from the only factor that contributed to this decline. In fact, developments in the secular world were most responsible for the demise of interchurch aid and global diakonia, particularly the increases in government funding, the needs of governments to channel their support through the nongovernmental sector, the proliferation of humanitarian actors (both faith-based and secular), and increasing professionalism within the humanitarian community. These trends are all related. More available funding for humanitarian work meant the emergence of more actors, which in turn raised concerns about the quality of aid being delivered, and ultimately led governments to demand higher standards of accountability. These global trends, coupled with a certain rigidity in ecumenical structures that limited the ability of the WCC to respond with more flexibility to these challenges, were responsible for the changes that took place over the course of the past two decades. This is a story of transformation, and while the jury is still out on whether the new ecumenical instrument, the ACT Alliance, will be able to overcome the pressures that destroyed interchurch aid, there are possibilities for a new instrument of ecumenical solidarity with those in need—possibilities that hold out the hope for new expressions of ecumenism itself and of a new relationship with the secular world.

A Word on Definitions

While the other essays in this volume may use the term philanthropy as "voluntary action for the public good," this is not a term used in the ecumenical movement. Rather, in international ecumenical circles, the term of choice has been *diakonia,* meaning Christian service. This term is widely understood and used in Europe and other parts of the world, but North American ecumenical organizations often used the term *service* as a stand-in for the poorly understood concept of diakonia (although its expression in terms such as *deacon* remains widespread). There are many books, articles, consultations, and reports that provide theological reflections on the term *diakonia.*[1] This essay, however, focuses not on the theological understanding of diakonia but on the way in which the churches have cooperated with each other in service to human need. The ecumenical movement "is committed to the search for visible unity, not as an end in itself but in order to give credible witness 'so that the world may believe,' to serve the healing of the human community and the wholeness of God's entire creation."[2] In other words, ecumenism is based not only on a commitment to unity between churches as a theological imperative but also on the conviction that, by working together, Christians will be more effective in mission and in service.[3]

Origins and the Era of Interchurch Aid, 1948–1961

The WCC was not the beginning of the global ecumenical movement. On different levels, individual Christians, missionary societies, and churches had developed ways of working together for decades through such instruments as the YMCA, YWCA, the Student Christian Movement, and ecumenical discussions around mission, faith, and order. A global mission conference in 1910 led to the formation of the International Missionary Council in 1921. The 1910 World Missionary Conference at Edinburgh is usually seen as the beginning of the modern ecumenical movement, as missionaries who had seen the negative effects of their competition in missions on Christian unity sought to develop ways of working together. Discussions about forming a global council of churches gathered steam in the years following World War I, and a provisional committee of the WCC was set up in 1942. Delayed by World War II, the WCC was formally established in 1948 as a fellowship of churches (not individual Christians, not ecumenical organizations, but churches). "The World Council of Churches is a fellowship of churches which confess the Lord Jesus Christ as God and Saviour according to the Scriptures and therefore seek to fulfill together their common calling to the glory of the one God, Father, Son and Holy Spirit."[4]

Even before the WCC was launched, however, the churches worked together in service to people in need. In 1944, organizers of the WCC created the Department of Reconstruction to help war-stricken Europe. This department set up or contacted councils of churches and their agencies which could offer help—first in the United States, the United Kingdom, Switzerland, Denmark, and Sweden. Then, it asked the non-Catholic churches in war-affected countries to set up national committees to discuss their common needs (e.g., France, the Netherlands, Poland, and Germany). Funds were given by churches and their related organizations to churches and their related organizations, with the WCC playing the role of "matchmaker" between donors and recipients. Gradually, the Department of Reconstruction took on pieces of work in its own name through funds sent directly to WCC headquarters. By 1945, the department was united with the older European Central Bureau for Inter-Church Aid (set up in 1922) and renamed the Department of Reconstruction and Inter-Church Aid. By 1949, it had taken on the work of the Ecumenical Refugee Commission, which had been set up in 1946, and given yet another name: Department of Inter-Church Aid and Service to Refugees (DICASR). By the early 1950s, it had expanded its scale of response to include regions beyond Europe.[5]

Names:
Department of Reconstruction, 1944–1945
Department of Reconstruction and Inter-Church Aid, 1945–1946
Department of Inter-Church Aid and Service to Refugees (DICASR), 1946–1960
Division of Inter-Church Aid, Refugee and World Service (DICARWS), 1960–1971
Commission on Inter-Church Aid, Refugee and World Service (CICARWS), 1971–1992
Unit IV: Sharing and Service, 1992–1998
Regional Relations and Ecumenical Sharing, 1998–2002
Diakonia and Solidarity, 2002–2006
Ecumenical Solidarity and Regional Relations (a project within the Justice, Diakonia and Responsibility for Creation Unit), 2006–

"From its inception, the World Council of Churches has considered diakonia as an inseparable component of the ecumenical vision, together with worship, fellowship, and witness to the world."[6] This is a bold statement and one that was largely true for the first four decades of the council's existence. The first general secretary of the WCC, Dr. Willem A. Visser't Hooft, made his acceptance of the position conditional upon the readiness of the council to become active in the field of mutual aid, "for there could be no healthy ecumenical fellowship without practical solidarity."[7] In the years immediately following World War II, the emphasis of ecumenical diakonia was on the reconstruction of Europe and especially on rebuilding and supporting the churches. Interchurch aid was intended to restore church buildings, to replenish human capital, and to support reconciliation between churches. The stories of interchurch relationships in the years immediately following the war are wonderful expressions of repentance, reconciliation, and commitment to maintaining ties between churches in countries that had fought a long, bitter, violent war. As initially formulated, interchurch aid was intended to support churches rather than to provide assistance to all those in need. This concrete expression of solidarity between churches supported ecumenism. Churches that received support through the ecumenical family saw that ecumenism had a practical—as well as a theological—dimension. Churches that supported reconstruction of European churches learned that they could do more by working together than they could do on their own.

In fact, it is hard to imagine what the ecumenical movement would have looked like without interchurch aid. Churches in Germany and elsewhere were desperate for support to rebuild. If they had not received international support, would they have been as committed to ecumenism, or would they have been more inward-looking and isolated? If they had received that support solely through individual denominational channels, would they have been as committed to ecumenism? Certainly, the commitment of the early WCC leaders and some of the major North American and European church leaders in reengaging with German churches was key to German reconciliation, the ecumenical movement, and broader political developments, such as the movement for European unity.

While interchurch aid was the rationale for the development of emergency relief programs, it did not take long for interchurch aid to extend beyond the churches. The churches and their communities were overwhelmed with refugees. Millions of people were displaced by World War II and subsequent Soviet consolidation of control of Eastern Europe. A particularly important component of the WCC's work was its support for church engagement with refugees and its direct service to refugees. Refugee work was inherently international; refugees fled one country for another, and cooperation between churches enabled those churches to help find solutions for the displaced. Even during the Second World War, churches were actively cooperating to assist Jewish and other refugees to escape Nazi persecution. After the war, it was natural for these churches to work to resettle refugees from the Soviet Union and Eastern Europe on a large scale. Indeed, by 1959, the WCC's Refugee Service had resettled 209,000 refugees.[8] In 1960, the WCC had five hundred field staff working in thirty countries around the world on refugee issues.[9] The WCC's Refugee Service was one of the first international organizations to work with the Office of the United Nations High Commissioner for Refugees (UNHCR) when it was created in 1950. Like both interchurch aid and UNHCR, what began as a focus on finding solutions for Europe's refugees soon acquired a global character in response to widespread displacement resulting from struggles against colonial rule.

In the ten years or so after World War II, interchurch aid expanded beyond support for churches themselves to support for the churches' programs to serve their communities. In the broader secular world, this was an era of hope for new multilateral institutions, particularly the United Nations (UN), where the churches had played a central role in drafting the UN Charter and later the Universal Declaration of Human Rights. This was a time when governments and citizens around the world hoped that multilateral instruments would overcome national interests and their resulting conflicts. In this context, the WCC was the multilateral instrument of its member churches, and it represented the hope that this instrument would be successful in overcoming the petty disagreements between churches in the quest for Christian unity.

This was also a time when the Protestant churches were powerful actors in North American and European societies. Particularly in North America, most political and economic leaders were members of mainline churches. Moreover, the churches were in a privileged position vis-à-vis the secular world. The UN's relief apparatus was just being set up, and most of the humanitarian relief agencies were either in the process of formation or were themselves dealing with the effects of the war on their own operations. Thus, 80 percent of the relief channeled through U.S. nongovernmental organizations (NGOs) in the immediate postwar period was sent through Church World Service (CWS), an early ecumenical service effort by U.S. churches later incorporated, for a time, into the National Council of Churches.[10] There simply was not much competition; the churches were way ahead of their secular counterparts in the scale of their organization, the strength of their institutions, and their commitment to international service.

As reconstruction work wound down in Europe, interchurch aid came to mean support for churches in their diaconal work in their communities. In addition to expressions of solidarity, expressed through letters, statements, and pastoral visits, supporting diaconal work also included financial support. The WCC, like many of its secular counterparts in the development world, structured this work as discrete projects. In 1956, the WCC published its first "project list"—a compilation of project proposals and budgets from churches around the world. Screened and recommended for funding by national councils of churches in the global South, the projects were listed and circulated to churches and their agencies in the global North for funding. Funders could pick and choose which projects to support—a system that suited the funders well, but one that some recipient churches did not like, particularly those that were not chosen by the donors. Less popular projects, such as support for theological education, tended to receive less funding than others, such as direct assistance to refugees. Beginning in 1971, the WCC came up with the idea of including "priority projects" along with the comprehensive listing of thousands of projects that were guaranteed funding from undesignated ecumenical funds. But the project system itself became increasingly controversial, as it was slow and bureaucratic, and the large church-related agencies increasingly bypassed the system. Over time, the project system came to represent less and less of the global transfer of ecumenical funds.

A somewhat different system for emergencies and humanitarian response developed in recognition of the fact that there simply was not time to wait for project proposals to be written. Rather, when an emergency occurred—for example, a typhoon or a war—the WCC emergencies desk would contact the churches in the affected area and issue an appeal, which churches around the world would then support. The WCC would monitor the expenditure of funds and, by working multilaterally, would prevent duplication of effort and ensure that small churches as well as large ones were supported.

Interestingly, by the mid-1950s, DICARWS had been "given permission to raise its own budget annually and therefore [was] not dependent on WCC's general budget."[11] At that time, the "service budget" was $1.1 million, of which $525,000 was for the refugee service, which in turn was used to mobilize an additional $2.5 million from other sources, mainly UNHCR, for its work with refugees.[12]

While there was not much competition between the churches and secular agencies in the 1950s, competition with missionary societies was fierce. In 1956, the International Missionary Council and DICARWS met in Herrenalb, Germany, to divide up responsibilities for channeling assistance. DICARWS agreed to limit its support to projects for emergencies and refugees, to projects requiring an "urgent" response, and to "churches not in regular contact with missionary societies." In other words, the mission societies were to provide the long-term support for mission activities and for development projects while the WCC was to concentrate its efforts on short-term emergency situations, refugees, and churches that were not in a relationship with mission societies. These Herrenalb principles, as they came to be known, were revised in 1964.[13] For many years, interchurch aid was expressed through support for projects. But global ecumenical concerns with issues of justice, development, peace, and, later, the environment were manifest in many ways beyond the project system and interchurch aid.

Solidarity with the World, 1961–1994

In 1961, the mandate of the WCC's diaconal work was changed to a focus on solidarity—and solidarity as service to the world rather than solidarity only between churches. Rather than rebuilding church buildings and strengthening the human resources of churches, aid was to be given to support churches' ministry to their communities, including health services, educational programs, and emergency relief when needed. Certainly, for the first twenty years or so of this period, diakonia was central to the council's engagement with the needs of the world. But this was also a period when new concerns with justice moved to the fore, when the churches became much more active in working for peace, and environmental issues came on the international and ecumenical agenda. The International Missionary Council was incorporated into the WCC in 1961, bringing with it a different assortment of projects as well as substantive contributions on the nature of partnerships. In fact, while mission societies are generally regarded today with great suspicion by the secular progressive community, the ecumenical mission agencies were far ahead of their time in engaging with justice issues in the world, in recognizing the strength of local organizations, and in their quest to develop relationships of partnership between global North and South that transcended a donor-recipient relationship.

This was a time when ecumenism itself was growing. The number of national councils of churches more than tripled between 1948 and 2001,[14] and regional ecumenical bodies were founded in all regions over the course of two decades.[15] The formation of these ecumenical bodies was encouraged by the WCC as an expression of ecumenism—the drive for Christian unity—but also as means for channeling assistance from northern churches and their agencies to meet needs in the South and East. A major WCC Church and Society conference in 1966 called on the churches to move away from direct aid (because such assistance often created new dependencies) and instead move to support development programs that were locally funded and administered. Transformation and social justice became central themes of ecumenical discussions. In fact, "justice not charity" was a keynote of the 1968 Uppsala Assembly, ushering in a period of intense reflection on the relationships among solidarity, development, mission, and justice. At the same time, the WCC played a leadership role in strengthening secular networks of NGOs to respond collectively to challenges in emergency response. The WCC was a founding member of both the International Council of Voluntary Agencies (ICVA) in 1962 and of the Steering Committee for Humanitarian Response (SCHR) in 1972.[16] While ICVA was (and is) the only global coalition bringing together northern and southern NGOs working in emergency response, SCHR was a smaller gathering of the largest NGO families working on humanitarian response. The WCC had a foot firmly in both camps.

In 1971, the Commission on the Churches' Participation in Development (CCPD) was formed to look at development from a progressive perspective with a particular emphasis on peoples' participation in development rather than economic indicators of growth. A decade later, this commission's work culminated in the ecumenical conciliar process on Justice, Peace and the Integrity of Creation. While the Commission on Inter-Church Aid, Refugee and World Service (CICARWS) concentrated on meeting immediate needs through existing church and ecumenical structures, the emphasis in CCPD was on linking and supporting people's movements.

With the benefit of hindsight, the separation of the progressive justice agenda from diaconal instruments was probably a mistake. CICARWS remained a powerful unit within the WCC—after all, it oversaw the disbursement of funds to churches in every region. But with the creation of CCPD, there was a perception that the creative thinking around development was taking place elsewhere, and CICARWS increasingly came to be seen as a utilitarian instrument for channeling money. CICARWS staff were organized as area desks (e.g., an Africa desk, a Latin America desk) with a few functional offices operating on a global level (e.g., refugee service, a migration desk, the emergencies office, personnel, material support). But the power in CICARWS—and, indeed, in the council—lay with the regional desks. The area secretaries played a key role in the council as a whole through their relationships with churches and ecumenical actors in the region. The main point of entry to global ecumenism for churches was usually the area secretary, who would refer them to other departments and staff responsible for different areas of engagement. But the area secretaries were also important because of the funds channeled through their offices. Although decisions on projects (and, later, priority projects) were made by regional groups, area secretaries could shape those discussions, advise churches on which projects were more likely to be funded, and, using their relationships with agency staff, often ensure that projects particularly important to specific churches received the funding they needed. The area secretaries were widely regarded as knowledgeable and essential to the ecumenical movement yet, at the same time, as presiding over little "empires" within the council. Their influence was strengthened by the fact that most of the agencies providing funds to the WCC were also organized along regional lines. Thus, the Africa secretary of Church of Sweden Aid had as counterparts the Africa secretary of CWS and the Africa secretary of the WCC.

After the WCC Assembly in Nairobi in 1975, the focus—and the language—shifted from giving and receiving to sharing of resources. The notion of resources, moreover, was redefined to include not just financial resources but also cultural, spiritual, theological, and human resources. In 1983, at the WCC Assembly in Vancouver, diakonia was both affirmed as central to the churches' ministry and challenged to go beyond traditional understandings:

> Diakonia as the Church's ministry of sharing, healing and reconciliation is of the very nature of the Church. It demands of individuals and churches a giving, which comes not out of what they have but what they are. Diakonia constantly has to challenge the frozen, static, self-centered structures of the Church and transform them into living instruments of the sharing, healing ministry of the Church. Diakonia cannot be confined within the institutional framework. It should transcend the established structures and boundaries of the institutional church and become the sharing and healing action of the Holy Spirit through the community of God's people in and for the world.[17]

That same year—1983—a new WCC Office for Resource Sharing was created as a separate entity from CICARWS, based on a vision that all would be givers and receivers. While CICARWS saw itself as the multilateral ecumenical instrument for sharing, this new Resource Sharing mechanism was poorly understood. CICARWS staff and constituency were confused. Was this an effort to limit the power of CICARWS? Was it to be another layer of bureaucracy? The regional groups established in the early 1970s by CICARWS were changed to become WCC-wide regional groups intended to screen and list projects for the council as a whole. While the progressive independent analysis on justice was being carried out by CCPD, now the mechanism of resource sharing was supplanting CICARWS's traditional role as the instrument for diakonia.

Even as CICARWS was struggling to find its role vis-à-vis CCPD and new resource-sharing instruments, the funds mobilized through the ecumenical movement were substantial. In March 1984, the WCC, together with Catholic partners, launched the

Churches' Drought Action in Africa (CDAA), an appeal to raise $100 million over five years. The target was met within a few months. By March 1986, the total amount raised by all participants in CDAA was $500 million.[18] These were impressive sums of money in the mid-1980s, but most of these funds were not transferred through the multilateral instrument of the WCC; they were sent instead directly by ecumenical agencies in the global North.

A major consultation on diakonia held in Larnaca, Cyprus, in 1986 emphasized prophetic diakonia rather than projects, stressed the importance of the local church, and called for the regional groups to devote more time to analysis and reflection and less to screening of projects.[19] In 1987, the World Consultation on Koinonia: Sharing Life in a World Community, held in El Escorial, Spain, highlighted the importance of sharing, reciprocity, and mutual accountability. Recognizing that increasing amounts of church funding for development were flowing outside of church and ecumenical channels, the consultation called for more ecumenical "discipline" and produced guidelines for sharing. These guidelines included "the implementation of mutual accountability and participation in decision-making between the South and the North."[20]

By the 1980s, however, the ecumenical and church-related agencies, or specialized ministries as they were called in some circles, began to chafe at the bit. These agencies had become major players in their own right, with increasingly larger budgets and independent identities. For the most part, the agencies had been set up in the same era as the WCC, the immediate postwar period, to respond to the same sorts of needs. Like the WCC, they worked to support the diaconal programs of local churches, councils of churches, and related organizations. They looked to the WCC for leadership, and the WCC expected them to follow its guidance, but they had no formal link to the WCC and no recognized "status" in the ecumenical movement.[21] Over the years, as they built up their resources, they began to wonder why they were simply sending money to the WCC rather than developing their own programs. In their own countries, secular organizations (and sometimes mission agencies) were engaging in development work on an operational level. The ecumenical and church-related agencies developed their own staff capacities, drawing from the professional world of development, and, by the mid-1980s, usually had far more staff capacity than the WCC.[22] Thus, an ecumenical development agency might have ten or twenty staff working on Africa while the WCC never had more than two Africa secretaries supported by several administrative staff. Yet the expectation was that the WCC was to play the leadership role in determining what the needs were of the churches—and societies—in the regions.

The agencies also began to chafe at the expectation that they would work exclusively or even primarily through the churches. Although this was what set them apart from their secular counterparts at home, they came to realize that churches and their related organizations were often not the most progressive elements of their societies. Nor were they the most efficient. Generalizations are always risky, but certainly many churches and related organizations in the global South had come to depend on their relationships with the WCC area secretaries for their financial well-being. It was a comfortable system for them and for the WCC but one that was challenged by the growing capacity and professionalism of the agencies.

Looking back, the Larnaca consultation provided an opportunity for a radical rethinking of ecumenical diaconal work, of discussing the possibility of new instruments for using the expertise of the agencies in supporting development work in the regions, and of building a capacity for progressive thinking on the burning issues of development. Instead, the Larnaca consultation emphasized the role of the local church in diakonia and called for more advocacy. But advocacy was not the strength of CICARWS. After the 1991 WCC Assembly in Canberra, CICARWS became one of four program units—now named Unit IV, Sharing and Service.

Advocacy was centered elsewhere in the WCC—in the Commission of the Churches on International Affairs (CCIA) and in CCPD. The agencies were supportive of more targeted, focused, and effective advocacy, and they were critical of the WCC's advocacy role. The WCC's model of advocacy was based on statements by church leaders, which could be powerful statements representing the position of the global church on the burning issues of the day. But because such statements represented consensus by church leaders, it generally took a long time and often quite a bit of "watering down" before the statements could be adopted. By the 1990s, new models of advocacy based on grassroots campaigning were emerging in the world. This was a time when the International Campaign to Ban Landmines and the World Social Forum were mobilizing young people on an unprecedented scale. The WCC's emphasis on formal statements by church leaders and its reluctance to engage with new models of advocacy were a source of frustration to the agencies.

It is difficult to date when the agencies decided to pursue a more independent course and to create their own structures apart from the WCC. The flow of money had started to bypass the WCC much earlier; certainly by the 1980s, most agency funds were directed bilaterally. In 1990, the European agencies created the Association of World Council of Churches Related Development Organisations in Europe (APRODEV) with an office in Brussels set up particularly to follow the European Union. In 1992, four ecumenical development agencies (Bread for the World, Protestant Association for Cooperation in Development, Interchurch Organization for Development Cooperation, and Christian Aid) started a process of reflection and discussion about their work and its direction, including CCPD and churches from the global South. The resulting publication, *Discerning the Way Together,* signaled that the "WCC was no longer the only space for reflection on ecumenical diakonia and development."[23]

Meanwhile, the WCC sought to adapt to changing times by introducing ecumenical round tables that largely replaced the discredited project system. By 1990, there were fifty round tables in which national churches or councils of churches would present their plans and programs, and funding agencies would indicate the extent of their financial support. In some cases, these were dynamic gatherings in which partners analyzed the political, economic, and social contexts of the societies they were working in and would argue over priorities in the church's total program. For example, there were opportunities for funding partners to encourage churches to include women's perspectives and work on interfaith issues—issues that sometimes did not come naturally to local churches. At the same time, national churches challenged agencies to engage in greater advocacy on the burning issues that affected the lives of their communities. Other round tables were poorly prepared and marked by resentment on the part of the national churches about the scrutiny they were undergoing by northern agencies, viewing it as a lack of trust. The round table system was reviewed in 1994.[24]

While the WCC's work with long-term development was coming under criticism and increasingly seen as irrelevant for the agencies, the most radical change came in the area of emergency response. The WCC's emergencies desk continued to respond to emergencies by working with churches in the affected region to issue appeals to support local partners' response to the emergencies. But by the early 1990s, emergency response had become big business on the global scale, increasing from around 3 percent of official development assistance in the 1970s to 12–14 percent in the mid-2000s.[25] Increasing amounts of money were being channeled for emergency response. For the church-related agencies (like their secular counterparts), raising funds for emergencies—and being visible in emergency response—was important to their other work. They needed reliable information about the situation on the ground that they could use in their fund-raising efforts. The WCC emergencies system relied on short messages from local churches and a letter from the emergencies desk (supplemented later with situation updates) outlining the needs. The churches were not very good at providing rapid, high-quality reports of how the money had been used. Consequently, the agencies became increasingly frustrated. The situation was complicated by the fact that the Lutheran World Federation (LWF), a confessional body to which most of the major financial supporters of the WCC were also related, also issued emergency appeals, often using the same local partners in the same situation. Thus, an ecumenical agency, such as DanChurchAid or Bread for the World, would receive appeals from both the WCC and the LWF for the same emergency (though the appeals were often different).

A 1993 review of the WCC's ecumenical emergency response found that, "due to the growth in the number and visibility of humanitarian crises, the system had become unwieldy and unsustainable."[26] In 1994, a new pilot structure, Church World Action, was put into place to respond to the widespread humanitarian needs in Rwanda. A year later, a new structure was created, Action by Churches Together (ACT) International, with a single common purpose, which was to act quickly and conform to secular humanitarian standards. But before discussing this new instrument—which marked the beginning of a new era—it is appropriate to look back at the trends in this long second period in the history of the WCC's diaconal work.

At the beginning of this period (1961 to 1994), CICARWS was at the height of its power; by the end, the signs of its decline were clear. In the early part of the period, there was an ecumenical commitment by the churches and their related organizations to work together in development and humanitarian response as well as a commitment to the WCC as the central multilateral instrument for doing this. Jenny Borden finds that this period—from 1968 to sometime in the 1980s—was the WCC's heyday for advocacy as well; the council played "a visible, prophetic and inspirational role in global advocacy, leading education, prayer and activity in churches all over the world."[27] CICARWS certainly strengthened ecumenism, and the flow of money to church partners in the global South ensured their loyalty to the WCC. While this sounds cynical and while financial transfers were important, this should not be seen as downplaying the genuine commitment of churches to church unity. But when church leaders could count on the WCC to provide the funds to support their work, they did not have to spend much time and resources looking for funds from other sources or cultivating relationships with secular funding agencies (as was the case for other civil society organizations in their countries). They could be assured that the WCC would accept them and their approaches to the issues. As funding through the WCC began to decline and bilateral funding from the ecumenical agencies increased—with more and stricter reporting requirements—southern churches became increasingly critical of the role of agencies and increasingly resistant to changing existing ecumenical structures.

Ecumenism itself was changing as ecumenical organizations proliferated, many of which depended on the same set of ecumenical and church-related agencies for funding. As mentioned above, many national councils of churches had been created or supported to serve as channels for funding development and relief projects. In some cases, these Christian councils developed their own service agencies, such as Christian Care in Zimbabwe. In other cases, such as Church's Auxiliary for Social Action (CASA) in India and the Social Assistance Foundation of Christian Churches (Fundación de Ayuda Social de Las Iglesias Cristianas, FASIC) in Chile, the churches set up ecumenical agencies that became increasingly professional. Ecumenical networks were created to deal with a wide range of justice issues, from children's rights to water to indigenous rights to HIV/AIDS. Ecumenical and church-related agencies supported these justice issues, which were, in many ways, more creative and attractive to funding partners than the ongoing social service programs of the churches and their social service agencies. Theological institutions, lay training centers, and a host of lay academies also required international support.[28]

While the ecumenical landscape was becoming increasingly crowded, the churches themselves maintained their own programs and agencies. Thus, Presbyterian World Service/Disaster Assistance was both an actor in international relief and a supporter of ecumenical structures such as CWS at the national level and the WCC at the international level. Sometimes, there was competition between these denominational structures and ecumenical ones. But the churches that provided financial support for these structures were losing members, funding, and energy. In North America, mainstream churches all faced sharp declines in membership and income between 1960 and 1990, and they reacted by cutting programs, staff, and support for ecumenical programs. In Europe, mainstream churches faced similar declines in membership, but most continued to receive funding through their national governments or through state taxes. In Europe, ecumenical and church-related agencies became favored instruments for distributing government funds.

Around 1990, CICARWS organized a briefing for the heads of agencies on its work. This was an opportunity for CICARWS to present its program and to garner support for its activities as well as to engage them in discussions of the burning issues of the day. These briefings became annual events and, over the course of the next nineteen years, changed in character from CICARWS (later Unit IV) briefings to the agencies to meetings jointly organized with agency representatives to a Heads of Agencies Network (HOAN), which developed its own agenda to meet the needs of the agencies.

The power dynamics during this era were characterized by the increasing power of the ecumenical agencies and the declining power of the WCC as a multilateral instrument. The WCC increasingly assumed the position of defending the churches vis-à-vis the agencies. Churches and service agencies in the global South found themselves developing bilateral relationships with agencies even as they defended their relationship with the WCC.

One of the major driving forces for change was the increasing professionalization of humanitarian work and the proliferation of humanitarian actors. In the immediate postwar period, as mentioned above, 80 percent of the relief and reconstruction funds sent to Europe was channeled through CWS. By 1990, there were dozens of secular and faith-based NGOs with far larger budgets than CWS: World Vision, CARE, Save the Children, Catholic Relief Services, etc. In its early years, CWS had enjoyed a comparative advantage because of its strong relationships with churches in all regions. But the trend in other secular organizations was toward developing global alliances. Thus, Save the Children USA was part of a global Save the Children Alliance with strong partners in countries such as the United Kingdom, Norway, and Sweden. World Vision was first created as an American evangelical NGO but in subsequent years was transformed into World Vision International with independent World Vision partners in many countries and a budget exceeding $2.5 billion.[29]

For their part, donor governments channeled increasing amounts of their development and relief funds through NGOs. It was cost effective for them to contract out the work, and often they preferred to work through NGOs that could bypass southern governments (and the complaints they generated of corruption, political influence, and bureaucratic delays). In contrast to the southern governments, NGOs were seen as flexible, cost effective, creative, and committed. The Iraqi displacement crisis of 1991, the anarchy of Somalia, and the deepening war in the Balkans led to still more funds for NGOs—and to a drive for more professional standards. In this era of heightened competition between NGOs, a greater flow of funds for humanitarian response, and a drive for professionalism, the standard WCC mechanism for emergency response seemed old-fashioned, slow, and rigid. The ecumenical agencies drew distinctions between southern ecumenical agencies that had developed professional approaches to their work and traditional church partners who seemed to expect unconditional support by virtue of their relationship to the churches. To be fair, WCC staff worked with these southern churches, encouraging them to develop more professional skills and to increase their capacity. WCC staff organized capacity-building workshops, training partners in such issues as financial management, report writing, and proposal development. But the WCC's capacity to train church officials was limited, and many more training opportunities were provided by secular organizations.

"Our mission is to help people in need," Daleep Mujari, former director of Christian Aid, often said, "and if the churches can do that most efficiently, we'll work with the churches. But if they can't, we'll find other partners." In contrast, a Kenyan pastor lamented the fact that "the church agencies come in and run their programs without even talking to us. I don't understand why they don't support the churches. We're in the community, we'll be here forever. Don't they realize that by strengthening our role in society, we can better serve the needs of our people?"[30]

A Time of Transition: 1994 to Today

The period from 1994 to the present began with the creation of Action by Churches Together (ACT) International in 1995 as a new ecumenical instrument of emergency response. Fifteen years later, the ACT Alliance was established, bringing together ecumenical partners to work together in development. The ACT Alliance largely replaced the WCC's diaconal work, whose area desks now focused on the important issues of relationships with member churches. In effect, ecumenical diaconal work—the practical solidarity of responding to churches facing earthquakes or assisting desperately poor people—has spun off from the WCC.[31] The center of gravity has passed from the WCC—as a council of churches—to agencies that represent a new form of ecumenical engagement, one that perhaps better reflects the needs of the world.

At the same time, increasing media attention to emergencies coupled with growing donor requirements for accountability have increased the pressure on international NGOs to implement more professional programs. In the global North, it is no longer enough for a local humanitarian organization to be church related; it has to be able to deliver measurable results and fulfill increasingly stringent reporting requirements. Northern church-related agencies increasingly are choosing to work with local secular and interfaith NGOs rather than churches, leading to questions from many local churches and church-related organizations that had relied on the support from agencies for many years.

For church-related organizations, questions of accountability between northern and southern organizations have been a major issue. In the 1980s, for example, there was great concern within the WCC-related network of church-related agencies about the concept of "ecumenical discipline," which was a common understanding about relations between churches and church-related agencies, especially focusing on solidarity and mutual accountability.[32] A process of consultation sought to develop guidelines for the ways in which northern and southern churches and related organizations would relate to one another in a way that would respect the central role of local organizations. However, the pressures of professionalism and the competitive marketplace were such that implementation of these guidelines never got very far. European Union institutions, for example, provide significant funding for humanitarian work by large European church-related organizations. Often, a condition of this funding is the presence of expatriate staff in a given country. This means that a church-related organization receiving such funds is under pressure to send expatriate staff to the country rather than channeling those funds through a local partner.[33]

ACT International sought to bring together ecumenical partners—both agencies and specialized ministries and emergency departments of churches—in one global instrument of emergency response. The creation of ACT was intended to meet several needs—the need for higher professional standards, for better and more modern communications, and for a common identity. In an increasingly competitive field (and a crowded one with hundreds—sometimes thousands—of NGOs in a particular emergency response), there was no visual marker identifying the fact that Finn Church Aid, the United Methodist Committee on Relief (UMCOR), and Christian Care were part of a global ecumenical family. Each church or agency used its own name. As Jenny Borden explains:

> The secular families of agencies were growing and becoming stronger and more visible, whilst the church-related agencies, representing in many ways a more legitimate global expression of civil society, were continuing to act in disparate and invisible ways. There was a sense at that time that whilst the churches—both related agencies and local churches—were contributing massively in many of the emergency situations, the lack of coordination diminished the effectiveness of the response. Furthermore the level of involvement, coming as it did from a variety of agencies and churches within the ecumenical family all using their own names with no common visible thread linking them, was felt to be unrecognized by the international community, by government funders and by the UN humanitarian actors, and hence the ability to raise funds and have influence was diminished.[34]

Catholic humanitarian actors had Caritas as a global umbrella, the Red Cross/Red Crescent movement had long had a unique identity or brand, but the churches and related agencies in the WCC family had no common identity. The agencies resisted a formal identity linked to the WCC, perhaps fearing that a closer link to institutional churches would make them subject to church decisions or, equally important, give the impression that they were controlled by the WCC. Action by Churches Together was a good name for the new alliance—the emphasis was on action, on churches, and on churches working together (without the often misunderstood term ecumenical). Membership in ACT International was initially automatic; all WCC and Lutheran World

Federation (LWF) member churches and related agencies were automatically members of ACT by virtue of their relationship to the WCC and LWF. (This was later changed as a membership application process was implemented; while all WCC- and LWF-affiliated bodies were eligible for membership, it was not automatic. Applicants had to apply for membership and indicate that they had signed the Red Cross/NGO code of conduct and were willing to abide by ACT policies.)

ACT International represented a new kind of global ecumenical instrument. Made up of members from both global North and global South, with a governance structure that represented a commitment to inclusiveness, ACT International had a small central office that moved quickly to establish clear policies in a range of areas, to improve the network's communications, and to establish highly professional ways of working. ACT faced a tough time in its early years as expectations were high—and varied. There was still resistance in parts of the WCC to ACT and to the council's lack of control over ecumenical emergency response. There was also some resentment of the dominant role played by the LWF, which, together with the WCC, was one of the two parent bodies of ACT. While the WCC disbanded its emergency office, recognizing that ACT was now its emergency response arm, the LWF maintained its separate emergency office. LWF no longer issued emergency appeals on its own, but its office stood ready to help Lutheran churches and partners with their proposals and submissions while there was no one at the WCC who could provide this level of assistance to non-Lutheran churches seeking support from ACT.

Over the years, ACT International became more and more recognized as an important actor in emergencies, developed increasingly professional standards and policies, and constantly struggled with the issue of power dynamics within its membership. ACT's strength—in comparison with most other humanitarian NGOs—lay in its vast network of churches and related agencies in all regions. While some secular emergency NGOs could respond more quickly and effectively when an emergency occurred, ACT had local partners, rooted in their communities, who could provide both an effective initial response and long-term support—long after international agencies had departed. ACT devoted considerable energy to programs of capacity building but, as a 2004 external evaluation concluded, it was an incomplete process, and ACT's full potential remained unrealized.[35] There were also tensions between northern agencies and, occasionally, between northern agencies and the ACT secretariat. In particular, the use of the ACT "brand" was erratic. The need for a common visible identity had been a major factor in the formation of ACT, yet agencies were inconsistent in the way it was used. For some, the ACT logo was included on their websites and business cards. For others, it remained very much in the background or seemed to be another bureaucratic layer. As one CWS staff member explained to me in the late 1990s, "Much of our funding comes from community contributions who really don't understand how Church World Service relates to their denominations and who aren't big supporters of ecumenism. So first we have to explain what CWS is—and often that brings up painful discussions of its relationship to the National Council of Churches. For us to then add another layer of bureaucracy to explain what ACT is and why we don't just transfer the money to people on the ground—well, that gets too complicated."

ACT seeks to build capacity of local church-related organizations in responding to emergencies in their countries. In spite of this capacity-building component for local organizations, of the $80 million or so channeled through ACT every year for emergencies, approximately two-thirds goes through northern church-related agencies (including the one-third passed through the LWF). The need for comprehensive and timely reports, particularly when government funds are mobilized, means that northern church-related donors often prefer working through large professional organizations over smaller church organizations based in developing countries.

While ACT was struggling to invent itself, the WCC was struggling to find its place in the new ecumenical landscape. In 1996, Unit IV attempted to recast its work in the context of Jubilee—the vision of a fairer world—and tried to place the work of diakonia at the heart of the council. But the notion of Jubilee—while interesting on a theological level—did not catch on. After the 1998 Assembly in Harare, the WCC engaged in another round of restructuring. Unit IV: Sharing and Solidarity became the Regional Relations and Ecumenical Sharing team. This represented a shift away from the WCC's operational involvement and role in multilateral resource sharing toward a recognition of the importance of the area secretaries in maintaining relationships with churches and ecumenical actors in the region. It was also a shift toward enhancing the WCC's roles in facilitation, coordination, networking, and capacity building of ecumenical organizations. While multilateral sharing continued in a reduced form, and WCC staff continued to facilitate and support round tables, funding dropped off. In 2002, the WCC consolidated its diaconal work in a new Diakonia and Solidarity team, whose stated aim was to "empower marginalized groups, including uprooted people, in their struggles for dignity and sustainable communities." Within this overall aim, the team's activities were directed toward five specific objectives: sustaining relationships among member churches and related organizations, creating spaces for reflection, empowering communities, building the capacities of member churches and partner organizations, and developing a coherent and holistic approach to meet human needs.[36]

Meanwhile, the WCC constituency and staff were struggling with the issue of the WCC's role in the ecumenical world. In September 1997, the WCC had adopted "Towards a Common Understanding and Vision of the World Council of Churches" (CUV), the product of more than eight years of study and consultation. The document notes that, while nearly two-thirds of the founding WCC churches came from Europe and North America, today, nearly two-thirds come from Africa, Asia, the Caribbean, Latin America, the Middle East, and the Pacific. The CUV proposed the concept of a "polycentric" ecumenical movement in which the "WCC is no longer the center, but a privileged instrument with the role of fostering the coherence of the movement."[37]

The early 2000s were a time of crisis for the WCC as a whole. Its budget and staff were reduced by up to 50 percent, income dropped, and the council was forced to cut some of its major program areas. There was a feeling among many of the WCC's member churches, particularly its Orthodox members, that the WCC had gotten away from its "roots" and needed to refocus its energies on relations with its members. As one WCC staff member reported,

> One source of WCC's difficulties has been its perceived priorities. A disproportionate attention to social and political issues, and the attention that WCC has given to a "third world" and liberal agenda, and to related movements, networks and NGOs, has tended to marginalize the theological, doctrinal and other priorities of the inter-church body, and has resulted in a weakened commitment of a number of traditional churches, distancing the WCC from local parish reality.[38]

Specifically, there was a crisis with the Orthodox churches that were particularly affected by the demise of communist regimes. On the one hand, there were opportunities for church renewal. But on the other, Alexander Belopopsky reports, "Insecurity and threatened identity have led to defensiveness and fear of 'the other.' Many churches in Central and Eastern Europe, Orthodox and Protestant, have experienced a growth in anti-ecumenical sentiment over the last years, resulting in the withdrawal from WCC of two Orthodox churches, the churches of Georgia and of Bulgaria, as well as of the less-publicized Russian Baptist church."[39] A Special Commission on Orthodox Participation in the WCC was mandated at the WCC's Assembly in Harare in 1998.

While ACT was developing its new professional ways of working and deepening its relationships with the secular humanitarian world, the WCC's energy was focused on deepening and improving relations with its members, particularly repairing damaged relationships with the Orthodox member churches. If the WCC was to have a role in multilateral sharing of resources or concrete expressions of diakonia, it needed to devote attention and political capital to the issue. But the attention of the governing bodies and of the leadership was devoted to managing the larger crisis. Any available energy went into discussing ways of strengthening relationships with the churches and discerning a new place for the WCC in the broader ecumenical world. In 2002, WCC general secretary Konrad Raiser initiated a discussion on a new "architecture" or "configuration" of the ecumenical movement in response to the decline of existing models of institutions and the multiplication of ecumenical and confessional church structures. Recognizing that the present system was simply not sustainable, he called for a new, more flexible multilateralism.[40]

Ecumenical Advocacy Alliance

Meanwhile, the discussions within the agencies, organized as the Head of Agencies Network, focused on the need for a new ecumenical instrument for advocacy. Ecumenical advocacy—or public witness—had been central to the WCC's work since its establishment in 1948. In fact, the Commission of the Churches on International Affairs had been created in 1946 as the churches' collective instrument for both speaking out on global issues of concern and conducting quiet diplomacy, particularly at the United Nations. It was a respected institution with an impressive history. But by the mid-1990s, its office in New York had declined as funding shortfalls meant a redirection of energy.[41] Where once the council had mobilized impressive teams to bring forward the churches' concerns at the Commission on Human Rights in Geneva and indeed all major UN world conferences, the delegations began to get smaller, and the important ongoing monitoring role declined. The WCC governing bodies continued to issue statements on important issues of the day, and staff mobilized processes of reflection and analysis in support of some of these statements, such as on the use of sanctions. In particular, the WCC was instrumental in raising the issue of climate change and in leading the United Nations to adopt the concept of responsibility to protect.[42]

Developing WCC statements and study processes centered on the CCIA staff and on the churches, however, because there was not much room for the agencies who themselves had developed impressive capacities for carrying out advocacy on the national level. They were eager to use their capacities and their collective identity to work on the global level. Agencies were represented in the CCIA and occasionally participated in the drafting of statements, but this was not enough. They argued that it was right and proper for churches to have their own processes for developing statements as churches, but the agencies, too, needed a way to conduct advocacy on the global level. A process, including WCC representation, was set up in the late 1990s to begin thinking about a new ecumenical instrument for advocacy and, in 2000, the Ecumenical Advocacy Alliance (EAA) was created. The EAA went beyond the WCC's traditional constituency and opened participation to a variety of groups, from World Vision to Catholic orders to churches and agencies in all regions. With more than sixty members, the EAA agreed from the beginning to concentrate on two priority issues in order to focus its work and to increase its impact. In its initial period, these issues were HIV/AIDS and trade; working groups were set up to conduct research and agree on strategies for action. The EAA was deliberately structured not to compete with the WCC and developed a campaign style of working that was quite different from the WCC's deliberative and consultative processes with the churches.[43]

Broadening the Ecumenical Movement

Meanwhile, there were initiatives to create new ecumenical structures to reflect the Christian landscape better—which include, for example, the Roman Catholic Church and the "newer independent, charismatic and non-denominational churches [that] have stayed away from the organized ecumenical movement."[44] The Global Christian Forum, initiated in 1998, seeks to be a different kind of ecumenical body than the WCC—looser in structure, more inclusive in membership, and serving as a forum for dialogue rather than an organized implementer of programs. Following an intensive process of regional consultations, an international founding meeting was held in Limuru, Kenya, in 2007, which drew 240 delegates from seventy-two countries.[45] About half of the participants in the various consultations came from evangelical/Pentecostal churches with the other half from mainline churches. The Global Christian Forum recognizes the changing ecumenical demographic where Pentecostals today are estimated to number 600 million persons, while the churches of the WCC number some 550 million persons, and the Catholic Church includes more than a billion people.[46]

In the United States, a similar process of broadening the base of ecumenical dialogue led to the formation of Christian Churches Together (CCT). Like the Global Christian Forum, it eschews structure; rather, there is an annual meeting, a steering committee to act between meetings, and two staff members. For its first two years, two themes were at the heart of CCT: poverty and evangelization. CCT is in dialogue with both the National Council of Churches in the United States of America (NCCUSA) and the National Association of Evangelicals.[47]

It is striking—and deliberate—that neither of these two new ecumenical initiatives uses the word "ecumenical" in its name; rather they emphasize their "Christian" nature. Both have insisted that they do not intend to replace either the WCC or the NCCUSA but rather want to provide a broader forum for Christian churches to dialogue on issues of concern. Neither seeks to recreate the programmatic work of the two councils. As one supporter of the Global Christian Forum explains, this new initiative is seen as a forum that can welcome new realities in a way that traditional ecumenical structures cannot. "Those who have invested their lives into building and maintaining these [ecumenical] structures are at times blind to the challenges of the newer forms of Christianity, assuming that the newcomers, once they have learned the 'ecumenical grammar' will fit into and contribute to the old. Furthermore, the old is often blind to its impotence, this in spite of reduced budgets and vacant buildings."[48]

By 2007, the WCC's project on "Ecumenical Solidarity and Regional Relations" was established—now as a project within the Justice, Diakonia, and Responsibility for Creation unit (itself one of six programs in the once-again reorganized WCC). The description of this project is telling:

> This project reflects the ecumenical commitment to sharing resources amidst growing poverty and polarization, displacement, exclusion, etc. It provides practical solidarity in response to the needs of the WCC's constituency, while keeping in mind the principle of mutual accountability. Such solidarity can take various forms: pastoral visits to churches facing difficult situations, working with churches to strengthen their organizational capacities, and providing timely resources to support strategic initiatives.[49]

It goes on to say, "This project facilitates WCC's involvement with ACT Alliance at the global level. Relationships with and between ecumenical partners working in the field of diakonia and justice will be strengthened as a result of this project."[50]

The last multilateral funding instrument—the Ecumenical Solidarity Fund—was discontinued in 2010. Financial support had been shrinking, which meant that many applications had to be refused and related administrative costs had become comparatively expensive. The WCC concluded that "the staff time involved can be invested more effectively for the benefit of churches in other activities of the Council" and suggested using funds remaining for other projects and redeploying staff in other areas of work.[51]

ACT Alliance

While ACT International responded to emergencies and the EAA provided sophisticated advocacy on two specific issues, the agencies and specialized ministries wanted more. They wanted a global instrument to address the full range of issues on which they were working, which are frequently lumped together as development (including work on long-term community organizing and empowerment), issues of particular concern to women and youth, microfinance, the environment, and a host of other issues. Again, working through Heads of Agencies Network and with the WCC's participation, the agencies embarked on a process to come up with a new instrument for bringing together the work and enhancing the visibility of the ecumenical family in the area of development. Given the success of the ACT name, they urged that the name ACT be expanded to include not only emergency response but also long-term development. They also suggested that the new body include the work of the EAA as a new advocacy arm. Discussions in Geneva and the regions were held over the course of several years and, at a meeting in December 2005, there was agreement to create a new ACT Development with the goal of eventually merging it with ACT International to form a new ACT Alliance that would work on both development and humanitarian response. It took four years of discussions and negotiations to reach this goal.

Merging ACT Development and ACT International proved to be a difficult undertaking on many levels. ACT International was concerned that broadening its mandate would weaken its work in emergency response—a process still being consolidated. Merging governance structures and staffing proved to be a time-consuming task. Given the difficulties of merging these two bodies (which at least shared a common membership of WCC- and LWF-related bodies), a merger with the EAA was postponed. If it was this difficult to bring together two bodies with roughly similar membership, how could the new alliance coordinate with World Vision and the Catholics?

The ACT Alliance was formally created in January 2010 and is currently made up of more than one hundred member organizations working in long-term development and humanitarian assistance. More than seventy of these members are based in the global South. Members work in 130 countries, employ around 30,000 staff and volunteers, and mobilize approximately $1.5 billion each year. The ACT secretariat has a staff of eighteen, and its members are all related to the WCC and/or the Lutheran World Federation.

The alliance brought together the work of ACT International (created in 1995) and ACT Development (created in 2003). Its mission statement of the alliance states:

> Members of the ACT alliance work together for positive and sustainable change in the lives of impoverished, marginalised and vulnerable women, men, girls and

boys through coordinated and effective humanitarian, development and advocacy work. . . .

We work with and for people of all faiths and none. We give priority to the poorest and most vulnerable people in areas of the world with the greatest need for external assistance. And we work to enable and strengthen existing capacity and resources, putting communities at the centre.

We work to uphold ethical and professional standards of transparency and accountability to the communities we serve, to those whose resources we are asked to be stewards of, and to each other. In all of this, we are committed as an alliance to learning, coordinating and collaborating with each other and others to increase the difference we make.[52]

The creation of the ACT Alliance was intended to increase the effectiveness of the work as well as the visibility of the ACT family within the increasingly diverse and crowded world of NGOs. Toward this end, the issue of branding—and co-branding, in which each agency includes the ACT Alliance logo with its own name and logo— became a central feature of members' commitment to the new entity. One of the objectives of the ACT Alliance is that the alliance will "promote, under a shared family name, the visibility of the development work, humanitarian assistance and advocacy initiatives being undertaken by the alliance." And the co-branding policy states that, "upon the launch of the ACT Alliance, members should begin using the new ACT Alliance name and logo and work under this co-branding policy."[53] However, a quick check of the websites of a dozen ACT Alliance members in August 2010 found that only two have displayed the ACT Alliance logo on their home pages, suggesting that the issue of co-branding continues to be a difficult issue.

In terms of power dynamics, it seems the WCC accepts that the ACT Alliance needs to be accommodated and supported. In the years of consultations leading up to the formation of the ACT Alliance, the WCC feared that this was an effort by northern agencies to take control and to bypass churches in both the North and the South. Many of those tensions have either been overcome or submerged, perhaps, in part, because the ACT Alliance has made an effort to ensure the full participation of southern (and eastern) partners in its operations and has struggled to overcome the inevitable power dynamics of donor-recipient relationships.[54]

Concluding Thoughts

Interchurch aid was central to the development of the World Council of Churches in its formative years and served to build and consolidate relationships within the ecumenical family, initially in war-torn Europe and later in the world. As ecumenical relationships became stronger, the WCC expanded its work of "solidarity to the world," developing large-scale programs of service to refugees and channeling large amounts of money to support projects developed and run by churches in all regions. The reflection and analysis carried out on issues ranging from partnership to justice was, in many regards, path-breaking. For example, the suggestion that rich countries channel 0.7 percent of their

GDP in assistance to the global South has its roots in the WCC's Uppsala Assembly in 1968, which called for 2 percent of GDP to be allocated for development work. Similarly, the call for "justice not charity" was a theme in the same 1968 WCC Assembly—it would take several decades before this theme was seriously discussed in the secular world.

By the mid-1980s and early 1990s, the world was changing. The ecumenical agencies, largely created after World War II with support from their churches, were becoming more professional in their approach to development, humanitarian response, and advocacy. In part, this was a reaction to the increasing governmental resources available for development and emergencies, the expanding role of the media in shaping humanitarian response, and the proliferation of NGOs that created an increasingly competitive environment. The agencies attracted creative, committed (and, often, young) staff who wanted to change the world and who saw possibilities of doing so through global advocacy campaigns. Perhaps because most of the agencies had to raise funds from the general public, they developed skills in public relations, in telling human interest stories, and in new forms of communication. In this environment, it was not enough for agencies to raise funds by saying, "We're passing the money on to the WCC to distribute to long-standing church partners who are doing good things." The agencies developed their own partnerships and their own programs in all regions, sometimes working with church partners and sometimes developing new relationships.

Michael Taylor describes the professionalism dilemma as one of ecumenism versus efficiency.

> Ecumenism, we are told, requires us to respect the special relationship which binds together the ecumenical family through thick and thin, and to choose to stay with ecumenical partners even where they are judged to be less than efficient when it comes to aid and development and the struggle against poverty and for life. Efficiency, it is said, declares that our first loyalty is to the poorest of the poor and that we must work with whomever we judge will most effectively address our overriding concern, whether they are ecumenical partners or not.[55]

The new competitive environment for all NGOs, including faith-based organizations, is evident in all regions. Before 1989, for example, churches in Central and Eastern Europe were one of the few expressions of civil society. Rooted in the local context, they provided humanitarian assistance to people in need and were supported by church-related agencies from abroad as well as by their own constituencies. With the proliferation of NGOs in the following decade, their unique position was challenged. New, often more professional, NGOs were created to respond to particular social needs. For example, many new Romanian NGOs were created after 1990 to provide services to orphans and street children. Faith-based Romanian organizations that had worked for years with children now found themselves competing for foreign funds with new Romanian NGOs.

The glory days of the 1960s–1980s meant that the WCC had been well resourced to carry out hundreds of programs, but the flow of ecumenical funds had also enabled the establishment or growth of dozens, perhaps hundreds, of ecumenical bodies—ranging from national and regional councils of churches to student movements to issue-specific coalitions to educational and training institutions. All of these required funding, however, by the agencies who were beginning to balk at the assumption that their support was required and yet not conditioned by performance.

Funds for traditional multilateral ecumenical institutions dried up. Institutions such as the World Council of Churches were caught in a bind. Its history, culture, and constituency predisposed it to continue working as it had always done, while the growing power of the agencies was insisting on new ways of working. There might have been a moment in the mid-1980s where the WCC could have introduced radical changes in its diaconal work that would have reengaged the agencies, incorporated professional, innovative ways of working, and maintained its leadership role. But the conditions were not right for the WCC to be open to those changes. And so the decline of diakonia—at least as expressed through multilateral sharing—began. This is not to say that the WCC does not continue to make contributions in other areas, such as theological reflection on diakonia or analysis of global issues, but its role in channeling financial support to churches has disappeared. At the same time, it seems that the WCC has become more introspective, more concerned with interchurch relations (which was always its essence as a fellowship of churches), even as alternative forums for ecumenical dialogue gain strength. It is almost as if the council has come full circle: from a preoccupation with interchurch aid in the early years to an expansive focus on solidarity with the world to a return to concentrating on interchurch discussions and dialogue.

New ecumenical instruments have been created that respond to new power dynamics in both the ecumenical and secular worlds. Are people in need better served by the new instruments? Although such evaluations would probably be impossible to carry out, my hunch is that beneficiaries are indeed better served through the more professional approaches of the new instruments. Assessments are more carefully performed, and more attention is paid to issues of participation, accountability, and evaluation. The rights-based approach used by most ACT Alliance members affirms the dignity of recipients, and members are particularly careful to stay away from anything smacking of missionary activity or proselytizing. The losers in the new system are the churches who are not "professional" enough to participate in the work of the ACT Alliance and who have lost the opportunity to be transformed by diaconal work. The imperative to respond to people in need is central to the Christian tradition (and, indeed, to all religious traditions). Millions of Christians do so as individuals with no financial support from anyone, and that will, of course, continue. But small churches that used to receive a small amount of money to support this work—to run a preschool for Chechens in Moscow or to provide transport to a pastor to go to a refugee camp—may find it more difficult to do so.

The wineskins—and the wine—are, indeed, new.

Notes

Thanks to Michael Taylor, Dawn Ross, and Dwain Epps for their thoughtful comments on an earlier draft of this essay. I also drew from my own active participation in many discussions for more than twenty years as a staff member of the World Council of Churches and, for six years, of Church World Service.

1. See, for example, the articles in *Ecumenical Review* 46, no. 3 (July 1994); International Theological Commission, *From the Diakonia of Churches to the Diakonia of the Apostles* (Mundelein, Ill.: Hillenbrand Books, 2007); and Paul S. Chung, *Churches' Mission and a Diakonia of Reconciliation: A Global Reframing of Justification and Justice* (Minneapolis: Lutheran University Press, 2008).

2. World Council of Churches (hereafter referred to as WCC), *Towards a Common Understanding and Vision of the World Council of Churches* (Geneva: WCC, 1997), 2.8.4.

3. The World Christian Database (www.worldchristiandatabase.org/wcd) estimates that there are more than 9,000 different Christian denominations in the world, with 635 in the United States alone.

4. WCC, "Who Are We?" http://www.oikoumene.org/en/who-are-we.html.

5. Michael Taylor, *Not Angels but Agencies: The Ecumenical Response to Poverty—A Primer* (Geneva: WCC, 1995), 4.

6. "From Inter-Church Aid to Jubilee, World Council of Churches, 2002," 5, http://wcc-coe.org/wcc/europe/diakoniahistorybook.pdf.

7. Kenneth Slack, *Hope in the Desert* (Geneva: WCC, 1986), 9.

8. WCC, *Minutes, Central Committee Meeting, 1959* (Geneva: WCC, 1960), 26.

9. WCC, *From Evanston to New Delhi, 1954–61* (Geneva: WCC Report of the Central Committee at the Third Assembly of the World Council of Churches, 1961), 110.

10. Ronald E. Stenning, *Church World Service: Fifty Years of Help and Hope* (New York: Friendship Press, 1996), 3.

11. WCC, *From Evanston to New Delhi*, 109.

12. Ibid., 113.

13. WCC, *From New Delhi to Uppsala, 1961–68* (Geneva: WCC, 1968), 119.

14. The earliest National Council of Churches was the Protestant Federation in France in 1905. By 1910, there were 2 councils, 23 by 1928, 30 by 1948, and 103 in 2001. Nicholas Lossky, Miguez Bonino, and John Pobee, eds., *Dictionary of the Ecumenical Movement*, 2nd ed. (Geneva: WCC, 2001), 257.

15. Conference of European Churches, 1959; East Asia Christian Conference, 1959 (renamed Christian Conference of Asia in 1973); All Africa Conference of Churches, 1963; Pacific Conference of Churches, 1966; Caribbean Conference of Churches, 1973; Middle East Council of Churches, 1974; Latin American Council of Churches, 1982. Lossky, Bonino, and Pobee, *Dictionary of the Ecumenical Movement*, 257.

16. "From Inter-Church Aid to Jubilee," 10.

17. Report of Vancouver Assembly, cited in "From Inter-Church Aid to Jubilee," 14.

18. Thomas Best, ed., *From Vancouver to Canberra* (Geneva: WCC, 1990), 165.

19. Klaus Poser, ed., *Diakonia 2000: Called to Be Neighbours: Official Report, WCC World Consultation, Inter-Church Aid, Refugee and World Service, Larnaca, 1986* (Geneva: WCC, 1987).

20. *Guidelines for Sharing* (no. 6), World Consultation on Ecumenical Sharing of Resources, El Escorial, Spain, October 30, 2007.

21. It was not until the 2006 WCC Assembly in Porto Alegre that the WCC established the category of "Specialized ministries in working relationship with the WCC," which permits the twenty-four specialized ministries and mission agencies that accepted this status to send observers to WCC governing bodies. Specialized ministries are now also given seats on various international ecumenical bodies, such as the Assembly Preparation Committee, Ecumenism in the 21st Century Continuation Committee, Working Group on Governance, etc.

22. See, for example, Jill Hawkey, *Mapping the Oikoumene: A Study of Current Ecumenical Structures and Relationships* (Geneva: WCC, 2004).

23. "From Inter-Church Aid to Jubilee," 18. This "Discerning the Way Together" initiative was followed by a project to explore Christian approaches to poverty. See Michael Taylor, *Christianity, Poverty, and Wealth: The Findings of "Project 21"* (London: SPCK, 2003).

24. For a summary of the review as well as an overview of round tables, see http://www.wcc-coe.org/wcc/what/regional/round.html and http://www.oikoumene.org/fileadmin/files/wcc-main/documents/p4/P401/manual.pdf.

25. Peter Walker and Kevin Pepper, "The State of Humanitarian Financing," *Forced Migration Review* 29 (December 2007): 33, http://www.fmreview.org/sites/fmr/files/FMRdownloads/en/FMR pdfs/FMR29/33–35.pdf.

26. Jenny Borden, *Responding to Emergencies with the World Council of Churches: A Report Based on One Month with the Emergencies Desk, Unit IV* (December 1993), available at the WCC Library, Geneva, Switzerland.

27. Jenny Borden, "Prophetic, Pragmatic, and Practical: A Review of Global Advocacy Undertaken by the World Council of Churches, Ecumenical Advocacy Alliance, ACT International and ACT Development" (Geneva: Ecumenical Staff Working Group on Global Advocacy, 2007), 9.

28. See Jill Hawkey, *Mapping the Oikoumene,* rev. ed. (Geneva: WCC, 2005), for a summary of the diverse ecumenical organizations, http://www.oikoumene.org/fileadmin/files/wcc-main/documents/p1/mapping-the-oikoumene-revised-21-2-05.pdf.

29. http://www.wvi.org/wvi/WVIAR2009.nsf/0D0BC6D2A56F63AF882576DC00252534/$file/wvi_ext_ar_A4_2009_0210_d07.pdf.

30. Interview with author, 2000.

31. A similar process of spinning off is evident in the Ecumenical Church Loan Fund (ECLOF), which was set up as a program in the WCC in 1946 to provide loans to support church rebuilding efforts. Just as the WCC broadened its interest beyond reconstruction of churches, so, too, ECLOF expanded into loans for a wide range of programs and set up ECLOF committees in many countries to review and process the requests. In 2002, ECLOF was renamed the Ecumenical Microfinance Fund for Development and spun off from the WCC. Now it works in thirty countries with a loan portfolio of $22 million, serving more than 100,000 active clients. http://www.eclof.org/index_UK.php?p=about.

32. *Sharing Life: Official Report of the WCC World Consultation on Koinonia, Sharing Life in a World Community* (Geneva: WCC, 1987).

33. For an early discussion of the pressures of government funding, see Jenny Borden, "Government Funding and the Ecumenical Sharing of Resources—Ecumenical Diakonia: New Challenges, New Responses," *Ecumenical Review* 46, no. 3 (July 1994): 311–15.

34. Borden, "Prophetic, Pragmatic, and Practical," 19.

35. John Eriksson and John Borton, "Unlocking the Potential Within: Evaluation of the ACT Alliance in the International Response to Crisis" (Geneva: ACT International, 2004).

36. http://www.wcc-coe.org/wcc/what/regional/index-e.html.

37. Alexander Belopopsky, "WCC in Crisis? A View from Geneva," paper presented at the Hofgeismar Academy, May 19, 2003, 3.

38. Ibid., 1–2.

39. Ibid., 3.

40. See *Consultation on Reconfiguration of the Ecumenical Movement, Antelias, Lebanon, 17–21 November 2003* (Geneva: WCC, 2004).

41. Currently, there are priorities to strengthen the United National Liaison Office with agency support through secondments.

42. See Elizabeth Ferris, "A Faithful Case for Intervention: Our Common Responsibility to Protect Humanity and Prevent Atrocities," in *Pursuing the Global Common Good,* ed. Sally Steenland, Peter

Rundlet, Michael H. Fuchs, and David Buckley (Washington, D.C.: Center for American Progress, 2007), 73–90.

43. See Borden, "Prophetic, Pragmatic, and Practical," 15–20.

44. Huibert van Beek, "Editorial," *Transformation: An International Journal of Holistic Mission Studies* 27, no. 1 (January 2010): 3. (The entire issue is devoted to the Global Christian Forum.)

45. John A. Radano, "Global Christian Forum: A New Initiative for the Second Century of Ecumenism," *Transformation: An International Journal of Holistic Mission Studies* 27, no. 1 (January 2010): 29.

46. Ibid., 34.

47. Interestingly, one of the problems with the CCT has been the reluctance of African Americans to participate fully, seeing that the NCC as has been one of their main supporters in the struggle against racism. See Leonid Kishkovsky, "Following Christ with Great Joy: Christians Called to Reconciliation," *Transformation: An International Journal of Holistic Mission Studies* 27, no. 1 (January 2010): 57.

48. Cheryl Bridges Johns, "When East Meets West and North Meets South: The Reconciling Mission of the Christian Churches," *Transformation: An International Journal of Holistic Mission Studies* 27, no. 1 (January 2010): 48.

49. "Ecumenical Solidarity and Regional Relations," *World Council of Churches,* http://www.oikoumene.org/programmes/justice-diakonia-and-responsibility-for-creation/ecumenical-solidarity-and-regional-relations.

50. Ibid.

51. WCC, "Programme Plans 2011–2013, Summary" (Geneva: WCC, 2010).

52. "What Does the ACT Alliance Do?" http://www.actalliance.org/about.

53. The co-branding policy specifies that all full members are expected to co-brand with the ACT Alliance name and logo, that observers are not permitted to co-brand, and that the ACT Alliance name and logo should not be associated with work that falls outside the objectives of the ACT Alliance. Only ACT Alliance members are allowed to use the logo—a member's constituent churches/agencies or partners may not co-brand. At the same time, advocacy related to specific country situations should respect communities and organizations living and working there, and, "wherever possible," consultation should take place with national ACT members. ACT Alliance, "Co-Branding for Members of the ACT Alliance," 38, available from http://www.actalliance.org/resources/policies-and-guidelines/communications/CoBranding_Book_Eng.pdf.

54. For example, the governing body is composed of twenty-three members, including a permanent set for the WCC and the LWF. The remaining twenty-one members—three each from Africa, Asia, Western Europe, and Latin America and the Caribbean; two from North America (United States and Canada); one from Eastern/Central Europe; one from the Pacific nations, Australia, and Aotearoa/New Zealand; and one from the Middle East, with four other members elected from the membership—ensure balance and professional expertise on the board.

55. Taylor, *Not Angels but Agencies,* 141.

2 Religious Ambivalence in Jewish American Philanthropy

Shaul Kelner

Passover 1967. After an outcry of protest in the West, the Soviet Union had eased restrictions on the baking and import of unleavened bread, restrictions that had been designed to stamp out the last vestiges of Russian Jewry's observance of the springtime festival of the matzoh. Responding to the policy change, the American Jewish Conference on Soviet Jewry (AJCSJ), an umbrella group of twenty-five of the largest Jewish nonprofit organizations in the United States, revised the Passover seder supplement that it had first published the year before. The new text, written to be read aloud in homes and synagogues during the meal in which Jews ceremonially recount the biblical Exodus story, dropped all reference to the Soviets' ban on matzoh. Instead, it invoked Passover's general theme of liberation from bondage to contrast the religious freedoms enjoyed by American Jews with the religious and cultural oppression that the Jews of the USSR were being forced to endure. With millions of copies circulated in the national media and through synagogues across the country, the 1967 text read as follows:

> *This is the Matzoh of Hope*
> The leader of the service adds the following comments when distributing the matzoh
> after the blessing over the matzoh. He lifts a matzoh, sets it aside and says:
> This matzoh, which we set aside as a symbol of hope for the 3 million Jews of the
> Soviet Union, reminds us of the indestructible link that exists between us.
> As we observe this festival of freedom, we know that Soviet Jews are not free to learn
> of their Jewish past, to hand it down to their children. They cannot learn the
> languages of their fathers. They cannot teach their children to be the teachers,
> the rabbis of future generations.
> They can only sit in silence and become invisible. We shall be their voice, and our
> voices shall be joined by thousands of men of conscience aroused by the wrongs
> suffered by Soviet Jews. Then shall they know that they have not been forgotten,
> and they that sit in darkness shall yet see a great light.[1]

In retrospect, American Jews' use of the Passover ritual to frame the plight of Soviet Jewry seems logical. After all, Jews were trapped inside the Soviet Union, oppressed, denied the right to live as Jews, and yet not free to leave. When the walls finally did come down as the Communist regime collapsed, the exodus was swift and massive: More than a million Jews emigrated in the course of a decade. Although, at first glance, the

Passover framing may seem unsurprising, a closer examination of the Matzoh of Hope campaign raises perplexing questions that, in turn, point to deep-seated tensions within Jewish American philanthropy over the place of religion in the enterprise.

First, the AJCSJ, which sponsored the campaign, analogized the Soviet Jewish plight to Egyptian slavery not simply through words but also through a religious ritual that it created and promulgated. For some of its twenty-five member organizations, like the Synagogue Council of America and the Rabbinical Assembly, such work in the ritual sphere may have been *de rigeur,* but for others, such as the socialist Labor Zionist Movement and the expressly nondenominational National Community Relations Advisory Council, it was a departure, to say the least.[2] How and why did an American Jewish nonprofit umbrella group, whose work did not specifically apply to the congregational realm, come to see ritual work as something under its purview?

Second, although the AJCSJ was willing to employ ritual to frame the Soviet Jewish cause in Jewish religious terms, this engagement was hardly an embrace. A closer look at the Matzoh of Hope text of 1967 reveals something startling: Nowhere in this ceremony that analogizes the plight of the Jews under the Kremlin to the plight of the Israelites under Pharaoh was a call made to "Let my people go." In the litany of freedoms that the text says are denied to Soviet Jews, "freedom of exit" was never mentioned. It is a strange omission and one that demands accounting. Nor is it the end of the puzzle, for, in 1970, the AJCSJ's Matzoh of Hope statement was revised yet again. This time, freedom of exit, which warranted nary a mention in the years prior, appeared at the top of the list: "As we observe this festival of freedom, we know that Soviet Jews are not free—*not free to leave,* not free to learn of their Jewish past or to hand it down to their children."[3]

Why the initial reluctance to carry the Exodus frame to an obvious conclusion? Why the subsequent change? One explanation that can account for both choices is that the AJCSJ was guided by an instrumentally rational, strategic calculus that weighed the costs and benefits of calling for emigration rights, not by a value-rational commitment to enacting biblical narrative. In 1967, the AJCSJ leadership believed that the political environment militated against calling for emigration rights. Soviet Jews were not publicly demanding to emigrate; the likelihood that the Kremlin would bow to Western pressures on the issue seemed remote. There were concerns that efforts to achieve the unattainable would prevent the movement from achieving what it could attain—namely, the amelioration of the Jews' condition in the USSR. Pressure on the issue also risked exacerbating tensions in Soviet-Israeli relations. Under these circumstances, the AJCSJ made no reference to exodus. By 1970, however, the situation had changed. Soviet Jews themselves had begun demanding emigration rights. The Soviet Union's severing of diplomatic relations with Israel in the wake of the June 1967 Six-Day War also removed the issue of Soviet-Israeli relations from the considerations. These political developments altered the AJCSJ's calculus. It changed course and revised its Passover ritual. Both before and after the change in the text, the religious ritual was subservient to the demands of politics.[4]

The tensions manifest here in the AJCSJ's relationship to the religious ritual that it led, but refused to be led by, have roots that stretch back to the late nineteenth-century beginnings of federated American Jewish philanthropy and branches that extend onward to the present day. This essay traces these tensions, arguing that much of the ambivalence about religion within the American Jewish philanthropic network stems from the fact that these philanthropic institutions understand themselves to be not only agents of voluntary action for the public good but also agents of internal governance for an ethnic community whose corporate status is not formally established by law. As the philanthropies have come to understand themselves as taking on state-like functions for the American Jewish community, American notions of "church-state separation" have led to ongoing debates about the proper role, if any, of Jewish religion within the philanthropic system. After providing a brief history of the federation system in American Jewish philanthropy, I explore how the ambivalence about religion has manifested itself at three different moments in the federation's history: in the original move toward federated philanthropy a century ago, in the utilization of ritual in the Soviet Jewry movement in the 1960s, and in the efforts of the 1990s to redefine the relationship between federations and synagogues.

The Jewish Federation System

Federated Jewish philanthropy in the United States and Canada functions as an international organizational network that involves locally based fund-raising and fund-allocating community chests (known as "federations"), their recipient agencies, continental umbrella organizations for federations and for the different grantees, and coordinating bodies linking these continental umbrellas. Within each community (typically a greater metropolitan area), the local Jewish federation raises money, largely from Jewish donors, and distributes the funds primarily to serve local, national, and international Jewish welfare and educational needs. Federations operate an annual campaign whose proceeds are allocated by a lay-governed and professionally staffed community board. Commonly, a set proportion of the campaign, usually between a quarter and a third, is directed to the local federations' continental umbrella organization (the Jewish Federations of North America, or JFNA), which pools the money and reallocates it to national and international Jewish nongovernmental organizations in Israel, North America, and elsewhere in the world.[5] The largest of these recipients are the Jewish Agency for Israel and the American Jewish Joint Distribution Committee.[6]

Of the remaining two-thirds to three-fourths of the campaign, most is distributed locally, primarily to a fixed set of social service, community relations, and educational agencies that are said to constitute the federation's network. The core of this network in each community is typically made up of a Jewish Family and Children's Service organization, a Jewish community center, an independent Jewish day school, the local campus Hillel foundation, and a Jewish community relations council. Although federations may support synagogue programs on a case-by-case basis, they generally do not treat synagogues as federation agencies and do not allocate funds to cover the congregations' regular operating expenses. In addition to the annual campaign, federations also raise funds through emergency campaigns, planned giving, endowments, and foundation gifts. In recent years, the federation system has been raising between $2 and $3 billion annually.[7]

The federation model for organizing local Jewish philanthropy first emerged in Boston in 1895 and, within a decade, had spread to eleven other cities, including Chicago, Philadelphia, Detroit, and Atlanta. From 1906 through 1932, new federations were being established in Jewish communities across North America at the annualized rate of one every seven months. The largest spurt of federation creation came between 1933 and 1949, when more than two hundred were created, one every month and a half. This rate leveled off after 1950, with about one new federation being created every nine months through 1980.[8] Recent decades have seen a decline in numbers as smaller federations have closed or merged with their neighbors. As of 2011, the total number of local Jewish federations stood at 157.[9]

One of the many efforts to systemize philanthropy in the United States in the late nineteenth and early twentieth centuries, the federated model for Jewish philanthropy was introduced in the hope of bringing greater efficiency to the community's charitable work.[10] Competing fund-raising campaigns, duplication of effort, and lack of coordinated planning among the various synagogues and charitable groups had been seen as problematic for decades. Earlier efforts to rationalize Jewish philanthropy in the 1860s and 1870s had resulted in the outright merger of Jewish welfare agencies in a number of communities. Yet even with these reforms, American Jewish charitable agencies soon found themselves struggling to meet needs that had grown to unprecedented levels as the 1880s ushered in the first waves of the largest Jewish migration to American shores in history. Over the next four decades, more than two million impoverished Eastern European Jews would arrive in the United States, many settling in the crowded tenements of New York and other cities. New charitable efforts proliferated, exacerbating the problems of duplication and lack of coordination even as they failed to keep pace with the growing need.[11]

In contrast to the agency mergers of the 1860s and 1870s, the federation model that was introduced during the period of mass migration preserved the independence of the different charitable societies. At first, it linked the nonsynagogue welfare agencies under a single umbrella for the purposes of a unified community fund-raising campaign.[12] The late political scientist Daniel Elazar, still the most prominent scholar of the federation system, emphasized the importance of the federal character of the organizational arrangement, seeing it as reflective not only of its American context but also of premodern patterns of Jewish political organization:

> The covenant, or federal idea, emphasizing the development of contractually defined partnerships based on mutual obligation, was translated into concrete political institutions and embedded in Jewish tradition to become part of the political culture of

the Jews. . . . These federal arrangements are not necessarily the same as those in modern, territorially based polities, where constituent entities are united under an overarching government in such a way as to maintain the unity of the whole . . . while preserving the integrity of all of the partners. Frequently there are no overarching bodies, or only weak ones, to link the constituent units, but there is the linking of individuals and institutions in contractual relationships designed to foster partnership on several levels. Moreover, those partnerships take on a character of their own that is more than the sum of their constituent units.[13]

What began as an effort to streamline duplication in fund-raising efforts quickly evolved into something greater. The federations soon found that not only did they exercise control over considerable financial resources, but they also occupied a crucial position linking otherwise disconnected local welfare agencies. This strategic position as a central node in an interorganizational network stemmed from the federations' fundraising and fund-allocating activities and from the fact that its lay leadership brought together, around a single table, representatives of the various beneficiary agencies. In the language of social network analysis, federation centrality was established through the overlapping resource flows, information flows, and personnel flows.

As leaders of the various federations reflected on the role that the institution might play in local Jewish communities, they increasingly began to conceive of philanthropy not merely as a mode of achieving public good but also as an arena in which an ethno-religious community could come together and establish a modicum of self-governance.[14] This reconceptualization of philanthropy as a means to establish a polity is of particular significance in the American context.[15] Unlike in countries where religious corporations are legally established and granted state recognition, law establishes no formal governing bodies to manage the affairs of ethno-religious communities in the United States.

By the mid-1910s, some federations had come to understand themselves as coordinating bodies for their network of philanthropic agencies.[16] By the time of the Great Depression, a more ambitious vision had begun to take shape. Writing in the *American Jewish Year Book* of 1934–1935, the executive director of Boston's Associated Jewish Charities argued that the "Federation must be made the authoritative agency of the Jewish community," a "governing body" with communal planning responsibilities and in which "all groups of the Jewish community will be represented."[17] New York City's Federation for the Support of Jewish Philanthropic Societies had begun to move in this direction a decade earlier when it organized a community-wide survey in 1926. More than a needs assessment, the survey was, in the words of its director, "conceived as an instrument . . . for community organization."[18] It was not only the findings that were of importance to the sponsors. Rather, as historian Deborah Dash Moore shows, the process of developing and fielding the study was itself also understood as a means of redefining the boundaries of Jewish community in broadly embracing terms that transcended differences of class, ethnicity,[19] politics, and denomination and of simultaneously asserting the central governance role of the federation in this expanded community.[20]

Expansion of the federation system's role beyond coordination of welfare efforts and into broader issues of communal governance became especially evident in the federations' absorption of responsibilities for community relations work. Who speaks for American Jews? On what basis do those who claim to speak on their behalf assert the legitimacy of this claim? American Jews have no overarching governing body of elected representatives whose legitimacy rests on the democratic process. In the absence of this, the responsibility for representing Jewish interests to government, to business, and to other ethnic and religious communities has been assumed by a variety of voluntary organizations. Among these have been fraternal groups like B'nai B'rith, which established the well-known Anti-Defamation League; the American Jewish Committee, which represented the elite of America's German Jews;[21] and the American Jewish Congress, originally envisioned as a standing parliament for American Jews but quickly becoming but one more actor in a crowded organizational landscape. Significantly, local federations also entered into the arena.[22]

By the 1930s, demands for greater coordination and planning in the community relations sphere were being voiced, which were similar to the calls in the 1890s to better integrate American Jewish efforts in the social welfare arena.[23] Taking up the cause, the federation system convened the major community relations organizations. In 1944, at the annual assembly of the Council of Jewish Federations and Welfare Funds (CJFWF), the participating groups established the National Community Relations Advisory Council (NCRAC) under CJFWF sponsorship.[24] The NCRAC was a coordinating, planning, and policy-formulating body for its constituents, which included the Anti-Defamation League of B'nai B'rith, the two AJCs (Committee and Congress), the Jewish Labor Committee, Jewish War Veterans, the Reform movement's Union of American Hebrew Congregations, and the community relations councils of eighteen local Jewish federations. Here again, the federated model did not merge organizations but rather allowed the constituent groups to coordinate efforts while maintaining their independence and autonomy.[25]

The aspirations of federation leaders to establish the philanthropic network as the central mechanism of American Jewish communal governance were most fully realized during the decades of the Cold War. In its 1965 annual report, the Philadelphia Federation of Jewish Agencies proclaimed itself to be "drastically different from the Federation of twenty years ago." No longer limited to "matters of philanthropic service to the minority," the federation and its agencies were, it claimed, "now instrumentalities of the *total community* in acting for the welfare of its *entire* populace."[26] This was not an idle boast, nor was it a development limited to Philadelphia. Indeed, the federation system had consolidated power to such an extent that, in 1969, when student activists in the Jewish counterculture movement wanted to protest against the Jewish establishment and demand action on priorities like Jewish education and the campaign to free Soviet Jewry, they chose to picket the annual convention of the Council of Jewish Federations and Welfare Funds.

Affirmation of the federation network's power came from other sources, too. Scholars devoted books to the federations, portraying them as the "central address" of an American Jewish polity and as the bearer of a Jewish "civil religion" to rival traditional Judaism.[27] Adulatory press accounts suggested that the Jewish federations were a model of philanthropic success against which other American charities paled in comparison. The *Wall Street Journal,* for instance, in a 1983 article, established the federation's credentials by writing that it "raises more money each year than the American Cancer Society, the American Heart Association, the Muscular Dystrophy Association, the March of Dimes, and the National Easter Seal Society *combined.*"[28] In the 1980s, annual campaign revenues averaged $750 million a year, up from an average $450 million a year in the 1970s, $125 million in the 1950s and early 1960s, and under $50 million during the years of the Depression and World War II.[29]

The decades since have witnessed divergent trends. Since the turn of the millennium, annual campaigns have raised between $800 million and $1 billion a year. Adjusting for inflation, however, this represents a continuation of the secular decline in annual campaign revenues that began in the 1970s. Yet overall, even with this decline, real revenues have increased because the federation's income streams have diversified. Just before the economic crisis of 2008, federations received a record $2.6 billion in contributions to endowment funds, more than double the amount raised by the annual campaign. The contributions brought the size of federation endowments to approximately $15 billion prior to the market's downturn.[30] Although this has contributed greatly to the financial well-being of the system, it has not alleviated the sense that the federations are in decline.[31] In part, the malaise has to do with the perception of generational attrition, in which the young have been less likely to give to the same extent as their elders.[32] It is also connected to a redistribution of American Jewish philanthropic power away from the federations and into the hands of independent foundations. For most of the twentieth century, federations had been accustomed to setting the agenda for the Jewish community. Since the 1990s, the federation system nationally has increasingly found itself in the novel position of having to respond to priorities set by foundations.[33] With the loss of its agenda-setting power has come a crisis of confidence.

Religious Ambivalence in the Federation System

The Ideology of Separation

Jewish charitable federations were, in part, born out of dissatisfaction with synagogues. Addressing the National Conference of Jewish Charities in 1916, Boris Bogen, the director of the United Jewish Charities in Cincinnati—the seat of American Reform Judaism, home to its rabbinic seminary and congregational union—laid out the brief against the houses of worship with an exasperation that devolved into analogies to Heinz-brand condiments:

> Though still adhering to the monotheistic conception of the Deity the Jews of today are not altogether unanimous as to their affiliation with the Synagogue. . . . Social differences, [such] as minor disagreements over the mode of worship, led to the disintegration of the Synagogue . . . into fifty-seven varieties. . . . When Jewish philanthropy in the United States came face to face with the problem of mass immigration in the eighties it became apparent that the isolated, uncorrelated agencies for relief, the different groups connected with the Synagogue, were unable to cope with the situation. A more efficient organization became a necessity and the idea of co-operation arose. It was evident that the Synagogue was unable to achieve the purpose.[34]

Divided and divisive, incapable of channeling collective efforts and unable to meet dire needs, such was the charge against the synagogues. Philanthropic reformers recognized and valued the religious tradition as the ethical basis of their charitable enterprise. They distinguished between Judaism and the synagogue, however, seeing the factionalized houses of worship as an obstacle to the realization of Judaism's injunctions to do justice to the widow, the orphan, and the stranger. What the reformers sought was an institutional framework that could remove Jewish philanthropy from the purview of the congregations, transcend confessional differences, and unify the social welfare efforts of a religiously balkanized Jewish population. The goal, in Bogen's words, was "the separation of practical philanthropy from the Synagogue." This, he declared, "found its highest expression in the movement known as the Federation."[35]

Later in his speech, Bogen would suggest a "new possibility for real co-operation between Synagogue and Federation." His mention of this gives some indication of the prevailing state of affairs. Tension and turf battles between rabbis and social workers were common.[36] Federation volunteer and professional leaders "tried to steer apart from anything that might be considered Synagogue affiliations."[37] Using the synagogue as a foil, they had quickly come to define the new federation movement's identity via the contrast. As a result, federation was spoken of, by those involved with it, as a "secular" institution, whose professionals, for better or worse, have "no great use for the ideas for which the rabbi stands" and for whom "the synagogue is not an essential institution."[38]

The notion that the synagogue and the federation respectively represented "religious" and "secular" arms of the Jewish community, and that neither should interfere in the domain of the other, found additional grounding in the American ideal of church-state separation.[39] The equation was being drawn explicitly in the federation's earliest years. "For some time," Bogen said in 1916, "it was thought that the analogy of separating the State from religion or the school from the Church holds good in this case."[40]

The church-state analogy legitimized the federation's attempts to hold the synagogues at a distance.[41] But it did more than this, for it suggested a far broader scope of authority to which the federation might aspire. It is important to note that the analogy took hold at a time when the federation system's primary work was largely limited to the consolidation of fund-raising, the administration of allocations, and the coordination of efforts among relief agencies. Yet, once it became thinkable that the federation served in the capacity of "state" for the American Jewish community, it became thinkable that this institution could and should assume other roles and responsibilities associated with a state, such as in matters of governance, planning, defense, and diplomacy. This is precisely the direction that the system would later take. The examples given earlier of the New York Federation's 1926 community survey and the CJFWF's 1944 establishment of the NCRAC are merely illustrative of the broader dynamic that unfolded throughout the twentieth century.[42] The notion of federation as state also repositioned the philanthropic gift such that it was popularly spoken of as a "tax" levied by the Jewish community on its members.[43]

Two points here are worthy of our attention. First, in assuming a state-like role for the American Jewish community, the Jewish federation system complicates common understandings of the nature and scope of the philanthropic enterprise. Definitions of philanthropy have tended to emphasize the institutionalization of private voluntary action for the common good—an organized, collective effort as opposed to individual acts of charity or benevolence.[44] Consideration of federated Jewish philanthropy, however, makes clear that such a definition hardly succeeds in recognizing the full breadth of the phenomenon. Whatever else it may intend or accomplish, philanthropy—as an institutional sector—can also constitute a mechanism for the self-governance of religio-ethnic communities.[45] In the present case, federated philanthropy is as notable for its organization of the American Jewish community as for the many social goods that it has delivered.

Second, the power of the "state" analogy grew as the federation system took on more of a governance role, for the analogy found validation through realization. This reinforced federation leaders' tendencies to think of their relations with synagogues in terms of the American ideal of the separation of church and state. Over the course of the century, the notion of strict separation would be challenged at many points. Religious seminaries would assume responsibility for training many of the professionals who would come to staff the federations and their agencies. Recurring debates would take place decade after decade about federation funding of Jewish education and culture.[46] Notwithstanding their successes, these challenges have always been challenges. Ambivalence about the place of religion in the federation has been an enduring feature of the federation system from its beginnings and to the present day. This ambivalence is rooted, in part, in the power of an analogy to structure thought. So long as American Jews understand their federations to serve in a state-like capacity, American principles of church-state separation are likely to continue to generate ambivalence about the role that the institutions should play in the affairs typically handled within the synagogue walls.

Yet it should be clear that ambivalence is just that—a mixture of contradictory tendencies, not a singular antagonism. For all that federations have fancied themselves in the role of state, with an attendant rhetoric of secularity, they have refused to abandon fully a claim to religion. The assertion of the secular character of their enterprise was certainly a point of principle in the federations' earliest years, as the new philanthropic organizations sought to wrest control over Jewish social welfare efforts from the synagogues. By mid-century, however, federation leaders would be far less willing to relinquish the mantle of religious legitimacy to the synagogues as Bogen had relinquished it in 1916 when he suggested that "the Federation is in dire need of inspiration" and that only cooperation with the synagogue could give a "soul to the charity organization."[47] Three decades later, no external sources of inspiration or validation were needed when a celebration of the New York Federation's twenty-fifth anniversary extolled "the deep hold that the Federation institutions have on the affections and devotion of New York Jewry." All the religious legitimacy that federation required could be found within. In the words of the testimonial, the deep commitment to federation institutions

> cannot be explained by merely saying that they stand in the forefront of medical and social welfare institutions in the country, nor even that they constitute the largest network of voluntary philanthropies in the world. . . . More important than size is the spiritual meaning of Federation. . . . It is an important link, nay more, a guiding light in the way of life that we as Jews are building in America, as an expression of our deepest ideals and highest aspirations.[48]

This appropriation of a religious idiom to speak of the federation's work complicated the dichotomous framing that mapped federation and synagogues onto opposite sides of a religious-secular divide, but it certainly did not eliminate it. Indeed, the very next line of the anniversary article reasserts the federation system's old claim to transcend confessional differences and to offer unity where synagogues fostered division: "There is no reckoning how great a role this common-shared concern for our local philanthropic institutions has played in solidifying us as a group, in giving us a banner and rallying ground to which every Jew may render loyalty, whatever his walk of life or individual ideology."[49] In the decades to follow, the place of religion within the federation system would continue to evolve. Rather than bring about any resolution of the deep tensions at the heart of the enterprise, however, the changes would only add layers of complexity.

Political Activism and Religious Ritual

The American Jewish Conference on Soviet Jewry's rituals of the late 1960s, beginning with the Matzoh of Hope, signaled another convolution in the federation system's ambivalent relationship with religion. AJCSJ, it will be recalled, was the federation system's national instrumentality for mobilizing support on behalf of the oppressed Jews of the Soviet Union. Its offices and professional staff were donated by the National Community Relations Advisory Council, which itself had been created under federation auspices in 1944. As a coordinating body, the AJCSJ brought the federation system, through the NCRAC, into partnership with two dozen other national organizations, including the umbrella bodies of the Conservative, Orthodox, and Reform synagogue movements.[50] The Matzoh of Hope ritual was one fruit of this partnership, its text having been drafted by the NCRAC professional responsible for coordinating the AJCSJ, Albert Chernin, in consultation with four rabbis and lay leaders from the conference's Orthodox and Reform constituent organizations (as well as with one leader of a Labor Zionist group).[51]

The Matzoh of Hope represented a departure for the federation movement. Federations had long before abandoned the early position that held that they engaged in "secular" work while synagogues held responsibility for "religious" matters. Yet the philanthropy's claim to the Jewish religion had been premised on a notion of religion that framed it solely in ethical terms—i.e., federation work as "an expression of our deepest ideals and highest aspirations." In this religion of universal ethics and good works, which harked back to German Jewish Reform ideology of the 1800s, ritual had no standing. Rather, ritual was the aspect of Jewish religion that federation leaders had willingly left to the synagogues for one of the very same reasons that they had established the federation as separate from the synagogues in the first place. More than any disagreements about belief, it had been disagreements over proper practice that had caused the sharpest religious divisions among Jews. Although American Jews could not agree on the need to avoid pork or to worship with heads covered, they could agree that helping the poor and serving other Jews in need was a religious imperative. With the Matzoh of Hope, the federation system, through the NCRAC and the AJCSJ, broke with its tradition of bifurcating religion into separate ethical and ritual realms.

This move was possible, in part, because of broader changes in the American Jewish ethnic and religious landscape, having to do with the evolution of the Reform movement's position on ritual and the integration of Orthodox and Conservative Jews into institutions like federations. But the move occurred because a religious protest movement had arisen outside of the synagogues and the federations alike, challenging the very notion of dichotomized religious and secular realms, each housed in its own separate institution. In the movement to free Soviet Jews, the mobilization of Jewish ritual and its symbols was pioneered by the Student Struggle for Soviet Jewry (SSSJ), a New York–based grassroots organization that sought, among other things, to prod the AJCSJ to greater action.[52] In the summer of 1964, the year that both it and the AJCSJ were founded, SSSJ had organized clergy in New York City to undertake a public fast and had sounded the ram's horn (shofar) at a prayer-service-cum-protest-rally on the boardwalk outside the Democratic National Convention in Atlantic City (the same convention known in civil rights movement history for refusing to seat the integrated delegation of the Mississippi Freedom Democratic Party). In May 1965, in Manhattan, SSSJ marchers donned prayer shawls, took up Torah scrolls and shofars, and proceeded to encircle the Soviet mission to the United Nations seven times, a "Jericho march," they called it, to bring down the walls of oppression. A few weeks later, the SSSJ did the same at the Soviet embassy in Washington, D.C.

SSSJ's protests brought Jewish ritual out of the synagogues and into the streets and quickly established it as a signature form of Soviet Jewry movement protest. By expropriating Jewish ritual from the synagogue, the SSSJ redefined ritual from a religious matter that should be contained in the private sphere to a mode of Jewish political action that had a place in the civic arena.[53] This, of course, struck at the core assumptions of the ideology of separate secular and religious spheres on which the federation-synagogue division of labor was based. In this way, the SSSJ made ritual available to a federation system seeking to rally American Jews to the Soviet Jewish cause. The AJCSJ took up ritual creation with the Matzoh of Hope. Soon after, it began promoting the efforts of local federations and community relations councils to develop Soviet Jewry movement rituals associated with the holidays of Hanukkah, Rosh Hashanah, Tisha B'Av, and Simchat Torah, among others.[54]

Although the Matzoh of Hope campaign represented a departure for the federation system, in that it involved its community relations agencies directly in developing and prescribing religious ritual behavior, it also reasserted the central governance role that the federation system had traditionally claimed. Not only did the AJCSJ bring the NCRAC into partnership with the national synagogue bodies, it also enabled federation system professionals to orchestrate a remarkable cross-denominational collaboration between Reform Judaism and Orthodoxy, developing a Passover ritual that would be used by members of both denominations and by Conservative Jews as well.

With the AJCSJ's Matzoh of Hope campaigns, the federation system intervened in the private home ritual behaviors of hundreds of thousands, if not millions, of individual Jews. Through its calls to publicize the campaign in sermons from the pulpit, it also intervened in the worship services of synagogues across the nation. Ritual, once deemed purely religious, was now also a civic or political act. Yet this seeming secularization of the sacred was also a sanctification of the secular. By blurring the symbolic boundaries dividing the "religious" from the "political" and the "private" from the "public," the Matzoh of Hope campaign further eroded the already problematic distinction between religious and secular spheres that had informed the creation of the federation system.[55]

Such changes did not mean federations had finally resolved their historical ambivalences about the place of religion in their work. As noted earlier, at the same time that the AJCSJ was calling on Jews to perform the Matzoh of Hope ritual at their Passover seders, it was calibrating the ritual's script to include or exclude the holiday's central theme of exodus, depending on whether the organizational strategy of the moment was emphasizing amelioration or emigration. Had the AJCSJ been governed by a logic generated by the holiday itself, the calls for exodus would have been made irrespective of political considerations. Yet the AJCSJ's embrace of religious forms did not imply that it was prepared to embrace religious logics. Religion remained a site of tension and negotiation, as it had from the beginning and as it would continue in the years to follow.

Federation-Synagogue Relations

With the Matzoh of Hope and subsequent AJCSJ/NCRAC activities around the holidays of Hanukkah, Tisha B'Av, and Simchat Torah, the federation system became a creator and promoter of Jewish holiday ritual. Yet these activities did not necessarily inform the federation's self-understanding. Paying no heed to the forays into ritual work that it had been indirectly sponsoring on the Soviet Jewry front for the better part of a decade, the Council of Jewish Federations and Welfare Funds, in 1975, reiterated the principle that it might be "useful to distinguish between the ritualistic, private activities of the synagogue," on the one hand, and "communal or public programs," on the other.[56]

The occasion for reasserting a distinction between private ritual acts and public communal affairs and for using that distinction to define the appropriate boundaries of federation work was a report of the CJFWF's Task Force on Synagogue-Federation Relations. The fact that such a task force was created indicates that not all was smooth in the relationship. This, of course, was nothing new. The federation system's establishment in the late nineteenth century was partially an attempt to marginalize the synagogues in American Jewish social welfare efforts and to relocate this work in institutions whose guiding ethos would be that of professionalized social work and scientific philanthropy. Conflict was thus built into the relationship from the outset, and it persisted over the decades. At mid-century, federations continued to argue that synagogues placed parochial interests over the greater Jewish good and were structurally incapable of delivering social services as efficiently and effectively as the federation's professionalized agencies could. Synagogues, for their part, turned the federation system's early claims to being the secular arm of the Jewish community against it. Pointing an accusing finger at Jewish hospitals with Christmas trees in their lobbies and Jewish social service agencies that failed to maintain kosher facilities or observe the Sabbath, synagogues charged federations with a lack of commitment to Jewish values. The conflict was exacerbated by the financial stakes involved, as federations sought to enlist synagogues' help in fundraising for the annual campaign and as synagogues saw federations as competitors for their congregants' charitable dollars.[57]

Beginning slowly in the 1970s and gaining momentum in the 1990s, federation and synagogue leaders found grounds for rapprochement over shared concerns that assimilation was threatening the long-term well-being of the American Jewish community, including the viability of federations and synagogues alike. For evidence, they pointed to federation-sponsored community surveys that revealed generation-related declines in Jewish affiliation and commitment, coupled with increases in interfaith marriages, the children of which, the surveys also showed, tended not to affiliate as Jews.[58] Understanding themselves to be facing a shared problem, federations and synagogues became increasingly convinced that the key line of distinction in the American Jewish community was not the distinction between secular and religious institutional spheres but the distinction between people who maintained any type of Jewish connection and people who maintained none. In the federations, this led to the creation of "continuity commissions" charged with supporting programs to strengthen Jewish identity.[59] Some of these programs were located outside of the synagogues in camps, private schools, and Israel experience tours. Others, including preschools, youth groups, adult education programs, and family education programs, were synagogue based or involved synagogues as partners.

Over and above the programmatic and financial partnerships was a symbolic closing of the gap, with federations coming to define their mission in community-building terms that allied them with synagogues as agents of cultural preservation, cultivation, and transmission. By the first decade of the new millennium, the change in tone was such that the professional leading Boston's Combined Jewish Philanthropies would open an article on federation-synagogue partnerships by declaring that "*the synagogue* is the most critical institution in Jewish life." Drawing unapologetically on the Hebrew-language terminology of the Bible, he would go on to frame the federation's mission as working with synagogues to "transform the spiritual life of our people and create real communities of *Torah, Tzedek* and *Chesed*—learning, social justice and caring."[60]

Even this effort to articulate a new paradigm for federation-synagogue relations, however, would invoke the century-old rhetoric distinguishing between community-minded federations and turf-oriented houses of worship: "Synagogues and other gateway communities need federations to create a community of communities in order to broaden their vision, preventing them from becoming narrow and parochial. They need umbrella institutions that symbolize K'lal Yisroel, the community [of] Israel."[61] The fact that this polarity could cast shadows even on an attempt to transcend the historical divisions between federations and synagogues raises the question of why the binary has remained so salient throughout the decades.

Underlying the tensions between the two institutions, and indeed a main source of their persistence, is an interplay between social structure and symbolic structures. Federations and synagogues exist as two autonomous institutional spheres. Because the institutional field has a dichotomous structure, it enables and even encourages people to think about institutions as standing in opposition to one another and as representing opposite sides of conceptual pairs. The binaries of parochial/communal, religious/secular, and spiritual/technical have been mapped onto the synagogue/federation dichotomy, with synagogues associated with the parochial, religious, and spiritual and federations with the communal, secular, and technical. Needless to say, such conceptual binaries are not simply reflections of an objective reality; rather, they are also acts of mental boundary work, undertaken precisely because the reality is not neatly divided in two. The attempt to make complex reality conform to an either/or model is inherently problematic and inevitably doomed to fall short of the work it is being called on to do. Yet it is the default approach because of the social fact that two institutional structures thought about them in terms of binary oppositions.

This is the structural-conceptual trap that has plagued attempts to set federation-synagogue relations on a more constructive footing. For decades, many people have tried to pronounce the problem away, declaring the secular-religious split to be a false dichotomy. In 1996, the federation system's Jewish Education Service of North America put out a 120-page report calling for a "closer and more encompassing partnership" between the institutions. "Until fairly recently," it said, "synagogues were perceived as 'denominational' and 'religious,' federations as 'communal' and 'secular.'"[62] This perception had persisted, notwithstanding the declaration a full two decades earlier by the 1975 CJFWF Task Force on Synagogue-Federation Relations that "the designation of the relationship in terms of secular versus religious is a false issue. Federation and its agencies are expressions of Jewish religious impulses."[63] Even there, however, one may ask why, three decades after the 1944 *American Jewish Year Book* celebrated the "spiritual meaning of Federation . . . as an expression of our deepest ideals and highest aspirations," the 1975 task force could not simply take the federation's religious character for granted.[64] In part, the answer is that there were voices in both the federation system and the synagogues that persisted in affirming the federation system's early self-designation as "secular." More than this, however, the secular label has had to be disowned repeatedly, generation after generation, rather than only once, because the notion of the federation's secular character is rooted not in its activities or ethos but in its relational position as the opposite element to the synagogue in the federation-synagogue pair. So long as synagogues and federations exist as two autonomous institutional spheres, it is likely that the binary concept of religious versus secular will continue to structure discourse about their relationship.

The Civil Religion Thesis

For most of the twentieth century, federation leaders' claims that their community chest organization played a governance role in American Jewish life had served to legitimize a policy of nonintervention in matters religious, a policy modeled consciously on the American paradigm of church-state separation. In the 1970s, however, the notion of philanthropy as a governance system was taken up and elaborated by scholars in dialogue with that era's new work in the sociology of religion, resulting in a novel alternative perspective on the religion-state relationship being inserted into Jewish communal discourse.

In 1976, political scientist Daniel Elazar published *Community and Polity: The Organizational Dynamics of American Jewry*. As its title suggests, this book, seminal in its field, theorized the network of American Jewish nonprofit organizations as a political system that allocated resources, managed conflict, and organized collective action. In this polity, Elazar argued, the local charitable federations provide "the most clear-cut examples of government-like institutions in the American Jewish community."[65] Elazar's argument was picked up by Jonathan Woocher, a sociologist active on the federation scene, who combined it with Robert Bellah's contention that political systems can

Shared religious values

find legitimation through a "civil religion" that ascribes transcendent significance to the secular political order. The notion of civil religion had been introduced by Bellah in a 1967 article. It quickly became an influential critique of the secularization thesis, which had long argued that modernity's disenchantment of the world entailed the retreat of religion into the institutional realm of the church (and a weakened church, at that). Drawing on Émile Durkheim's conception of religion as beliefs and practices around shared symbols that sustain social order by uniting people into a moral community, Bellah made a compelling case for the "religious" underpinnings of "secular" political orders. But as these religious dimensions of political life were concerned with the meaning of political institutions rather than with questions of God, existence, and the nature of the universe, he suggested the term "civil religion" to indicate its delimited scope.[66]

With Elazar suggesting that the federation was the governing agency of an American Jewish polity, and with Bellah suggesting that polities find legitimation in a civil religion that expresses the transcendent meaning of the political order, Woocher reasoned that the federation system might find legitimation in an institutionally grounded "civil Judaism" that was distinct from traditional Judaism.[67] In his 1986 book, *Sacred Survival: The Civil Religion of American Jews,* Woocher looked to the rhetoric, calendar, and activities of Jewish federations to identify what he called the major tenets of a civil Jewish faith that asserted the transcendent meaning of the federation system and its work. Foremost among these tenets were the interconnected moral imperatives of Jewish unity, mutual responsibility, and Jewish survival in a post-Holocaust world.[68] These articles of faith were buttressed by core myths, especially the ashes-to-redemption narrative that moved from the depths of the Nazi annihilation to the heights of national resurrection in a sovereign State of Israel. "The myth of 'Holocaust to rebirth' is," Woocher wrote, "a myth of life triumphant over death, and the civil religion has used the power of its imagery to mobilize Jews for the tasks it deems to be life-giving."[69] Civil Judaism also mobilized Jews through the rituals that it offered. Mission trips to Israel and to other sites of the federation's overseas work, the annual campaign "with its banquets and speakers, card calling and phonathons," leadership retreats, and the annual pilgrimage of thousands of donors, volunteers, and professionals to the Council of Jewish Federations' General Assembly all served as opportunities for American Jews to express and reinforce their commitment to the federation's values and mission.[70]

Woocher was insistent on the fundamentally religious character of this interlocking system of beliefs, myths, and rituals. Although it made no particular claims about God, it drew from the deepest wells of religious sensibility:

> The structure is built out of classic polarities—between Jew and non-Jew, survival and disappearance, community and individual, exceptionalism and normality, renewal and destruction, life and death. The dynamic is one of passage—from passivity to activity, from victim to maker of history, from death-witness to life-giver. Civil Judaism is a religion of tensions recognized, confronted, held in the balance, and thereby transcended.[71]

Civil Judaism, Woocher asserted, was not "a Judaism of the home, the synagogue and the school" but, rather, a "Judaism of the historical-political arena, of an elaborated polity and of public activism."[72]

By taking the federation seriously as the bearer of an authentic religious meaning system, Woocher reframed the issue of federation-synagogue relations. What was commonly thought of as a conflict between two domains, religious and secular, might be better understood, Woocher suggested, as a conflict between two alternative forms of Jewish religious expression:

> Civil Judaism legitimates a way of being Jewish and a program of Jewish activity within which the role of the synagogue and the rabbinate—the life of study, prayer, and ritual observance—are no longer primary. . . . [T]here are other *mitzvot* [religious commandments] equally sacred for the Jew. The federation campaign lends its own rhythm to the Jewish year. . . . Service on federation or agency boards, attending to the urgent needs of the Jewish people, takes on the character of a sacred calling. "We Are One" [the federation's slogan] becomes a more immediate and compelling watchword than "*Hashem echad*" ("the Lord is One").[73]

Conclusion

What does consideration of the Jewish federation system have to offer to a broader conversation about religious philanthropy in America? If nothing else, it offers the service of problematizing taken-for-granted notions about the two key terms at the heart of the conversation and about their relationship. For here we have a Jewish philanthropy that wrestles with the question of whether it is a religious enterprise, or a secular one, or a civil religious one, or one that enacts religious values but eschews religious rituals, or that embraces religious rituals only to the extent that it can keep their commanding power in check, and so on. We also have here an instance in which philanthropy is not thought of simply as an effort to mobilize private action to serve the public good but is understood explicitly as the basis for managing the politics of a voluntary ethnoreligious community. Raising and distributing funds and serving populations in need are only a partial aspect of what Jewish federations do and, from some perspectives, hardly the most important aspect.[74]

It is not coincidental that the case of the Jewish federations raises questions not about one term alone in the phrase "religious philanthropy" but about both, for the problematics of the one are linked to those of the other. Insofar as American Jewish philanthropic institutions have come to serve as agents of communal governance, their state-like role has been deeply implicated in the complexities of the "religious question" within these organizations. In the American Jewish case, the notion that the federation serves as a state-like governing body has led even to the contradictory outcomes of asserting the fundamentally *secular* character of the federation (per the analogy, "synagogue is to federation as church is to state") and of asserting the fundamentally *religious* character of the federation (per the civil religion thesis). Whereas the former posits a religious/secular divide, the latter transcends it.

For more than a century, ambivalence over the place of religion in the philanthropic enterprise has been a defining tension within the Jewish federation system. Although recent federation discourse has sought to reconcile the tension or to minimize its significance, such a tendency is better seen as a reflection and product of the tension than as a sign that the federation is somehow escaping it. The ambivalence over religion has structural roots that are intimately connected with the federation's governance role and its existence as an institutional sphere separate and distinct from the synagogues. So long as these structural features remain in place, the federations are likely to continue to struggle with difficult questions about the role of religion in American Jewish philanthropy.

Notes

The author wishes to thank Tom Davis, Deborah Dash Moore, Richard Pitt, Laurence Kotler-Berkowitz, the Berman Jewish Policy Archive, and the participants in the October 2010 conference on religion and philanthropy at IUPUI.

1. Israel Miller to Member Organizations, memorandum, "Matzoh of Hope," March 15, 1967, National Conference on Soviet Jewry Records, I-181/1/2, American Jewish Historical Society, Center for Jewish History, New York.

2. By "nondenominational," I mean not affiliated with the Orthodox, Conservative, or Reform branches within American Judaism.

3. American Jewish Conference on Soviet Jewry, "In the Name of Humanity . . . ," *New York Times,* April 17, 1970, 26, emphasis added.

4. Albert D. Chernin, "Making Soviet Jews an Issue: A History," in *A Second Exodus: The American Movement to Free Soviet Jews,* ed. Murray Friedman and Albert D. Chernin (Hanover, N.H.: Brandeis University Press, 1999), 54–56; Edward R. Drachman, *Challenging the Kremlin: The Soviet Jewish Movement for Freedom, 1967–1990* (New York: Paragon House, 1992), 179–95; Fred A. Lazin, *The Struggle for Soviet Jewry in American Politics: Israel versus the American Jewish Establishment* (Lanham, Md.: Lexington Books, 2005), 32.

5. The umbrella organization has been restructured several times over the past century. For most of the twentieth century, it was known as the Council of Jewish Federations and Welfare Funds, or just the Council of Jewish Federations (CJF).

6. In the past, some communities held separate campaigns for local and overseas needs. The federations supported the network of local agencies, and the United Jewish Appeal (UJA) supported Israel and Jewish communities abroad. In 1999, the CJF merged with the UJA to form the United Jewish Communities, now known as JFNA.

7. Annual reports of the United Jewish Communities and the Jewish Federations of North America are available at www.jfna.org.

8. Harry L. Lurie, *A Heritage Affirmed: The Jewish Federation Movement in America* (Philadelphia: Jewish Publication Society of America, 1961), 39–41; Daniel J. Elazar, *Community and Polity: The Organizational Dynamics of American Jewry,* rev. ed. (Philadelphia, Pa.: Jewish Publication Society of America, 1995), 212–17.

9. Jewish Federations of North America, "About the Jewish Federations of North America," 2011, www.jewishfederations.org/section.aspx?id=31.

10. The federation system predates the introduction of "scientific" philanthropy by foundations such as those of Rockefeller, Carnegie, and Sage. Although it shares a rationalizing thrust, in its origins, the federation system is better understood as an attempt to coordinate "traditional distributive philanthropy" than as an effort to reimagine the philanthropic enterprise wholesale. Judith Sealander, "Curing Evils at Their Source: The Arrival of Scientific Giving," in *Charity, Philanthropy, and Civility in American History*, ed. Lawrence J. Friedman and Mark D. McGarvie (New York: Cambridge University Press, 2003), 225.

11. Lurie, *A Heritage Affirmed*, 30–32.

12. Ibid., 44–49; Daniel J. Elazar, *Community and Polity: The Organizational Dynamics of American Jewry* (Philadelphia: Jewish Publication Society of America, 1976), 160–62.

13. Elazar, *Community and Polity* (1976), 86–87. Elazar's writings on Jewish federalism tended toward the essentialistic, reading the biblical narratives of Sinai and the twelve tribes as history and claiming that this established a Jewish political culture that manifested itself more or less consistently throughout the ages. One need not accept the claim of a transhistorical Jewish penchant for federalism to recognize the applicability of the federalist label to the case of the American Jewish philanthropic community chests.

14. B. M. Selekman, "The Federation in the Changing American Scene," *American Jewish Year Book* 36 (1934–1935), www.ajcarchives.org.

15. The use of the term *polity* follows Daniel Elazar. See note 45.

16. Boris D. Bogen, "The Federation and the Synagogue," *Bulletin of the National Conference of Jewish Charities* 6, no. 6 (1916): 88, www.bjpa.org/Publications/details.cfm?PublicationID=1536.

17. Selekman, "The Federation in the Changing American Scene," 87.

18. Deborah Dash Moore, *At Home in America: Second Generation New York Jews* (New York: Columbia University Press, 1981), 165.

19. At the time, ethnic differences based on country of origin were still the basis of important lines of division separating Jews in America from one another. To speak of the population in the early twentieth century as "Jewish Americans"—as if they constituted a single ethnic group—is somewhat anachronistic.

20. Moore, *At Home in America*, 148–74, esp. 162–72.

21. Jewish immigration to the United States came in several waves, each from different parts of the diaspora. When Russian and Polish Jews began arriving *en masse* in the 1880s, they found an established Jewish American community comprised mostly of Jews of German descent. The bulk of the German Jewish immigration took place from the 1820s to 1850s. That population experienced rapid acculturation and economic mobility.

22. Ralph Segalman, "Community Organization in the Small Jewish Community," *Jewish Social Service Quarterly* 22, no. 2 (1945), www.bjpa.org/Publications/details.cfm?PublicationID=5745.

23. Selekman, "The Federation in the Changing American Scene," 79–80.

24. In the 1970s, the word "Jewish" was added to the organization's name (National Jewish Community Relations Advisory Council). In 1997, NJCRAC was renamed the Jewish Council for Public Affairs.

25. Joshua Trachtenberg, "Religious Activities," *American Jewish Year Book* 46 (1944–1945): 97–98, www.ajcarchives.org; Harry L. Lurie, "Jewish Social Welfare," *American Jewish Year Book* 47 (1945–1946): 261, www.ajcarchives.org; American Jewish Committee, "Thirty-Eighth Annual Report," *American Jewish Year Book* 47 (1945): 680–81, www.ajcarchives.org; Louis J. Segal, "Jewish Community Relations," *Jewish Social Service Quarterly* 24, no. 1 (1947), www.bjpa.org/Publications/details.cfm?PublicationID=6015.

26. Quoted in Jonathan S. Woocher, *Sacred Survival: The Civil Religion of American Jews* (Bloomington: Indiana University Press, 1986), 53, emphasis added.

27. Elazar, *Community and Polity* (1976), 181; Woocher, *Sacred Survival.*

28. Quoted in Stephen J. Whitfield, "In Defense of Diversity: Jewish Thought from Assimilationism to Cultural Pluralism," in *Charity, Philanthropy, and Civility in American History,* 301, emphasis in Whitfield.

29. Elazar, *Community and Polity,* rev. ed., 408.

30. United Jewish Communities, *2008 United Jewish Communities Annual Report: The Voice of One. The Power of Many* (New York: United Jewish Communities, 2008), http://www.bjpa.org/Publications/details.cfm?PublicationID=3808.

31. For good treatments of the federation system's crisis of confidence, see Gary A. Tobin, "Talking Truth about Jewish Federations" (San Francisco: Institute for Jewish and Community Research, 2007), www.jewishresearch.org/PDFs/FederationPolicyPaper.pdf; and Jack Wertheimer, "Current Trends in American Jewish Philanthropy," *American Jewish Year Book* 97 (1997), www.ajcarchives.org.

32. Egon Mayer, "Intergenerational Philanthropic Slippage: The Case of Children of Major Jewish Philanthropic Families in New York City," in *Contemporary Jewish Philanthropy in America,* ed. Barry Kosmin and Paul Ritterband (Savage, Md.: Rowman and Littlefield, 1991).

33. Shaul Kelner, *Tours That Bind: Diaspora, Pilgrimage, and Israeli Birthright Tourism* (New York: New York University Press, 2010), 39–44; Jeffrey R. Solomon, "Jewish Foundations" (Jerusalem, Israel: Center for the Study of Philanthropy in Israel, Hebrew University of Jerusalem, 2008), www.sw.huji.ac.il/upload/Salomon2008_foundations.pdf (in Hebrew); Gary A. Tobin, "The Transition of Communal Values and Behavior in Jewish Philanthropy" (San Francisco: Institute for Jewish and Community Research, 2001), www.jewishresearch.org/PDFs/Transition_Phil_2001.pdf.

34. Bogen, "The Federation and the Synagogue," 87.

35. Ibid.

36. George Fox, "The Rabbi as Social Worker," *Bulletin of the National Conference of Jewish Charities* 4, no. 4 (1913), www.bjpa.org/Publications/details.cfm?PublicationID=1424; "Religion and Social Work," *Bulletin of the National Conference of Jewish Charities* 4, no. 4 (1913), www.bjpa.org/Publications/details.cfm?PublicationID=69.

37. Bogen, "The Federation and the Synagogue," 88.

38. "Religion and Social Work."

39. Moore, *At Home in America,* 151.

40. Bogen, "The Federation and the Synagogue," 88.

41. Hasia R. Diner, "Jewish Self-Governance, American Style," *American Jewish History* 81, nos. 3–4 (1994): 281–82.

42. NCRAC and its constituents work in the areas of defense and diplomacy. Defense need not imply the use of physical force. Typically, Jewish Americans have fought anti-Semitism through the legal system, the court of public opinion, and through recourse to law enforcement.

43. Wertheimer, "Current Trends in American Jewish Philanthropy," 14.

44. Lawrence J. Friedman, "Philanthropy in America: Historicism and Its Discontents," in *Charity, Philanthropy, and Civility in American History,* 6–8; Peter Dobkin Hall, "The History of Religious Philanthropy in America," in *Faith and Philanthropy in America: Exploring the Role of Religion in America's Voluntary Sector,* ed. Robert Wuthnow and Virginia A. Hodgkinson (San Francisco: Jossey-Bass, 1990).

45. This was the insight upon which political scientist Daniel Elazar built his oeuvre. The representative works of his scholarship are Elazar, *Community and Polity;* and Daniel J. Elazar, *People and Polity: The Organizational Dynamics of World Jewry* (Detroit: Wayne State University Press, 1989).

46. Lurie, *A Heritage Affirmed;* Gary Rosenblatt, "The Life and Death of a Dream," *Baltimore Jewish Times,* November 7, 1980; Elazar, *Community and Polity,* rev. ed., 270; Barry Shrage, "Sacred Communities at the Heart of Jewish Life: 20 Years of Federation/Synagogue Collaboration and Change in Boston," *Agenda: Jewish Education* 15 (2002), www.bjpa.org/Publications/details.cfm?PublicationID=950.

47. Bogen, "The Federation and the Synagogue," 89.

48. George Z. Medalie, "New York Federation—after Twenty-Five Years," *American Jewish Year Book* 45 (1944): 133–34, www.ajcarchives.org. See also Moore, *At Home in America*, 151.

49. Medalie, "New York Federation," 133–34.

50. AJCSJ was not unique in this sense. NCRAC itself included among its founding members the Reform movement's Central Conference of American Rabbis.

51. Israel Miller to Constituent Organizations of the AJCSJ, "Project re 'Matzoh of Oppression,'" February 18, 1966, National Jewish Community Relations Advisory Council Records, I-172/86/8–10, American Jewish Historical Society, Center for Jewish History, New York.

52. Jacob Birnbaum to Abraham Joshua Heschel, letter, November 22, 1965, personal papers of Jacob Birnbaum.

53. Shaul Kelner, "Ritualized Protest and Redemptive Politics: Cultural Consequences of the American Mobilization to Free Soviet Jewry," *Jewish Social Studies* 14, no. 3 (2008): 1–37.

54. Shaul Kelner, "Social Movements and Ritual Innovation: The Ritual Cycle of the American Mobilization for Soviet Jewry," in *Jewish Cultural Studies*, vol. 3: *Revisioning Ritual: Jewish Traditions in Transition*, ed. Simon Bronner (Oxford: Littman Library of Jewish Civilization, 2011), 360–91.

55. Kelner, "Ritualized Protest and Redemptive Politics."

56. Draft Guidelines, Task Force on Synagogue-Federation Relations, Council of Jewish Federations and Welfare Funds, quoted in Ted Kanner, "Federation and Synagogue: A New Partnership for a New Time," *Journal of Jewish Communal Service* 53, no. 1 (1976): 23.

57. National Conference of Jewish Communal Service Committee on Public Issues, "Respective Roles of Synagogal and Other Jewish Agencies," *Journal of Jewish Communal Service* 40, no. 2 (1963), www.bjpa.org/Publications/details.cfm?PublicationID=5339; Isaac Trainin, "Federation and Synagogue Relationships," *Journal of Jewish Communal Service* 34 (Summer 1958).

58. Barry A. Kosmin et al., *Highlights of the C.J.F. 1990 National Jewish Population Survey* (New York: Council of Jewish Federations, 1991); Sylvia Barack Fishman, *Double or Nothing? Jewish Families and Mixed Marriage* (Hanover, N.H.: Brandeis University Press, 2004), 6–7.

59. Federations had been supporting Jewish education since the 1910s and 1920s, but it was frequently a point of contention, raising concerns about the proper scope of federation responsibilities. By the 1940s, federations were directing approximately 10 percent of their allocations to Jewish education, typically to an umbrella Bureau of Jewish Education. The proportion of monies directed to Jewish education doubled in the 1970s and rose to approximately 25 percent in the 1980s. Lurie, *A Heritage Affirmed*, 73–75, 200, 206–207; David Shluker, "The Federation and Jewish Education," *Journal of Jewish Communal Service* 72, nos. 1–2 (1995); Wertheimer, "Current Trends in American Jewish Philanthropy."

60. Shrage, "Sacred Communities at the Heart of Jewish Life," 3–4, emphasis added.

61. Ibid., 12.

62. David Saperstein et al., "Planning for Jewish Continuity: Synagogue-Federation Collaboration: A Handbook" (New York: Jewish Education Service of North America, 1996), 11, http://www.bjpa.org/Publications/details.cfm?PublicationID=2457.

63. Quoted in Kanner, "Federation and Synagogue," 23.

64. Medalie, "New York Federation," 133–34.

65. Elazar, *Community and Polity* (1976), 180.

66. Robert N. Bellah, "Civil Religion in America," *Daedalus* 96 (1967); Émile Durkheim, *The Elementary Forms of Religious Life*, trans. Karen E. Fields (New York: Free Press, 1995); Charles S. Liebman and Eliezer Don-Yehiya, *Civil Religion in Israel: Traditional Judaism and Political Culture in the Jewish State* (Berkeley: University of California Press, 1983), 4–5, 240n8, 240n10; James A. Mathisen, "Twenty Years after Bellah: Whatever Happened to American Civil Religion?" *Sociological Analysis* 50, no. 2 (1989): 129–46.

67. Woocher, *Sacred Survival*.

68. Ibid., 67–76.

69. Ibid., 135.
70. Ibid., 146–55.
71. Ibid., 155.
72. Ibid., 160.
73. Ibid., 163.
74. In one policy paper, serving populations in need was mentioned as a "basic value" of Jewish philanthropy but not as one of its main purposes. Rather, these purposes concerned such things as cultivating communal leadership and building bridges to other ethno-religious communities. The paper indicates the extent to which latent functions have been redefined as manifest ones. Tobin, "The Transition of Communal Values and Behavior in Jewish Philanthropy," 14–18.

3 The Price of Success

The Impact of News on Religious Identity and Philanthropy

Diane Winston

THE SALVATION ARMY'S current scale of operations and degree of respectability bear little resemblance to the circumstances of its modest start in London's slums, a transformation due as much to the Army's portrayal by the press as to its natural evolution as a religious movement. Founder William Booth launched the Christian Mission in 1865; thirteen years later, when he changed his organization's name to the Salvation Army, Booth was already known as "the General." Drawing on the prestige of the British military, he repurposed its trappings for a spiritual mission: "officers" (clergy) wore uniforms and preached to "soldiers" (laypeople) who practiced "knee drills" (prayers). A living metaphor, the Army's goal was to conquer the world for Christ, first mounting campaigns across Great Britain, then launching overseas invasions. Willing to try anything to reach the unchurched, Booth encouraged women to preach while male soldiers played barroom tunes on brass instruments. Troops engaged in street "warfare," "occupied" high-profile public spaces, and "invaded" dens of iniquity to save sinners. Deemed unchristian by conventional churchgoers, Booth's innovations sparked angry sermons, censorious editorials, and rowdy protests.

The General did not care about criticism as long as his methods gained attention. His single goal was to save souls, but he soon saw that sensational antics by themselves offered little succor to people who were hungry and homeless. According to Salvationist lore, Booth's commitment to social outreach began when he discovered a knot of homeless men sleeping beneath London Bridge. Appalled by this stark evidence of poverty's toll, the General ordered Bramwell Booth, his son and second-in-command, to "do something." Although the tale is apocryphal, it points to a larger truth about the Army's humanitarian mission: It is the manifestation of what Booth called "practical religion," a Christian response to human need.

The Army's entwined commitment to service and salvation manifests its understanding of a biblically based evangelical theology. Yet balancing and reconciling these two goals has been an almost constant challenge to its mission and identity. Early on, some members of Booth's inner circle expressed concern that the social side could overwhelm the spiritual. Others pressed for a bold religious program to reform the social sector. This debate did not remain internal to the Army. In the early twentieth century, some critics complained that money raised for material relief actually went to spiritual programs. Others said religious messages crept into what were supposed to be secular social services. Still others lamented that those social programs were rendered without any spiritual substance at all.

Did the Army, as some of its own members have charged, sell its birthright for a bowl of porridge (in this case, a present-day $3 billion budget)?[1] Or did it escape the fate of other nineteenth-century legacy institutions—the Women's Christian Temperance Union and the Young Men's Christian Association, for example—by evolving in ways that honor but update its core values? This essay suggests a third option. The Army's public identity is, in part, shaped by news depictions that reflect contemporaneous notions of religion and philanthropy. In the feedback loop of modern life, some of these notions, in turn, have colored the Army's self-perception and subsequent media strategies. But over the past century, its fundamental mission and identity have remained consistent with its evangelical roots, even when these have been hidden in plain sight.

For much of the twentieth century, news and entertainment media portrayed the Army as a highly regarded charitable philanthropy.[2] Before the 1910s, the Army had not always received positive press; religious and civic leaders roundly condemned its aggressive street-corner evangelism. Writing about women recruits in 1892, the *New York Times* opined, "Whoever joins the Salvation Army from the nature of the case bids good-bye to respectability."[3] But public opinion shifted as a result of the Army's relief work during the 1900 Galveston hurricane, the 1906 San Francisco earthquake, and World War I. The new perception was that the Army embodied an activist faith that put deeds before creeds. News stories identified the movement as "religious" in the 1920s and 1930s, but there were few references to its evangelical fervor. Mention of the Army's religiosity continued to decline through the mid-decades of the century, but the pattern shifted in the 1960s and 1970s. As religion increasingly became part of American public life, the Army's Christian character reemerged as an aspect of news coverage. By the dawn of the twenty-first century, the movement's evangelical commitments often *were* the news.

Would attention to its conservative beliefs jeopardize the Army's success as a charitable fund-raiser? For almost a century, public acceptance was predicated on the assumption that, notwithstanding its name, the Salvation Army did not compel clients to follow or even learn about its brand of militant evangelicalism. In the early 1900s, Salvationist leaders cultivated a nonsectarian image to woo the media and win public support. But by 2000, domestic and international events had propelled religion to the top of the news agenda, and the Army's faith-based mission and identity became part of a public debate over the role of religion in civil society—including the delivery of social services.

Seeking to tease out the complicated relationships between religion and philanthropy as well as the impact of the news media on religious philanthropy, this essay uses the Salvation Army as a case study. Moving back and forth between Army history and news coverage, it draws on the *New York Times* and the *Washington Post*—two preeminent national newspapers with slightly different orientations—to examine press representations of the movement. The essay begins with a short overview of the Army's history that contextualizes its notion of "practical religion." In the wake of World War I and the growing reality of pluralism, practical religion's emphasis on deeds over creeds was an apt formulation for a public Christianity. Salvationist leaders, despite their staunch evangelical faith, did not contradict this representation since it drove positive press coverage of the Army. Over the next several decades, the Army allowed its evangelical commitments to be downplayed to the public at large. That began to change significantly in the 1960s when Salvationists' conservative faith increasingly clashed with changing social mores as well as new government regulations, which they were obliged to uphold as recipients of public funds for social services. This essay focuses on the Army's evolving image in the last third of the twentieth century, when the era's contentious debates over the role of religion in public life brought fresh attention to the Army's evangelical commitments. In conclusion, it considers whether or not the Army's mission and message have remained constant over and against shifting media representations.

Practical Religion

William Booth first experimented with practical religion in the early 1870s, opening a string of inexpensive food shops to serve London's poor and working classes. But the enterprise proved costly to sustain, and he was forced to close the shops. After rechristening his mission "The Salvation Army," the group continued its focus on soul saving, but leaders took small steps to reintroduce a social program. In the 1880s, when the Army set up its first Training College for officers, Booth's daughter Emma took female "cadets" to work in the London slums. Rather than aggressively proselytize residents, the young women lived among them, seeking to win their trust through acts of compassion and service. Emma's younger sister Evangeline did likewise, opening a "hospital" for broken toys in the city's poorest neighborhood and posing as a flower seller to learn more about her neighbors' plight.

By 1890, William Booth decided a more systematic approach was needed to combat the problem of urban poverty, and he authored *In Darkest England and the Way Out.* Booth likely was inspired and assisted by Frank Smith, an Army officer and disciple of Henry George, and W. T. Stead, a crusading journalist. *In Darkest England,* which sold 115,000 copies in its first year, proposed the establishment of urban "salvage stations" to teach employment skills to the "down-and-out," as the Army called the poor. Once prepared for work, clients would (Salvationists hoped) find God before shipping out to farm colonies in rural England and overseas. The plan was never put into practice, but three short-lived, domestic farm colonies were attempted in the United States. The Army did set up a complex network of social services, including shelters, soup kitchens, salvage centers, hospitals, employment centers, and rescue homes, first in England and then worldwide.

After seeding the Army throughout Great Britain, Booth turned to overseas conquest. When a young soldier's family sailed for Philadelphia in 1880, the General gave tacit approval to starting a branch in the United States. Following the family's small successes, he sent an eight-member party to invade. Similar to its initial reception in England, the Army irked American clergy as well as local citizens. Its raucous parading, street-corner revivals, and female preachers were excoriated, as were its interracial worship services. Landing parties in continental Europe and India met similar resistance. Salvationists were jailed, jostled, and jeered worldwide. In response, officers went native, adopting local customs and cultivating indigenous leaders to offset criticism. When direct evangelism faltered, Army missionaries offered social services to their target population. Their plan was to establish a beachhead; by addressing material needs, they hoped to gain acceptance and create trust. This was practical religion in action since, for Salvationists, evangelical and humanitarian efforts were complementary. But both secular and religious critics were skeptical. Albeit with different motives, they accused the Army of siphoning contributions for social work into missionary efforts.

In the United States, Booth's son and daughter-in-law—Ballington and Maud, head of the American forces from 1887 to 1896—began a modest outreach program. In 1889, following the example of her sister-in-law Emma, Maud organized a brigade of "slum sisters" to minister in New York City's tenements. Lest they alienate the people whom they wished to serve, the young women wore plain clothes instead of Army uniforms; many slum dwellers were Jewish and Catholic immigrants who might have felt antipathy for Protestant missionaries. Others, including native-born Protestants, might dislike the Army's brand of militant Christianity. The slum sisters did not discuss religion unless they were asked about their motivation to serve. They trusted that their work would bear spiritual fruit, believing their presence itself was a ministry.

Not everyone was pleased by the development of the Army's social wing. Some Salvationists felt it was a distraction from their evangelical task. Catherine Booth, William's wife and the "Army mother," accepted the new direction with reservations. According to historian Norman Murdoch, she felt that "soup and soap were, at best, ancillary to soul saving. Catherine died in 1890; had she lived longer, she might have shared others' concerns about the gap between the Army's spiritual and its social work."[4] When George Scott Railton, Catherine's protégé and a member of the Army's inner circle, publicly criticized the social program, William Booth banished him to a series of small Army outposts.

During the 1897 depression, the Army opened a women's shelter in New York City that welcomed anyone who needed a bed. A few months later, Salvationist leaders established a men's shelter nearby, and they announced plans for housing the needy nationwide. The Army required a minimal fee or a few hours' work from those who had little or no money and encouraged "guests" to attend the nightly worship service. Proponents of scientific philanthropy, a school of thought that divided the deserving from the undeserving poor, opposed Army "hand-outs." From their perspective, the Army's activities reflected the worst kind of religious sentimentality: providing unsystematic aid in the hope of saving souls. But Salvationists believed their methods allowed the poor to retain their God-given dignity and improved their chances for redemption.

Salvationists knew they needed to appear "religious" as opposed to "evangelical" since contributors might not share their faith commitments. Describing their work to journalists, they stressed their intention to provide aid regardless of race, religion, or nationality, a message that enabled the Army to expand its philanthropic network with funding primarily from private donors. In 1902, Salvationists first received money from New York City when Frederick Booth-Tucker, a son-in-law of the General, requested support for work with "fallen women." Booth-Tucker reasoned that the Army deserved funding because it kept the women from becoming public charges.

The Army's profile rose significantly during World War I. Serving American troops overseas, "Sallies"—Army women who staffed hospitality huts in France—turned skeptics into supporters. The Army sent both women and men to the frontlines, but the Sallies were the troops' delight; they baked, sewed, and "mothered" the men. They also held religious services for those who wished to sing hymns and recite prayers. But their greatest ministry was day-to-day service. Wrote one correspondent, "They let the work of their hands do most of the preaching without ever for an instant forgetting that there's a big idea somewhere that inspires them."[5]

The Army's war work exemplified "practical religion." It responded to human needs, relying on action rather than words. After the war, Army leaders raised money more easily than before. They were no longer accused of diverting funds for proselytizing. Rather, community leaders, trusting them to get a job done, pressed them into service. Army leaders did not see their newfound popularity as a threat to their mission. As the movement's social service journal noted, anyone "who would understand the Salvation Army must first realize that its uncompromising aim is the salvation of souls."[6] According to Army historian Edward McKinley, even as Army officers pioneered new forms of social outreach, they recognized the need "for centering every welfare program on Christ."[7]

During the 1920s, the Army was one of the nation's most respected charities. When the Depression hit, its national network of services positioned the Army as an early provider of aid. Even after the federal government started its own outreach, it frequently partnered with the Army, which was caring for 20 percent of the homeless and transient population nationwide. By early 1933, Salvationists were giving New Yorkers 100,000 meals and 25,000 lodgings free of charge each week. When the city ran out of beds, it asked the Army to provide more, and when coffee stations were needed around town, municipal leaders turned to the Army for assistance. Still, throughout the 1930s and 1940s, Army funds were overwhelmingly from private sources.

The Price of Success

Grateful for the Army's help in the Depression and its work with the USO in wartime, private funders gave even more generously during the post–World War II boom. The increase in funds combined with the professionalization of social work had a significant impact on the organization. As programs expanded, so did the number of lay staff: Between 1951 and 1961, the number of non-Salvationist clerical and social workers doubled. Within a movement based on the link between belief and action, this new development troubled some. Similarly, some Salvationists saw the expansion of government funds for social service delivery, a trend that started in the 1960s and ballooned in the 1970s, as problematic since the monies came with strings—in the guise of regulations—attached.

The Army's reputation—as a service provider, an honest steward, and an efficient charity—made it a favored recipient for government grants. William Booth believed tainted money, given by public or private sources, was washed clean in God's service, an assumption that George Bernard Shaw ridiculed in *Major Barbara*. Just as Shaw's heroine questioned the wisdom of taking donations from distillers and munitions manufacturers, some Salvationists wondered if government funding would have deleterious effects. Accepting it entailed liabilities: Local and federal agencies wanted to control the programs they financed while Salvationists were accustomed to overseeing their own mix of religion and social service. Moreover, since the First Amendment was widely interpreted as prohibiting any federal funds for religious activity, Salvationists were asked to separate the religious from the social aspects of their work. This meant calculating how much office space, utilities, and staff time went into each—a requirement that undermined the holistic principles of Salvationist theology. Through the 1950s and 1960s, Army service providers and their government overseers hammered out the details, but their negotiations were not considered news.

Over the long run, the Army's desire to serve proved stronger than its members' concerns about secularizing influences. With government assistance, Salvationists either began or expanded work in probation supervision, low-cost housing, nutritional services, day care, and drug rehabilitation. Seeking to maintain their autonomy and confirm their primary mission, Army leaders issued a statement in 1972 that reaffirmed the corps officers' commitment. "There is nothing inconsistent about the Army receiving governmental funds so long as it would require neither denial of its Christian incentive nor a compromise of its evangelical intention."

Evaluating whether or not Salvationists compromised their identity is difficult since the historical record is unclear. On the one hand, the Army appeared to accept government regulations mandating strict church-state separation. On the other hand, the Army regularly acknowledged in statements for donors as well as communication to membership that it was committed to its evangelical mission. A 1981 internal communiqué mandated that government or private agencies contracting with the Army must be made aware that it is "an international religious and military movement" and "a branch of the Christian church." Reading between the lines indicates that the Army often improvised, seeking to balance faith commitments with federal requirements.

Still, as Army leaders and government officials became more comfortable with each other, their mutual trust grew. Salvationists learned just how far they could push the spiritual character of their programs while regulators learned to appreciate that Salvationists could not fully separate their faith from their service. This is not to say that the relationship between the Army and secular authorities was without tension. In fact, as changing social mores led to a reassessment of cultural norms, the Army found itself embroiled in charges of discrimination. An early and ongoing source of conflict was the Army's position on homosexuality; Salvationist leaders opposed any union or sexual behavior outside heterosexual marriage, but critics said their stance singled out homosexuals. The problem became public when New York City mayor Edward Koch signed Executive Order 50, a 1980 decree that prohibited contractors with the city from discriminating based on race, religion, disability, age, sex, or sexual preference. City officials told the Army that they could not refuse to hire homosexuals for city-funded jobs in child services. The press published many pieces on the disagreement as well as op-eds debating the right of religious groups to accept public funds and then flout government laws. Initially, the Salvationists stood alone, but their position improved when the Roman Catholic Archdiocese of New York, which held many more city contracts, announced its support. The two, along with an Orthodox Jewish group, sued to overturn the order and won. The tone of coverage and editorials reflected the nascent culture wars that would pit "true believers" against "secular humanists." The Army, which depended on both camps for funding, did not use the controversy to flaunt its conservative bona fides. Rather, it sought to refocus public attention on its work and, at the same time, bolster its spiritual side.

According to McKinley, the Army historian, Salvationists tried to ensure that programs funded by government monies were discrete: If one of these new initiatives should end, corps programs and the Army's own welfare work would be unaffected. The role and activities of the corps—local churches that are the movement's spiritual base—served as a counterbalance to the restrictions that accompanied public funding. Army leaders pushed the corps to be financially independent, initially as a statement of commitment and later as a protection from federal regulations. At the same time, the Army opened Adult Rehabilitation Centers (ARC), which provide spiritually based rehabilitation for substance abusers and do not take government money. While these developments were tracked in Army publications, they received little attention in the secular press.

In 1996, Congress passed legislation that made it easier for religious groups to have access to federal funding for certain social programs. "Charitable choice" and the Bush administration's subsequent support for faith-based funding made it possible for religious groups to compete for federal funds on a "level playing field." However, government monies were only for service provision, and faith-based recipients could not discriminate against clients on the basis of religion nor could they compel clients to participate in religious activities.

Since the Army had been receiving government funds long before 1996, its leaders did not expect the new provisions to have much impact on their work or their funding. To keep their mission intact, they had earlier decided that no more than 20 percent of their budget would come from public monies. Accordingly, in 1997, about 15 percent of the Army's annual budget came from federal funds and, in 2009, 14 percent did. In the late 1990s, some Salvationists did wonder whether the new legislation would spur a fresh round of internal debates over the balance between direct evangelism and social service provision. At the time, Captain John Cheydleur, social services secretary for the Eastern Territory, noted, "A lot of young evangelical officers are saying to old guys like me that we should get out of government work because they don't want to hear about one more restriction ever again."[8] Yet what proved to be most important about charitable choice and attendant public discussions about the Army were the ways in which the role of religion in public life became news. A movement that, for decades, had downplayed its religious specificities now contended with headlines about its position on domestic partnerships, faith-based legislation, and disaster aid. Just as the media had once enabled the Army to hide its evangelicalism in plain sight, it now forced the organization to go public with its religious beliefs.

News and Good News

The news media has long played a central role in getting information about the Army's mission and identity before the American people. From 1880 to World War I, the vast majority of Americans—those who did not come into contact with its street evangelism or were not direct beneficiaries of its services—knew about the Salvation Army through newspapers and magazines. Much of what they read was negative. The Army was portrayed as a movement of overenthusiastic rabble-rousers who confused sensationalism with evangelism. Was the Army allied with virtue or vice, an 1885 *New York Times* editorial asked and then answered, "The Salvation Army seems to be organized for the purpose of applying the methods of the variety show to the propagation of Christianity. It undertakes to minister to the same craving for vulgar modes of excitement."[9]

Newspapers disparaged Army parades, decried its female preachers, and derided its use of popular culture. Even when positive stories on slum ministries appeared in the 1890s, reporters mocked its fervent followers. When a *Chicago Tribune* reporter went undercover to write about the Army, she admitted at the outset that her subjects seemed "a class of fanatics, bizarre and picturesque, and exciting only wonder and ridicule." She signed up with a small corps in a working-class Chicago suburb and, to her surprise, was inspired by the commanding officer's beauty, compassion, and grace. But when she was transferred to another corps, she found coarse recruits yearning for worldly pleasures and an unattractive captain who falsified her financial records.[10]

Critics frequently questioned the Army's finances, demanding to know where its money went and whether its account ledgers could be trusted. They accused Army officers of investing in a mining company (which some did) and charged Salvationist leaders with using funds collected for social work to support its soul-saving crusades (which appears to be untrue). By the turn of the century, the Army found support among advocates of social Christianity, a movement that applied religious principles to social problems. But secular philanthropists, committed to scientific methods of charity, castigated Salvationist philosophy and programs as sentimental and unempirical. These and other critics were silenced by the Army's outreach during the 1900 hurricane in Galveston, Texas, and the 1906 San Francisco earthquake. Galveston was the first occasion for extensive Army emergency relief, and its subsequent work in San Francisco garnered further positive attention.[11] Although California Salvationists had not been prepared for widespread property damage and consequent human need, they had jumped into action with a zeal and determination that impressed the local citizenry and was widely and favorably reported.

Evangeline Booth may have had in mind the Army's past success at large-scale relief work when she decided, a decade later, to send her soldiers to serve in World War I. Despite the modest scale of their efforts, Salvationists reaped a public relations bonanza that culminated in an unprecedented ability to raise money and command media attention. Widely popular, the Sallies were praised in poetry and song, newspaper reports, and letters from the front. A good deal of that attention was directed at Army lassies, the once reviled now revered symbol of the organization.

The media depicted lassies as vibrant and appealing, but their religion was less so, inverting the emphasis that the Army would have preferred. News reports on the lassies' work—whether frying donuts on the front lines or tending slum children at home—was central to the Army's transformation from evangelical outcast to humanitarian icon. Following the familiar Mary/Martha trope that valued women who were silent servants above those who were loquacious leaders, Army lassies embodied a deed-over-creed faith that was old-fashioned in its practice but modern in its pluralist and activist orientation. It fit the postwar era and reflected journalism's own notions about what religion should be.

Throughout the nineteenth century, newspapers had reflected a positive view of religion, albeit as an element of a universe circumscribed by evangelical Protestantism. Tall-steeple ministers were frequent editorial commentators, particularly when their perspectives on social issues coincided with those of publishers. Within that context, reporters unmasked religious scamps and scalawags, but deviance, like the Salvation Army's "sensationalism," underscored a normative view of Christianity as a civilizing and stabilizing influence on society. After the Civil War, however, innovations in science, advances in scholarship, and changes in society began to loosen religion's grip on the public imagination. A secularist tide took hold of the professions, and its influence was felt both in news coverage and in the journalism profession more generally.

Between 1870 and 1930, changes in the news business, including the growing importance of advertising and the need to reach a diverse readership, mitigated against a moralizing Christian perspective. Writing in 1933 on recent social trends, researcher Hornell Hart noted that the most significant change had been the "shift from Biblical authority and sanctions to scientific and factual authority and sanctions." Hart's contention was based on quantitative surveys, including one that looked at trends in religion coverage. In 1905, 78 percent of stories in the *Reader's Guide to Periodical Literature* were positively inclined to "traditional Christianity." By 1931, only 33 percent were similarly predisposed, and the numbers were even smaller when elite publications were counted.[12]

Similar trends occurred in the *New York Times,* where, between 1875 and 1930, the diminution of religion coverage could be quantified in terms of total news stories, page-one stories, and percentage of total news space. Sociologist Richard Flory, looking at *Times* editorials between 1870 and 1930, discovered parallels in the paper's attitude about religion. Through the 1880s, editorials had "an explicitly pro-religion and, more specifically, pro-Protestant Christianity stance."[13] The paper's predilections were evident in editorials about the growing clash between science and religion. Initially, the *Times* sided with the latter, opposing attempts to jettison traditional orthodoxies for modern science. But the paper's position shifted, and, by 1900, the *Times* advocated the liberal vision of religion as a social force for good over and against the conservative campaign for theological rectitude.

Flory argues that the same confrontation between scientific and religious authority, played out in the universities, professions, and public debate, also occurred within journalism. Educators and professionals "portrayed journalism as a scientific, and scientifically organized, profession that was central to the well-being and moral structure of society."[14] They believed that journalism, not religion, was best suited to explain the world and to provide authoritative guidance for living. Moreover, they inculcated journalistic standards of objectivity and truth that gave newspapers an aura of omniscience and infallibility.

For many journalists, the post–World War I Salvation Army exemplified religion's role in the new era. Insofar as it could be portrayed as a nonsectarian, activist faith, the Army represented the kind of Christianity that newspapers liked. References to raucous revivals and street-corner services were replaced by stories of slum nurseries and soup kitchens. Throughout the 1920s and 1930s, reporters referred to the Army as a "charitable organization," a "social organization," a "benevolent and charitable corporation," and a "social service institution."[15] Articles describing its shelters, salvage work, summer camps, and Christmas dinners were interspersed with profiles of leaders and lassies. A 1920 *New York Times* editorial, supporting a fund-raising drive, made only a fleeting reference to the Army's religious work.[16]

Even when the group's religiosity was noted, it was linked to service provision: "Its militant evangelism has been an essential part of its character since its beginnings in this country in 1880. So has the intensely practical aid which it brings to every type of misery with which it comes into contact."[17] A 1934 *Washington Post* profile of Evangeline Booth, the founder's daughter, celebrated her promotion from head of the American Army to commander of the worldwide Army. The story notes her fund-raising and organizational skills, her physical attributes and daily activities, her acting and hymn-writing abilities—but says nothing about her personal beliefs or the religious mission of the global denomination that she would soon lead.[18] Likewise, a feature piece on a retired Army officer makes much of her working despite her retirement, yet it never mentions what inspired a seventy-two-year-old to sell Army newspapers on the street corner.[19]

The close fit between the activist faith and the spirit of the times was evident in reporting on the Great Depression. The Army's brand of humanitarian activism resonated with national calls for service. In 1933, when George H. Dern, the U.S. secretary of war, announced the fight against the "second great war of the twentieth century," Evangeline Booth was by his side. Addressing an Army fund-raising rally at the Seventh Regiment Armory in New York City, Dern called for defensive lines against "hunger, misery, nakedness and privation," noting, "of those defensive lines, moreover, none is of greater importance than those which are manned by the troops of the Salvation Army."[20]

Throughout the 1930s, the *Times* and *Post* published news of Army fund-raising and subsequent service provision to victims of the economic collapse. Whether covering the Army's Christmas programs, appeal drives, or employment opportunities, news stories rarely, if ever, discussed the group's evangelical moorings. Nor were members asked about their faith commitments. The outbreak of World War II changed little. In December 1941, when the United States joined the Allies, the American head of the Salvation Army placed his troops "on a war basis" as well.[21] The Army's war work—staffing Red Shield and USO clubs that served the troops at home and abroad—was reported with minimal mention of its religious mission. The differences were there for all to see; Salvationist clubs offered religious services instead of dancing. But these were rarely mentioned by the news media.

Coverage did not change after the war ended. A 1949 article on the Army's social services began, "Of the many requests the public receives to support worthy health, welfare, educational and philanthropic activities, there is one that few New Yorkers can conscientiously turn down. That is the Salvation Army's current maintenance appeal for $1,100,000."[22] The reason for the Army's service provision went unstated. When an article could not sidestep the subject of religion, descriptions were muted. In an in-depth profile of his thirty years of working with prisoners and ex-cons, Salvationist officer J. Stanley Sheppard referred to his vocation simply as "religion in action." Left to elucidate, writer S. J. Woolf explained, "There is a heartiness about him that removes restraint, inspires confidence and evokes confidences. When he speaks of holy subjects he seems to bring them close to earth." Woolf portrayed Shepherd as anything but sanctimonious; neither was he pious, reverential, or even contemplative. Rather, he was the salt of the earth, invoking behaviors that would be anathema to a teetotaling Salvationist: "Not in uniform, he would pass for just another good fellow, driving a truck, overseeing a crew or even resting his elbows in a bar."[23]

Sheppard, whose profile was illustrated by a sketch of a portly, middle-aged man in an Army cap and uniform, was the new face of the movement. By mid-century, staid men had replaced winsome lassies as the Army public image. The apotheosis of the change was *Time* magazine's 1949 Christmas cover, picturing Army commissioner Ernest Pugmire, gray haired and bespectacled, enwreathed by brass bells. The accompanying story explicitly detailed the movement's evangelical origins with a historical sketch of the Booths. Unlike most newspaper stories, the newsmagazine described the rationale for the Army's "religion in action," noting, "It proceeds on the down-to-earth theory that Christ gave clear instructions on what to do about the degraded, the abandoned and the poor. . . . Booth was after men's souls and his principal weapon was evangelism. The modern army still fights that war, but now its principal weapon is charity." According to *Time,* the Army sacrificed its old-timey enthusiasms for public support and respectability, and "the kind of social welfare program over which Ernest Pugmire presides is a sounder attack against the enemy than all the processions General Booth might lead . . . and sounder than street-corner revivals."[24]

Over the next two decades, little was added to this pithy summary. The Army's hard-won "respectability" made for sober, if generally appreciative, coverage. The *Times* captured the cultural quid pro quo in a 1960 article about the Army's annual appeal. Since the Salvationists' devotion to the needy is "important," readers should view donations as "an effective investment."[25] Yet its do-gooder stolidity and muted, middle-aged militancy evoked a bygone era. When the *Post* covered the 1969 election of the Army's first non-British head, the novelty of a Swedish commander was overshadowed by descriptions of his outdated style: "He is tall, bespectacled, with a rather old-fashioned courtesy. On being introduced, he gives the hint of a bow from the waist down." The article also differentiated the American Army from its counterparts worldwide. Outreach in Asia, Africa, and Australia focused on religious missions and ministries. American Salvationists addressed social ills: "In America, we're slum conscious. We're teaching that it's necessary to get the slums out of the people." Only at the very end of the piece did the reporter quote an Army leader on the work's spiritual dimension: "Getting the slum out of the man means getting the man committed to religious values."[26]

By the late 1960s, the Army's religious claims were creeping back into the news. At a time when headlines asked if God was dead, whither the Jesus People, and what the Age of Aquarius really meant, the movement's conservative faith seemed noteworthy. A 1967 *Post* piece about the Army's Christmas drive featured a large photograph of a lassie clasping an oversized tuba. From the bows on her bonnet to the "S" on her epaulet, soldier Virginia Lodge was an image from another era. She sounded like one, too. "'Like other Armies,' she explained last week, 'the Salvation Army is a way of life and a tradition that runs in the family.'" Lodge was a third-generation Salvationist who taught at an Army Sunday school, volunteered with an Army women's club, and worked as a secretary at a local Army headquarters. Her good looks and wide smile harked back to a time when attractive lassies symbolized the movement. Lodge's image and words did double duty; while "selling" the Army's social services, she also embodied its old-time religion. Unlike lassies from the past, her persona was explicitly linked to the Army's conservative religion (growing up, she was not allowed to drink, dance, or "date a lot of boys") as well as its redemptive message, which, explained the article, was "to preach the Gospel and 'save' men and women."[27]

The press paid increasing attention to Salvationists' faith during the 1970s. Religion coverage had experienced a renaissance: The 1976 election of Jimmy Carter brought evangelicals into the American political arena, and the 1978 Iranian Revolution and subsequent 444-day-long American hostage crisis did the same for Muslims. But unlike religious movements that engaged in affairs of the state, the Army was depicted as apolitical and charmingly picturesque. Reporting on Army advances into youth culture in the article "Salvation Army Experimenting with Rock," the *Times* noted, tongue-in-cheek, "It's unlikely that long-haired, modly dressed members of the Salvation Army will soon be playing the Beatles' 'Help' instead of 'The Old Rugged Cross.'"[28] Overlooking the parallels between William Booth's use of brass bands and young Salvationists' deployment of popular culture, older officers confessed that they couldn't "relate" to the new music.

An equally arch tone underlay two stories about the Army's Christmas kettles. A 1971 piece chronicled the vicissitudes of bell ringing. After being kidnapped and robbed, one Army volunteer went to the police, who not only doubted his story but also speculated that he was victimized because he was either a homosexual or a john. (The young man denied both.) Another volunteer—fortunate to be working outside a Saks department store rather than the Port Authority Bus Terminal—reported what the reporter treated as an equally thrilling experience. "'This morning I met an atheist,'" she told the *Times*. "'He was my first one and he was very nice.'"[29] Two years later, the paper profiled Diane Chesney, a Salvation Army cadet working the city's largest kettle outside Macy's. When a green Volkswagen splashed slush on her, Mrs. Chesney gamely smiled. Later in the day, two boys tried to steal money from her kettle before a nearby Santa Claus intervened. "'It's not easy,'" she admitted. "'We all pray together before we leave in the morning, and we try to go to the kettles with the right attitude.'"[30]

Reporting on the Army became an integral part of the news media's rediscovery of religion. Stories still covered the nuts and bolts of fund-raising appeals, Christmas kettles, and leadership changes, but they also included an ethnographic dimension that explored the intersection of belief and behavior. Unlike the nineteenth-century press, which portrayed a sensational ministry motivated by a scandalous sensibility, twentieth-century reporters depicted a quaint relic from a bygone era. When women's equality and the fight for the Equal Rights Amendment loomed large in the news, both the *Post* and the *Times* asked how the Army, the first Protestant denomination to give equality to women in mission and ministry, treated its distaff members today. According to the *Times*, "husband and wife are really equal," yet the movement's strict rules (couples had to receive permission to marry, and they had to be wed in uniform; women took their husband's rank, never vice versa; women worked mainly in women's ministries) mitigated against a progressive interpretation of the faith.[31]

The Army's conservative religion was no more than a curiosity until its convictions began to clash with contemporary mores. In 1980, Mayor Koch signed Executive Order 50, compelling any organizations with municipal contracts in New York City to end discrimination based on "sexual orientation or affectional preference." When the Army learned it was out of compliance (it did not hire homosexuals for some jobs), leaders announced their refusal to change their policy: The movement did not recognize sexual unions outside of marriage, nor did it sanction homosexuality. Using the press to clarify their position, Army leaders explained, "'We do not practice discrimination, but we feel we need to reserve the right to make decisions on employment in certain positions.'"[32]

The coverage was polarizing. For those who supported gay rights, the Army's religious position was an intrusion into civic affairs. But for believers across the theological spectrum, the coalition of Protestants, Roman Catholics, and Jews was a united front against the moral relativism of secular humanism. From the Army's perspective, it was an important battle with a public relations cost. The Army had only ten contracts at risk, but the Catholic Archdiocese of New York, one of New York's largest service providers, and an Orthodox Jewish group joined forces in a legal suit against the provision. When the New York State Supreme Court struck down Executive Order 50, subsequent city mandates allowed more flexibility for religious groups.

Increased media attention to the interplay between religion and politics led to new types of stories about the Army. Standard holiday pieces on bell-ringers still appeared, but so did news on contested social issues. Even when the Army won the day, coverage drew attention to its conservative social and political positions. The Army's evangelicalism, or, to some, its fundamentalism, became relevant because of public as well as governmental support for its programs. Avoiding controversy was often impossible, as in 1998, when the Army turned down a contract with the City of San Francisco because it would have required providing domestic partnership benefits to unmarried and homosexual employees.

The decision forced cutbacks in services to seniors, drug addicts, and the homeless—as well as the loss of sixty staff positions. Three years later, the Army's Western Territory switched its position, agreeing to provide benefits. But a loud and very public outcry from right-wing evangelical groups induced the Army's National Headquarters to reverse its reversal. According to local coverage, the rescission had ramifications far beyond the Army's position on gays. A local official told the *San Francisco Chronicle* that it was a "mean-spirited move" aimed at pleasing the religious right. "Not just domestic partners, but grandparents, adult children, and others who are living with Salvation Army employees may remain without health coverage," the official stated.[33]

The Army also took a hit when newspapers reported it paid workers at its facilities below the minimum wage. Although the Army countered that the workers were "clients" who worked as part of their treatment program, the U.S. Labor Department ordered it to obey the law. "Department of Labor officials see this as a question of equity and fairness," reported the *Times*. "They say that the Salvation Army's practice of providing only a small reimbursement for work and no overtime, combined with poor record keeping, amount to a kind of exploitation of workers."[34] The Army mounted a behind-the-scenes campaign, and, within days, the government changed its policy, allowing the substandard pay scale to stand. The Army likewise scored a mixed win when the U.S. Department of Housing and Urban Development permitted a picture of Jesus to hang in a Connecticut shelter, despite a ban on religious decorations in federally financed projects.

These incursions on church-state separation looked minor when, in 1996, the federal government announced "Charitable Choice," legislation that enabled religious organizations to receive government funding for social services. The goal was to establish a "level playing field" for faith-based service providers while also protecting clients from religious messages and preserving church-state separation. Although the legislation was aimed at helping local congregations rather than large organizations such as Catholic Charities, Lutheran Social Service, or the Army, all of which received federal support, it nevertheless fixed public attention on the central role played by large faith-based service providers.

Salvationists' dual role was captured in a 2000 *Washington Post* holiday headline, "A Church Better Known as a Charity; for Its Soldiers, the Salvation Army Is a Way of Faith and of Life." Summing up the conundrum, a teenage Salvationist said her friends think she worships in a thrift store. The misunderstanding was widespread. Throughout the 1990s, the Army, whose "ubiquitous red kettles, tinkling bells and brass band" telegraphed the Christmas message, was the nation's largest charitable fund-raiser. Yet, wrote the *Post*, "Few people realize that the Salvation Army is an evangelical Protestant denomination of more than a million members in 107 countries, with its own creed, ordained clergy, seminaries and spiritual mission." Rather, the movement was best known for "its dependable track record of serving the poor and afflicted."[35] Apparently, many Americans—or, at least, the *Post's* reporter—had missed news coverage about the Army's theologically based positions against hiring gays and for displaying religious symbols in publicly funded programs. If some supporters had already assumed a conservative religious context for the Army's work, others seemed not to care.

The 2000 election of George W. Bush to the presidency ratcheted up news coverage of religion and politics. Ever since the "born-again" faith of Jimmy Carter garnered headlines in 1976, every four years reporters rediscovered the pivotal role of religious voters. Yet the unexpected ascendancy of Bush, who named Jesus as his favorite philosopher and credited his success and sobriety to God, signaled a turning point. Evangelicalism was more than a passing fad; it was a hallmark of the new millennium's politics. Early in the Bush administration, two news stories underlined the changed reality. In January 2001, the new president established the Office of Faith-Based and Community

Initiatives to enhance and expand the work begun by charitable choice. Supporters saw this as central to Bush's vision of compassionate conservatism, the idea that faith-based social services could and should supplement government relief. Eight months later, on September 11, the second story exploded when militant Islamist terrorists hijacked American jets in coordinated suicide attacks that killed more than three thousand people in New York, Washington, D.C., and Pennsylvania.

New Media, New Millennium

Journalism in the new millennium underwent swift and dramatic transformation. During the previous century, radio and television had cut into newspapers' dominance and profits. Each innovation not only changed the speed of news delivery and, as a consequence, the style of its presentation but also reduced the revenues of family-owned companies that had monopolized the newspaper business. The Internet, however, presented far greater challenges than anything that had come before. Many small newspaper chains and even some larger ones found they could not compete in the mid-1990s when online advertising websites such as Craigslist and others began gnawing at their bottom line. At the same time, the Internet's ability to provide readers with instantaneous, worldwide news that could be culled and cut according to personal interests undermined radio, television, and newspapers' lock on information. Staffs shrunk, profits dipped, and historic news companies sold themselves to the highest bidder. Seeking to hold erstwhile print readers and reach new ones, news managers fell back on the familiar tropes of conflict, scandal, and sensationalism. In addition to politics and sex, religion was a salable and frequently salacious topic; combinations of any two were even better.

A century earlier, journalists had expressed loftier aims. In 1915, Walter Williams, the first dean of the Missouri School of Journalism, wrote "The Journalist's Creed," eight statements that defined the news profession.[36] Williams said journalism was a public trust that practitioners approached as "gentlemen." He expected reporters to be "unswayed by the appeal of privilege or the clamor of the mob," writing only what they knew to be true in the service of humanity. He and like-minded educators believed that journalism held the key to safeguarding democracy, promoting international relations, and leading society to a better tomorrow. As sociologist Richard Flory argues, journalism professionalizers believed their role was to supplant traditional religion as society's shepherd. To this end, reporters caricatured old-fashioned religions while commending modern ones. In the 1910s and 1920s, the press saw the Salvation Army as a modern faith that, admirably, was more concerned with providing social services than debating theological positions.[37] By 2000, few journalists harbored grand ideals about their profession's capacity to improve society. The notion that journalism could and should replace organized religion as an authoritative interpreter and inspirational storyteller seemed absurd. Similarly, the Army's once modern faith now appeared outmoded, and its evangelical moorings made it an appealing target for reporting on culture war issues.

Ever since William Booth's day, the Army has tried to avoid politics, concerned that controversy would distract from its primary mission. Leaders said little publicly when the Clinton administration introduced charitable choice and not much more when Bush unveiled his faith-based office. But in the summer of 2001, the *Post* revealed a secret deal between the White House and the Army. In exchange for supporting the new initiative, Army leaders asked the administration to "issue a regulation protecting such charities from state and city efforts to prevent discrimination against gays in hiring and domestic-partner benefits." According to an internal document, the Army was concerned about showing a side of itself "starkly different than that of volunteers ringing bells outside shopping malls at Christmas."[38]

That other side stayed in the news, however, long after the White House hastily announced that it would not meet the Army's terms. Five days after the first story broke, the *Post* published an account of the revelation's impact under the headline: "Charity's Image Shaken by Gay Bias Flap: Salvation Army's Social, Spiritual Efforts Collide." Noting that the Army's middle-of-the-road, Norman Rockwell-like image seemed at odds with positions that dovetailed with the religious right, the paper explained, "What the Army's Rockwellian association obscured is its evangelical mission, with its long-standing and firm objections to abortion and homosexuality."[39]

The Army's stance on gays remained newsworthy through the decade, though most of the coverage migrated online. Despite carefully parsing its position to show it was neither homophobic in principle nor discriminatory in its service provision, the Army's refusal to employ practicing homosexuals and condone gay marriage made news every December. In 2009 and 2010, several online media outlets claimed Christmas collections in San Francisco and Chicago were down due to campaigns against antigay organizations, an assertion that the Army denied. Gay activists and supporters used online and social media to publicize the Army's positions, which were attributed to the biblically based, conservative theology associated with the religious right. Most mainstream news outlets, however, blamed an initial shortfall in 2010 Christmas kettle collections on bad weather and the sour economy rather than mentioning the anti-Army campaigns that linked its religion to right-wing politics.

Perhaps mitigating against mainstream news' negative coverage of the Army was its front-and-center role in providing disaster relief. Less than two months after the *Post* revealed the secret deal between the Army and the White House, terrorist attacks on September 11 reframed news stories on religion and politics. The destruction wrought by Al-Qaeda pushed aside domestic quarrels over the role of the religious right, at least for a while. The immediate needs at Ground Zero, the former site of the World Trade Center, focused both the religious and the relief communities on finding the dead, helping the living, and supporting those who were tasked with an enormous clean-up effort. Within minutes of the first plane crash, the Salvation Army had workers at the site. Salvationists provided meals for the clean-up crews and offered emotional and spiritual counseling for survivors. As in the past, news stories glossed over the organization's evangelical beliefs, focusing instead on its actions. In addition to downplaying religion, coverage was generally positive: An article on the Army's offer to pay household bills for 9/11 families began with an Army employee explaining that he would not reimburse calls for "phone sex."[40] The anecdote assumed that readers would understand the incongruity. The article's only other mention of the Army's evangelical beliefs was a description of it as a "religious group." Reporting on Army efforts in post-Katrina New Orleans and in Haiti following the 2010 earthquake similarly emphasized service delivery rather than religious mission.

The movement's faith-based outreach also remained in the headlines. In 2004, Joan Kroc, the widow of McDonald's founder Ray Kroc, left $1.5 billion to the group in her will. It was the largest gift of its kind: According to news reports, no individual had ever given as large a donation to a single charity.[41] Associates said Mrs. Kroc appreciated the Army's ability to provide services even though she did not share its religious views. As the *Times* explained, the Army was "run by ordained ministers and has a quiet but strong evangelizing component to its activities, which has often placed it at the center of controversies about public financing."[42] Subsequent coverage reported on the Army's difficulties raising funds to match the Kroc bequest, which was targeted at creating state-of-the-art community centers, a goal that some Army leaders deemed tangential to their core mission.

Given newspapers' shrinking news role—as well as cultural sea changes about the role of religion in public life—contemporary coverage of the Army has focused less on the merit of its funding appeals and service provision and more on its incursions into matters of church-state separation. Reports of a religious renewal in the New York division led to a string of *Times* stories about "freaked-out" non-Army employees who were informed "that they've come to whip us into shape."[43] Their concerns assumed greater significance when a federal court judge upheld the Army's right to apply a religious litmus test to employees, even those who served in secular programs that received government money. His ruling went against eighteen Army employees who said they lost their jobs or were demoted "because they refused to pledge support to the Salvation Army's mission of 'proclaiming Jesus Christ as Savior and Lord,' disclose what church they attended or name gay co-workers."[44]

Thus, in the twenty-first century, a religion that hid its identity in plain sight was outed by a news media formerly complicit in the cover-up. News consumers now had ample opportunities to learn not only about the Salvation Army's evangelical beliefs but also of their implications for the hiring, firing, benefits, and salaries of non-Army employees engaged in its government-funded social service provision. News outlets also reported on the Army's outreach, emergency relief, and Christmas kettles (features tracked giving patterns as well as idiosyncratic gifts such as gold coins or very large bills), but the majority of the pieces were "gotcha" stories that caught the Army in church-state conflicts. Nevertheless, in 2012, the Army was, as it had been for the past two decades, among the nation's top three charitable fund-raisers.[45]

The Army's status is not unique. Two of the top five charities in 2012 were religious, and public support for their work may well reflect the sensibility of a population that claims to be almost 80 percent Christian. The news media's coverage of the Army as an evangelical mission may have strengthened its attractiveness at a time of increased religious awareness. According to several Army officers, the movement's evangelical foundation appeals even to those who do not share it. "Many of our donors appreciate [that] we do this with a spiritual motivation," said Commissioner Carol Seiler, who oversees Army work in eleven midwestern states. "Joan Kroc didn't give us $1.5 billion because she was aligned with our faith. She did it because she thought we were trustworthy."[46]

The Salvation Army's example illuminates the challenges faced by religious groups that take government funds to provide social services. Religious entities must not only negotiate between secular regulations and religious doctrine, but they also do so, at least in the twenty-first century, in full public view. People generally learn about the world from the news media, and, until very recently, its grip on information was total. In the early twentieth century, news managers, emboldened by a sense of mission and empowered by their hegemonic position, promoted an idea of religion that was devoid of theological specificity or creedal commitment. In search of a religion befitting a pluralistic, action-oriented society as well as one that would not challenge their own authority, they advanced the Army. The Army's need to promote a nonsectarian image, as its very survival depended on public support, made for a symbiotic match. The Army may have allowed its identity to be hidden in plain sight, but its members never deviated from their fundamental mission. Now, as it was in 1880, the Salvation Army is "an evangelical organization dedicated to bringing people into a meaningful relationship with God through Jesus Christ."[47] Or, as a Salvationist might say, those with ears to hear and eyes to see will understand their mission, notwithstanding the twists and turns of a secular news media.

Notes

1. Salvation Army, "2009 Financial Summary," http://annualreport.salvationarmyusa.org; http://annualreport.salvationarmyusa.org/_pdf/2012_Expenses.pdf.

2. Diane Winston, "The Angel of Broadway: Transformative Dynamics of Religion, Media, Gender and Commodification," in *Religion, Media, and Culture: A Reader*, ed. Gordon Lynch and Jolyon P. Mitchell with Anna Strhan (New York: Routledge, 2011), 122–30.

3. "The Salvationists," *New York Times*, February 2, 1892, 4.

4. Norman Murdoch, *The Origins of the Salvation Army* (Knoxville: University of Tennessee Press, 1994), 165.

5. *American War Cry*, August 17, 1918, 2.

6. *The Survey*, November 15, 1924, 195.

7. Edward H. McKinley, *Marching to Glory: The History of the Salvation Army in the United States, 1880–1992* (Grand Rapids: Eerdmans, 1995), 177.

8. Diane Winston, *Soup, Soap and Salvation: The Impact of Charitable Choice on the Salvation Army* (Washington, D.C.: Center for Public Justice, 2000), 14–15.

9. "Religion by Riot," *New York Times*, March 22, 1885, 8.

10. Nora Marks, *Facts about the Salvation Army* (Chicago: Rand McNally, 1889).

11. McKinley, *Marching to Glory*, 133–35.

12. Richard W. Flory, "Promoting a Secular Standard: Secularization and Modern Journalism, 1870–1930," in *The Secular Revolution: Power, Interests, and Conflicts in the Secularization of American Public Life*, ed. Christian Smith (Berkeley: University of California Press, 2003), 398.

13. Ibid., 400.

14. Richard W. Flory, "A New Religion for Modern Times: American Journalism and Religion, 1870–1930," in *Oxford Handbook on Religion and the News*, ed. Diane Winston (New York: Oxford University Press, 2012), 54.

15. The essay draws on the *New York Times* and the *Washington Post*, large metropolitan newspapers with national readership.

16. Editorial, *New York Times*, June 4, 1920, 12.

17. "The Salvation Army," *New York Times*, April 30, 1928, 30.

18. "Eva Booth Takes High Command," *Washington Post*, September 16, 1934, SM7.

19. "Salvation Army's Anna Strohl Retires but Doesn't Quit at 72," *Washington Post*, December 16, 1938, 5.

20. "Dern Sounds Call for War on Want," *New York Times*, April 4, 1933, 7, *ProQuest Historical Newspapers, The New York Times (1851–2007)* (document ID: 105122792).

21. "Salvationists to Serve," *New York Times*, December 9, 1941, 46.

22. Howard A. Rusk, "Salvation Army's Aid to Man Given through Many Centers," *New York Times*, January 23, 1949, 48.

23. S. J. Woolf, "'Religion in Action' in the Prisons," *New York Times*, February 15, 1948, SM 22.

24. "Religion: I Was a Stranger . . . ," *Time*, December 26, 1949, http://www.time.com/time/magazine/article/0,9171,801173,00.html.

25. "New York's Salvation Army," *New York Times*, February 5, 1960, 26.

26. John Gayle, "Salvation Army Elects First Non-British Head," *Washington Post*, August 2, 1969, B5.

27. Bernadette Carey, "Salvation Army Drive Needs a Boost," *Washington Post*, December 16, 1967, C5.

28. "Salvation Army Experimenting with Rock," *New York Times*, September 5, 1972, 39.

29. Joseph Lelyveld, "Good Will toward Men?" *New York Times*, December 23, 1971, 24.

30. Judy Klemesrud, "She Smiled Warmly through a Cold Day," *New York Times*, December 21, 1973, 24.

31. Judy Klemesrud, "In Salvation Army Family, Husband and Wife Are Really Equal," *New York Times*, December 11, 1970, 67.

32. Michael Goodwin, "Salvation Army Losing City Pacts for Stand on Hiring Homosexuals," *New York Times*, March 3, 1984, 46.

33. Christopher Heredia, "Salvation Army Says No Benefits for Partners," *San Francisco Chronicle*, November 14, 2001, http://www.usc.edu/schools/annenberg/asc/projects/soin/liveIssues/liveissues archive.html.

34. Anthony DePalma, "Salvation Army Is Told to Pay Minimum Wage," *New York Times*, September 16, 1990, A42, http://www.nytimes.com/1990/09/16/nyregion/salvation-army-is-told-to-pay-minimum-wage.html.

35. Caryle Murphy, "A Church Better Known as a Charity," *Washington Post*, December 17, 2000, 1.

36. Walter Williams, "The Journalist's Creed," http://journalism.missouri.edu/jschool/#creed.

37. Flory, "A New Religion for Modern Times."

38. Dana Milbank, "Charity Cites Bush Help in Fight against Hiring Gays," *Washington Post*, July 10, 2001, 1.

39. Hanna Rosin, "Charity's Image Shaken by Gay Bias Flap: Salvation Army's Social, Spiritual Efforts Collide," *Washington Post,* July 15, 2001, 5.

40. Joyce Wadler, "Public Lives: A Salvation Army Soldier, Drafted in the Terror War," *New York Times,* January 10, 2002, B2.

41. Thomas A. Fogarty, "Joan Kroc Leaves Salvation Army $1.5 Billion," *USA Today,* January 21, 2004, B4.

42. Stephanie Strom, "Salvation Army Receives $1.5 Billion from Estate Built on McDonald's Franchises," *New York Times,* January 14, 2004, 13.

43. Daniel J. Wakin, "A Religious Renewal at the Salvation Army Raises the Threat of a Church-State Dispute," *New York Times,* February 2, 2004, B1.

44. Alan Cooperman, "Bush's Faith Plan Faces Judgment," *Washington Post,* October 20, 2005, 25.

45. Emily Gipple, Peter Panepento, and Cody Switzer, "How the Top 100 Have Changed in Two Decades," *Chronicle of Philanthropy,* October 14, 2012, http://philanthropy.com/article/How-the-Top-100-Have-Changed/134962/#id=321092&cat=social_service.

46. Carol Seiler, telephone interview, September 23, 2010.

47. "The Salvation Army: Salvation and Service," *Salvation Army,* http://www.salvationarmyusa.org/usn/www_usn_2.nsf/vw-dynamic-arrays/7100A2893080C5238025732500315746?openDocument&charset=utf-8.

4 Heartbroken for God's World

The Story of Bob Pierce, Founder of World Vision and Samaritan's Purse

David P. King

As FOUNDER OF both World Vision and Samaritan's Purse, Bob Pierce may rank as the leading religious philanthropist of the twentieth century. He first visited China as an evangelist in 1947. Upon his arrival, a Dutch Reformed missionary, Tena Hoelkeboer, invited him to preach to her school of four hundred Chinese girls. Pierce agreed, but, the day after his short evangelistic sermon, one of Hoelkeboer's students, White Jade, informed her father that she had converted to Christianity. Her father's response was to throw her out of the house. Hoelkeboer, distressed at the prospect of taking on yet another orphan, demanded of Pierce, "What are you going to do about it?"[1] Pierce gave Hoelkeboer ten dollars, all the money he had, and promised to send more each month on his return to the United States. After his return home, Pierce recounted the story to his American audiences, and it continues to be retold as the origin of both World Vision and Samaritan's Purse. Pierce's initial overseas encounter changed him. He had gone as a young American evangelist but returned as a missionary ambassador, bringing both the spiritual *and* physical needs of the world to the attention of American evangelicals.[2]

Pierce soon founded World Vision in 1950 as a small American evangelical agency with a simple mission of evangelism and child care in Asia. World Vision grew in size, budget, and renown through the 1950s and 1960s under Pierce's leadership. He rooted the organization in an American evangelical subculture while focusing on supporting missionaries, promoting evangelism, and providing emergency relief to Christian refugees, widows, and orphans. As it grew, however, World Vision began to engage new partners, appeal to broader audiences, and transform its operations. It expanded beyond evangelical missions while also interacting with ecumenical and secular relief and development nongovernmental organizations (NGOs).[3] It pursued governmental support even as it embraced an international perspective counter to its past pro-American Cold War outlook. These tensions led World Vision to reinterpret its identity as more humanitarian than missionary, more mainstream than religiously sectarian, and, at times, more professional than pious. Lamenting the new direction of World Vision, Pierce resigned in 1967.

While World Vision was willing to deal with the new tensions it encountered, Pierce remained stubbornly committed to his initial vision. By 1970, he founded Samaritan's Purse on the model of the original World Vision. Centered in the evangelical subculture, supporting missionary projects, and meeting emergency needs through the support of individual donors, Pierce traveled the world again as a one-man ambassador until his death in 1978. He groomed current president Franklin Graham, his successor, to follow the same model.

Both organizations' present success has outgrown their humble origins. Both also maintain substantial differences from each other. Today, World Vision is the largest Christian humanitarian organization in the world. It maintains offices in nearly one hundred countries with around forty thousand employees and an annual budget of more than $2.6 billion. Gone are the days of crusades and orphanages. Now, the organization undertakes emergency relief, community development, justice, and advocacy. It maintains a broad Christian identity, but its leaders are no longer pastors and evangelists. World Vision now recruits professionally trained development specialists and CEOs from Fortune 500 companies. Samaritan's Purse is the United States' tenth-largest humanitarian organization with more than $320.5 million in annual revenue. It, too, has begun to embrace development work in recent years, but it predominantly continues to embrace Pierce's model of emergency relief, supporting missionaries and children, and promoting Christian education. It remains outside the elite international nongovernmental organization (INGO) community while attached to its American evangelical constituency.[4]

Despite the similarities and differences between these organizations, Pierce remains the chief common denominator. While neither institution can be fully understood solely through its founder, Pierce's personality, vision, successes, and foibles had an uncommon effect on the direction of each. This essay focuses on Bob Pierce as a leading evangelical mission philanthropist and acknowledges his role in the massive growth of evangelical relief and development organizations after World War II. It also uses Pierce's story to illustrate how the tensions and evolutions of philanthropies' particular religious identities have been and continue to be central in shaping the actual motivations, rhetoric, practice, and production among faith-based organizations.

Religious Identity

In recent years, religion has found its way back onto the agenda of the relief and development sector.[5] Some development scholars, however, continue to segregate religious and secular organizations into separate camps with little common practices or purpose. Others assert that, while faith-based organizations may claim religious motivation, their actual practice demonstrates a general trend toward shared secularization.[6] They posit that as INGOs come into increasingly closer contact with governments, international bodies, and one another, they exhibit a general homogenization of language, practice, and organization.[7] Following in the footsteps of sociologist Max Weber, they propose that the shaping power of religion declines as initial charismatic leadership evolves into a developed bureaucracy that becomes highly rationalized, production oriented, structured, and professionalized.[8]

As faith-based agencies have grown to become highly influential, the broader field of global development has come to appreciate their size, experience, and expertise. Many development scholars have come to embrace religion's role as an asset in local communities. They have also discovered religious leaders as fruitful dialogue partners in articulating notions of the common good.[9] From this perspective, development notices religion but most often simply uses it as an instrumental addition to its current agenda. Development also often idealizes religion as a static set of beliefs. In contrast to development's ignorance, instrumentalizing, and idealizing of religion, I argue that religious identity matters. Of course, all religious identities are not the same. They may even be at odds with one another. Sometimes even a shared faith perspective produces varying responses and greater tensions within a single organization. Religious identity, however, is essential to the shifts an organization undergoes over time, the tensions it encounters from both internal and external pressures, and the actual practices and production of its humanitarian work.[10]

Bob Pierce's story provides an opportunity to trace the evolving religious identity within the early histories of two particular evangelical INGOs, World Vision and Samaritan's Purse.[11] His own fluid faith perspective led to changes and greater tensions within himself, within his organizations, among his core American evangelical constituency, as well as in the larger public square. His faith also never functioned independently of the shifting religious, cultural, economic, and political forces he encountered. In this essay, I highlight particularly how Pierce interpreted his religious identity through debates between evangelical missions and development, the degree to which professionalism compromises faith, and the extent to which religious agencies partner with governments and secular NGOs.

Pierce before World Vision

To understand Pierce, one must also understand the American fundamentalist-evangelical subculture to which he belonged.[12] Born in 1914 and raised a Nazarene in Southern California, Pierce began preaching by age thirteen. In his early twenties, he became the associate pastor for his father-in-law's nondenominational megachurch while also serving as a traveling evangelist.[13] Pierce inhabited a separatist fundamentalist subculture permeated by complexities, tensions, and multiple traditions. Fundamentalists agreed, however, that theological modernism, the effort to adapt traditional theology to modern culture, was a catastrophe. By the 1920s, many had pulled out of the mainline denominations and mission boards. Their aim was to separate from "the world" and an apostate liberal church, but, even as they faded from public view, fundamentalists created their own network of institutions—Bible colleges, mission societies, and radio broadcasts—that coalesced into a way of life.[14]

By the 1940s, however, some fundamentalists were eager to reengage mainstream culture. Theologian Carl F. H. Henry's *Uneasy Conscience of Modern Fundamentalism* burst onto the scene in 1947 to exemplify a new spirit of American evangelicalism.[15] Henry chastised the isolationist and sectarian nature of an outmoded fundamentalism. The time was ripe for change. "New evangelicals" coming out of American fundamentalism optimistically embraced the spirit of the times. Parachurch organizations such as the National Association of Evangelicals, Campus Crusade for Christ, Young Life, and the Navigators all emerged in the 1940s and early 1950s to take up the challenge.[16]

One particular group, Youth for Christ (YFC), may best exemplify this reengagement. By 1944, as a traveling evangelist, Pierce had eagerly joined YFC and quickly became a vice-president in the organization. Alongside other new voices such as Billy Graham, Pierce garnered national attention as politicians, preachers, and newspapermen promoted the rallies' success.[17] Throughout the 1940s, revivals of thousands of young people gathered in American cities each Saturday night. As its motto, "Geared to the times, but anchored to the rock," claimed, YFC embraced popular culture, American civic faith, and a potentially global outreach. Torrey Johnson, YFC's first president, told *Time* magazine that his organization's goal was the "spiritual revitalization of America and the complete evangelization of the world in our generation."[18] Youth for Christ sponsored hundreds of "world vision" rallies promoting the work of international missionaries.[19] Evangelicals carefully excised any aspect of the modernist social gospel from their missions. In winning the world for Christ, concern for the social issues of the day often faded behind a greater commission to preach and make disciples.

In the wake of World War II, YFC established "invasion teams" that the organization deployed for three- to six-month evangelistic tours to win the world for Christ. In contrast to typical career missionaries, these international evangelists exported their style of American revivalism. Short evangelistic sermons alongside upbeat music, Christian celebrities, and massive promotion, coupled with America's new global cachet, heightened international curiosity. Evangelists reported conversions in the thousands and declared the time was ripe for "greater conquests for Christ."[20] With little internal dissonance, the YFC evangelists exported a largely American gospel and returned to interpret the world to their American audience at home. YFC became both a mission society and a model of American triumphalism.

In 1947, Bob Pierce spent the summer holding evangelistic crusades in China for YFC. Pierce admitted being quite naïve and ill-informed about Christianity overseas, but his revivals met with intoxicating success, recording more than seventeen thousand decisions for Christ.[21] Pierce left China, however, with a new burden for human need. He began to think of himself as a "man in the gap" after experiencing war, religious persecution, and poverty firsthand. He claimed, "I had gone there to preach the gospel, true enough, but I had also gone there to capture the need of the people and to bring that need back to America."[22] Pierce had envisioned himself as America's next Billy Graham, but he instead became known as the "Billy Graham of Asia."[23] When

Communist control closed China in 1949, Pierce followed American troops into Korea. Having obtained press credentials as a U.N. war correspondent, he commenced preaching along the front lines to Allied troops and Communist POWs alike. At the same time, he officially founded World Vision in 1950 as "an evangelical inter-denominational missionary service organization meeting emergency world needs through established evangelical missions."[24] He supplied emergency resources to Korea's hospitals, schools, and orphanages while also preaching to crowds throughout the country. From its beginning, Pierce infused World Vision with a dual mission of evangelism and social concern.

Pierce's Outlook for World Vision

Throughout the 1950s, World Vision grew slowly. Its diminutive status stood in stark contrast to the more established religious humanitarian agencies born out of World War II. The "three faiths consortium" of mainline Protestants, Catholics, and Jews had built close ties with the U.S. government to play the leading role in large-scale humanitarian projects and distribution of surplus goods. Religious philanthropies such as Catholic Relief Services, Church World Service, Lutheran World Relief, and the American Jewish Joint Distribution Committee dominated private and public support in the 1940s and continued into the Cold War theaters of Korea and Vietnam.[25] Mainstream relief organizations dismissed World Vision's relatively miniscule size and sectarian evangelical theology, but, as an evangelical missionary organization, World Vision operated in a different context. Fraternizing with ecumenical mainline Protestants—much less Catholics, Jews, or secularists—was anathema. Flirting with humanitarian organizations also bordered on promoting social welfare at the expense of evangelism.

Even as a popular evangelist, Pierce faced critique for his humanitarian work from within his evangelical subculture. He shrewdly sidestepped the constant evangelical debates between evangelism and social concern by feigning theological ignorance. While a handful of evangelical theologians began to ponder how to reverse the malaise of evangelical social concern, Pierce illustrated needs through firsthand accounts of suffering overseas. He tied evangelism and social concern together with insider evangelical language that avoided the social gospel that conservatives despised.

At the same time, Pierce remained a constant promoter of "foreign missions." By the late 1950s, a reverence for missionaries had begun to shift to negative portrayals of out-of-touch cultural imperialists. Outside the American evangelical subculture, a general humanitarianism often replaced the concern once reserved for foreign missions. Pierce, however, portrayed missionaries as forgotten heroes who met both the spiritual and physical needs of suffering people. As other relief organizations sought greater institutional capacity, Pierce insisted that World Vision was merely a bridge between American evangelicals at home and missionaries overseas. Pierce resisted creating his own programs and institutions, instead entrusting missionaries themselves with the funds.

Pierce's evangelicalism also took the form of a particular American Cold War ideology that understood the mission field as a spiritual and physical battleground. Pierce described his mission as a "battle for souls" against communism, "a godless religion spawned in hell." In a war between Christianity and communism, the battle would be fought with the gospel of Jesus Christ and acts of mercy, often supported by Christian civilizations like the United States. He followed the Cold War's hot spots as they moved from China to Korea to Vietnam—believing the battle with communism would determine the fate of the gospel in Asia. In the context of the Cold War, Pierce felt, if his prayers came true, the dominoes would fall not for communism but for Christ.[26]

Pierce's ministry also coincided with a distinct cultural moment in which Americans turned their attention eastward after 1945. Instead of simply containing communism, however, he portrayed commonalities between the East and the West, highlighting Asia's integration of shared democratic and Christian beliefs.[27] Pierce was not above exoticizing and demonizing aspects of Asian and non-Christian cultures, but he lauded examples of Christianity's influence throughout Asia.[28] While Pierce acknowledged missionaries as heroes, he also profiled "indigenous" Asian Christians. Often highlighting their sacrifice and martyrdom for the gospel, Pierce told their stories as a challenge to a complacent Western Christianity. He also pushed for greater indigenous leadership in missions because he feared Asia's door closing to the West. He remarked that "the day of the white man and his missionary work is coming to a close. . . . If Asia is to be won for Christ, it must be won by Asians."[29]

World Vision's Operations in the 1950s

In 1953, Pierce was distributing more than $100,000 of support to missionary causes in Asia; by 1956, World Vision's budget eclipsed $1 million. Even with steady success, the organization remained both relatively small and difficult to define. It was not exactly an evangelical mission agency, nor was it a religious humanitarian organization. Mainstream relief organizations like Catholic Relief Services and Church World Service, with budgets of $120 million and $38 million respectively, dismissed World Vision's relatively small size and sectarian evangelical theology.[30]

Pierce, however, cared little for institutional development. World Vision simply expanded as Pierce's own networks grew. In 1978, World Vision reflected upon its beginnings:

> There was something remarkably existential and unpremeditated about our origin. A vision of need in Asia! The passion to act in the meeting of that need. It was almost as simple as that. No long-range planning. No elaborate mechanism of administration. Emergency by emergency, crisis by crisis. It was a summons from Christ to act and to act now.[31]

Pierce remained first an evangelist, and, as he evangelized throughout Asia and encountered a need, he would pledge his financial support and pray in faith that the money would come. When he returned to America, he would raise the required support and return overseas to deliver it. By the end of the Korean War, World Vision began to support longer-term projects in addition to meeting emergency needs. In 1953, Pierce introduced the concept of "child sponsorship" for his work in Korea. For $10 a month, Americans could support an individual Korean orphan. Child sponsorship soon became the backbone of World Vision's fund-raising as World Vision financed hundreds of missionary orphanages.[32] Pierce funded anything and everything—from missionary salaries and hospital buildings to new underwear for lepers and training for indigenous Christian pastors.[33]

As the face of the ministry, Pierce knew that his own self-promotion benefited World Vision's bottom line. Throughout the 1950s, however, Pierce was far better known overseas than at home. Missionaries and local church leaders overseas celebrated his arrival at every stop. Foreign dignitaries also lauded his efforts. Pierce often led Chiang and Madame Kai-Shek in Bible study on trips to Formosa. He prayed with President Syngman Rhee on visits to Korea.

At home, Pierce began to achieve growing popular support. First, he succeeded among American evangelicals. Prominent evangelicals such as Billy Graham served on World Vision's board while Pierce also became a regular speaker on the National Association of Evangelicals' annual program. He headlined his own nationally broadcast missionary radio program, published the leading evangelical mission magazine, and produced films of his travels that he screened across the country at churches, mission conferences, and civic auditoriums for average crowds of five to six thousand.[34] In addition, he began to gain ground outside the evangelical subculture. Pierce garnered the support of celebrities such as Roy Rogers and Dale Evans, appeared on national television programs such as the *Today* show and *This Is Your Life,* and became the subject of a best-selling book.[35]

Even as Pierce's public appeal grew, he continued to have limited interaction with other leading humanitarian organizations. His context remained evangelical missions, and, while World Vision shared some overlapping objectives with CARE, Church World Service, and Christian Children's Fund, they operated in different worlds. Pierce did continue, however, to maintain good relations with the U.S. government and military leaders. As an ardent "Cold Warrior," Pierce supported America's global reach to contain communism in Asia. He became a field representative in the emerging International Christian Leadership (ICL) organization that networked American politicians and international Christian leaders in efforts to strengthen both foreign relations and worldwide Christian revival.[36] Yet even as he became better connected politically, he steered clear of government funding. The leading religious humanitarian organizations received 50 percent or more of their annual revenue from the U.S. government, but Pierce insisted World Vision's support have no governmental strings attached.[37]

World Vision's identity mimicked its founder's personality as Pierce's energetic, entrepreneurial spirit defined World Vision's first generation. His charisma and restlessness relished the adventure of traveling to the war-torn and outer reaches of the world. Pictures of Pierce at home showed an iconic battered suitcase kept by his front door, always ready for the next emergency and evangelistic adventure. The airline industry dubbed him one of the world's ten most-traveled men.[38] He earned the reputation as both firefighter, first on the scene of a global emergency, and incorrigible cowboy, set on doing things his way. He never supported work he had not investigated personally, but he often committed funding on the spot with a prayer and a handshake. He subscribed to the "faith missions" principle promoted by fundamentalist missionaries that God alone could provide the necessary resources. Pierce called it his "God room" principle. He worried that "faith isn't required as long as you set your goal only as high as the most intelligent, most informed, and expert human efforts can reach."[39] World Vision's board, however, worried how to cover checks Pierce had already written "in faith." The organization constantly ran in the red with all-night prayer sessions to meet expenses. Pierce attributed a lack of institutionalism to living by faith, but this led World Vision to neglect its oversight of budgets and programs.

Pierce's charisma also harbored a shadow side. His overwhelming compassion was matched by an explosive temper. His constant travel and commitment to work left him estranged from his family. On several occasions, he worked himself into intense depression and exhaustion, taking extended medical leaves. He often abdicated day-to-day responsibilities, relying on a few devoted co-workers, but refused to abide by decisions of his board.[40]

Shifting Contexts—World Vision in the 1960s

World Vision emerged from the 1950s as a dynamic evangelical mission agency, but it faced new contexts by the 1960s. Pierce remained an institutional outsider to the governmental aid and humanitarian communities as he continued to promote evangelical missions and an ardent anticommunism. In 1958, *The Ugly American,* by William J. Lederer and Eugene Burdick, put American foreign policy in the forefront of popular culture. The book headed the best-seller list for seventy-eight weeks, selling four million copies while also being serialized in the *Saturday Evening Post.*[41] It noted the dangerous progress of communism while criticizing the incompetence and laziness of State Department officials and aid workers. Pierce went on record as agreeing with the book's analysis, publicly sharing his own encounters with Americans living comfortably overseas while unwilling to learn the local language and customs. He used the book to juxtapose the "ugly Americans" with "America's best ambassadors," sacrificial missionaries who served as "highly effective combatants in the fight against communism."[42] Pierce sought to remind the American public of the political benefits of missionaries who lived among the people building trust and meeting needs. Pierce argued that, because the United States benefited from missionaries' positive portrayal of American democracy, missionaries should receive the same privileges and prestige as aid and military workers.[43]

Throughout the 1960s, Pierce continued to advocate for a proactive anticommunism even as the American public's optimism of a post–World War II global engagement waned. If patriotic support for the Korean War marked the 1950s, malaise for

Vietnam defined the 1960s. By the mid-1960s, Vietnam had captured the attention of the American public, but Americans were less willing to accept a clear-cut Cold War ideology. Skepticism and apathy replaced past optimistic internationalism.

By the late 1960s, Americans had begun to question their role in the world, and this uncertainty extended to American evangelicals. New voices began to emerge to advocate for greater evangelical engagement in social issues. While still a minority within the evangelical community, the voices of activist Jim Wallis, theologian Ron Sider, community organizer John Perkins, and Oregon senator Mark Hatfield all called for a new type of engagement. World Vision's work overseas led some of its staff to sympathize with the social and political issues championed by a new generation of evangelicals at home. Yet, as a growing organization appealing to a broad constituency, World Vision attempted to walk along a tenuous tightrope in the middle of evangelicalism.

If the term *evangelical* was up for grabs in the 1960s, so, too, was *mission*. Even as evangelical missions grew numerically, evangelicals themselves debated the direction of the missionary enterprise. What was the relationship between evangelism and social action? Could they associate with nonevangelical Catholics or mainline Protestants? What was the role of Western missionaries in a postcolonial world? Internally, World Vision began to reexamine its identity as a missionary organization. While World Vision kept one foot firmly planted within evangelical missions, it also ventured slowly outside an exclusively evangelical orbit. In fields like Vietnam, it began rubbing shoulders with mainline and secular NGOs that it had previously ignored. At the same time, the aid community also began to shift its own focus away from macro structural issues toward smaller individual and community needs where evangelical groups felt more comfortable operating.[44] World Vision was still more missionary agency than humanitarian NGO, but new interactions allowed it exposure to new conversations and vocabularies that slowly began to chip away at its insular evangelicalism and reshape its practice to fit that of the leading NGOs.

World Vision Responds to Changing Contexts

Pierce's charisma led World Vision's steady growth, but that same untamed energy became an organizational liability. Even Pierce saw the need for greater professionalization and institutional stability. He hired Ted Engstrom as World Vision's executive vice-president in 1963. A fixture in evangelical parachurch networks, Engstrom had the managerial gifts Pierce lacked. Upon arrival, however, Engstrom discovered World Vision to be a half million dollars in debt and delinquent in paying its monthly bills. Under Engstrom, projects could no longer simply rely on prayer. Budgets also mattered. Adapting principles from the corporate world, he would conduct hundreds of seminars on time management and systems-thinking for both Christian pastors and executives in evangelical nonprofits. World Vision became known for creating a style of "Christian management."[45]

World Vision's early professionalization harnessed technology for fund-raising. It became one of the first Christian organizations to use an IBM computer to organize mailing lists. It personalized direct mail appeals to solicit greater financial support. In contrast to the spontaneous faith of Pierce's "God room" principle, World Vision now grew as it perfected its fund-raising techniques.[46]

World Vision also harnessed professionalization for global missions. In 1966, World Vision partnered with evangelical Fuller Theological Seminary to establish the Mission Advanced Research and Communication Center (MARC). Headed by Edward Dayton, a former aeronautical engineer turned Fuller seminarian, MARC served as both a clearinghouse and think tank for world evangelization. MARC sought to convince other mission agencies that research and development did not take the "Spirit" out of missions but, rather, enhanced the efficiency of evangelism. Anthropological, sociological, and census data became necessary information in order to evangelize a particular culture.[47]

At the same time, World Vision increasingly adapted the current practices of professional humanitarian organizations. Beginning in the early 1960s, in order to provide basic relief supplies like food, water, and clothing more effectively, World Vision established sophisticated delivery networks that featured storage, transportation, and distribution systems. These new networks moved away from working directly with local churches and mission agencies that World Vision found often lacked sufficient competence and efficiency for large-scale projects. Instead, its own delivery structures sometimes hired away the best local Christian talent at higher salaries. By 1962, World Vision registered with the U.S. Agency for International Development (USAID), which enabled it to receive commodities and grants to be used for humanitarian relief. Pierce remained cautious about any dependence on government, but he pursued limited connections in order to capitalize on available resources.[48]

Pierce's Reaction to World Vision's Changes

Pierce publicly embraced World Vision's progress, but he realized these new directions would fundamentally change the nature of *his* organization. As it professionalized, World Vision's board could no longer afford to rubber-stamp Pierce's unilateral actions. A broadening constituency as well as government grants demanded greater accountability. World Vision felt it could no longer raise support simply by appealing to the faith of its supporters. It also had to demonstrate responsibility and results. Pierce supported new technology, but he worried that progress would dampen the passion for traditional evangelism. He also feared increased association with government. Pierce relied on personal relationships for political access, often calling on U.S. secretary of state Dean Rusk for entrée into areas like Vietnam, but he worried that taking government funds would temper World Vision's evangelical mission.[49]

Pierce faced a changing World Vision even as his own physical and mental health deteriorated. He remained estranged from his wife and children as well as many friends. By 1964, he took a yearlong medical leave to undergo psychological treatment while also dealing with diabetes and staph infection. Pierce wandered alone through Japan, Vietnam, Korea, and Hong Kong to visit familiar cities and former friends. In his absence,

World Vision learned it could survive without him. When he returned to the presidency of World Vision in late 1965, he attempted to reinstate unilateral control, but the board was now willing to fight back. The direction, identity, and control of World Vision remained in flux.[50]

Vietnam

Many of the shifting contexts that Pierce encountered in the 1960s came to a head during World Vision's work in Vietnam. Pierce had visited and supported individual missionaries in Vietnam since 1955, but, as the country increasingly became a hot zone for American troops and the focus of American interests, World Vision turned its attention and resources to growing humanitarian needs. By 1967, Vietnam outdistanced Korea as the largest recipient of World Vision relief goods and quickly became the center of World Vision's public appeals. Vietnam captured the attention of the American public even as America's role in the world was now less clear cut. Similarly, World Vision's own operations in Vietnam illustrated its hesitant future. Pierce's actions and rhetoric in Vietnam demonstrate a man in between two World Visions: an older evangelical missionary agency and an increasingly sophisticated Christian humanitarian organization. He often appeared trapped, trying to hold these disparate influences in a single World Vision.

From the beginning, Pierce loved to profile individuals he met overseas. Most often, the "heroes" he would spotlight were forgotten missionaries, indigenous Asian Christians, American soldiers, and military chaplains who served as sacrificial models of Christian service. By the mid-1960s, Pierce also began to highlight USAID employees and other humanitarian agencies. In the late 1950s, he contrasted heroic missionaries with the "ugly Americans," State Department officers, and aid workers. Now, Pierce made a point to list the many mainline Protestant, Catholic, and secular voluntary agencies working together to meet needs in Vietnam. Without dismissing his own missionary identity, Pierce portrayed World Vision alongside conventional humanitarian organizations.

World Vision also expanded its projects in Vietnam. Pierce continued to raise funds for typical work: sponsoring children in missionary orphanages, distributing crutches and wheelchairs through local churches, and providing medical supplies and evangelical literature for local hospitals. He also commissioned large-scale endeavors such as "Christian refugee centers" to shelter displaced Vietnamese civilians and a proposed "Christian embassy" in Saigon that he hoped would coordinate all Christian work in Southeast Asia.[51] World Vision's expanding projects in Vietnam partnered for the first time with USAID resources. World Vision bought one community a John Deere tractor and depended on USAID support to teach farming techniques to the local population.[52] Even as it worked closer with the U.S. and Vietnamese governments, World Vision moved further away from reliance on the local churches. The size and growing complexity of World Vision's humanitarian commitments, its initial reliance on government support, as well as the limited size of Vietnam's local Christian population forced World Vision to develop its own delivery structures that began to sideline the church's direct role in relief efforts.

Vietnam also forced World Vision to reconsider its relationship with the U.S. government. The image of the United States as liberator in the wake of World War II had been replaced with a growing resentment of America as a new colonial power. Pierce, however, continued to rely on a Cold War ideology—Christian America at war with godless communism. In his appeals for support, Pierce acknowledged heated debate over war in Vietnam but claimed World Vision took a nonpolitical stance and only desired to meet the physical and spiritual needs that arose. His depictions of the war, however, remained unabashedly pro-American. He challenged his supporters to pray for American troops who were defending freedom and rescuing the innocent. Yet he never romanticized war. Often embedded with the military, he graphically recounted the horrors he experienced even while depicting soldiers' sacrifice in categories akin to Christian martyrdom.[53]

Vietnam led other humanitarian organizations to distance their work from American foreign policy. Since World War II, agencies such as Catholic Relief Services, CARE, and Church World Service viewed their work either as supportive of America's anti-Communist position or at least neutral in the face of international need. By 1965, however, as protest to the war escalated at home, many agencies realized that apoliticism was impossible. Any participation in Vietnam had become a politically partisan act. Vietnam ended the notion of apolitical humanitarianism and cozy church-state partnership overseas. Several ecumenical agencies pulled out of Vietnam while others sought to protest and influence U.S. military action. As a result, they lost millions of USAID dollars.[54]

World Vision was not dependent on USAID funds like other agencies, but it was tied to an American civic faith that mirrored the majority evangelical response. At first, it saw the war as the frontline to halt Communist advance. Later, as the war dragged on, evangelicals largely felt the need to stay the course—to achieve Nixon's "peace with honor."[55] Other relief agencies chastised what they considered Pierce's naïve apoliticism. Pierce never changed, but, as the war grew more unpopular at home, World Vision, as an organization, realized the impossibility of neutrality. Apoliticalism had become a political position. In order to become an international organization, World Vision began to reexamine its relationship with America.

New types of actors, projects, and government relations resulted in a mixed message of World Vision's purpose, at times highlighting evangelism while at others promoting large-scale humanitarian relief work. By the early 1960s, World Vision had begun to revisit its language and practices as a missionary organization. It began to accept government aid; it paid greater attention to the criticism of its work from ecumenical and secular humanitarian groups; and it also engaged an evolving conversation around missions among American evangelicals.[56] Sometimes, World Vision segregated evangelism and humanitarian work into distinct divisions. At other times, it articulated an emerging holistic understanding it called "total evangelism."[57] Most often, however, Pierce's stories merged both into his typical folksy evangelical piety. In taking supplies to a Vietnamese hospital, he witnessed Christian nurses evangelizing patients. Missionaries leading agricultural training alongside USAID officials in local villages also offered Bible classes. Despite the horrors he witnessed, he affirmed the war as Vietnam's greatest evangelistic opportunity. While not naïve to the theological and logistical changes under way in his organization, Pierce's personal stories trumped World Vision's otherwise uncertain transitions.[58]

Pierce Resigns

Pierce initially left America to evangelize China in 1947, but he returned to establish what would become the world's largest Christian humanitarian organization. He relentlessly promoted missions among American evangelicals while also persuading them to put the physical suffering of the world on their agenda. Pierce thrived on a lust for adventure, personally crisscrossing the globe and unilaterally promising funds for those in need, relying on God to provide the resources. He always welcomed a challenge, but he balked when those challenges confronted his own organization.

By the 1960s, World Vision began to rephrase its language of mission while also slowly venturing out of its American evangelical subculture. It began to interact with other NGOs, governments, and donor constituencies. It began to professionalize— embracing the vocabulary, practices, technology, and funding sources of other leading NGOs. It slowly distanced itself from a stridently pro-American bias. As future World Vision president Graeme Irvine wrote:

> Anyone looking at World Vision would see an organization that was action-oriented, centered around Bob Pierce himself, strongly evangelical, innovative, and progressive. As with most things, there was another side to the coin. The apparent strengths had corresponding weaknesses: instability, dependent on the idea and personality of one person, narrow relationships and limited international perspective.[59]

By 1967, the strain became too much for Pierce. He was physically and mentally unhealthy. His uncontrollable temper had cut ties with family and friends. His authoritarianism had bulldozed World Vision to organizational growth, but, when the board pleaded for more stability, he stubbornly refused. He tendered his resignation in a fit of rage, and the board accepted it. From founding the organization in 1950 until his departure in 1967, Pierce *was* World Vision, but World Vision had outgrown him.

World Vision's Second Generation

The 1970s marked a turning point for World Vision. Stan Mooneyham, World Vision's second president, was an evangelist and charismatic leader recruited from the Billy

Graham Evangelistic Association. In many ways, he shared the hard-driving entrepreneurial and evangelical spirit of Pierce, but he also pushed World Vision to change in ways unacceptable to Pierce. Those changes led to massive growth. World Vision's annual income grew from $4.5 million in 1969 to $94 million by 1982.[60] It had evolved from a small evangelical mission agency to a leading Christian humanitarian organization.

World Vision's greatest success was bringing its religious message to the new medium of television. It soon specialized in multihour hunger telethons. Images of poverty and starvation alternated with upbeat musical numbers by celebrities such as the Muppets and Julie Andrews. In the words of one producer, "World Vision productions couched the organization's Christian motivation in language the average person could understand. We did not want to hide the Christian purpose, but to express it in general terms more appropriate for a television audience."[61] World Vision consciously extended its message outside the evangelical orbit. Explicit language of mission broadened to general religious humanitarianism.

As it expanded, World Vision's ministry also evolved from funding individual orphans to large-scale relief and development. Eager to gain legitimacy among other NGOs, World Vision received a USAID grant in 1975 to establish its development capacity. By the end of the decade, relief and development defined the organization's direction. World Vision referred to its employees no longer as missionaries but as aid workers. This transition, however, required specialists trained in fields such as public health and agricultural development.[62] While World Vision insisted that all employees profess a Christian faith, fewer now came with degrees from evangelical seminaries or Bible colleges. A new class of technocrats entered the ranks of World Vision, often speaking a language distinct from Bob Pierce's fiery sermons.[63]

The INGO humanitarian community often continued to keep World Vision at arm's length, skeptical of its evangelical identity and the overlap between its missionary and relief/development work. Media, foreign governments, and other NGOs sometimes accused World Vision of blatantly pro-American policies and Western biases. World Vision's own field personnel complained at times of its paternalistic and controlling tendencies.[64] While Pierce had fought to keep World Vision grounded as an evangelical missionary agency distinguishable from other NGOs, new leadership sought to adapt new practices in order to become a leader in the humanitarian industry, albeit a clearly Christian one. As a result, World Vision debated internally how to be both sufficiently evangelistic and humanitarian. It also expanded to other countries, and an increased international presence tempered its past pro-American biases while demanding a need for a new organizational structure of shared international leadership.[65] It also began to rely less on American expatriates and more on an indigenous workforce. After Pierce's departure, World Vision sought to prove it could remain Christian while gaining newfound respect as a leading humanitarian NGO. While the tensions of balancing both its religious and professional identity persisted, World Vision emerged out of its founder's shadow to become a leading humanitarian agency.

Pierce Founds Samaritan's Purse

Pierce regretted the direction of the new World Vision. After his resignation, he continued to travel the world, finding release in a nomadic lifestyle free from responsibility. Pierce's charisma, however, despised the idea of retirement. In 1969, as his physical and mental health slowly returned, the board of a struggling evangelical mission organization, Food for the World, approached him to become president. The organization had only $12 in the bank, but Pierce accepted the job. In 1970, he renamed it Samaritan's Purse and set out recreating the World Vision he originally established in 1950.[66]

At Samaritan's Purse, Pierce reclaimed his identity as missionary adventurer, being the first on the scene ready to meet individual emergency needs. Rather than channeling resources through institutions, he personally delivered funds to the suffering. Instead of development projects, he highlighted heroic missionaries. He reminded his supporters, "I'm going to spend my life backing up people [who have] proved they care about people and God. When I could no longer do that through World Vision, that's when I resigned and started Samaritan's Purse."[67] As he encountered a pressing need in his travels, Pierce would promise funds and rely on his "God room" principle—that, in faith, God would provide. The board of Samaritan's Purse never officially met. As Pierce's friends, they simply rubber-stamped his decisions.[68] He solicited support through personal letters filled with "on-the-scene" stories of need, and, having taken World Vision's mailing list and the loyalty of many missionaries with him when he resigned, he depended on their personal support.

In establishing Samaritan's Purse, Pierce often explicitly argued against what World Vision had become. He felt professionalization diminished World Vision's reliance on faith. He told the *Los Angeles Times*, "World Vision has a new complex computer system which diagnoses the failures of Christianity and prints them on a data sheet. . . . I can't stand it. I love the early days when I was walking with widows and holding babies. When I began flying over them and being met by committees at the airport it almost killed me."[69] He often drew on the biblical Good Samaritan to differentiate his new organization from others. On occasion, he identified the priest and Levite, the two characters indifferent to the wounded traveler on the side of the road, as representing the "organizational machinery of relief agencies, charities, and even churches with vast sums of money and effort tied up in committee-controlled specialized funds and property, which often delays concrete action." He cautioned, "You can get your life and business down to where you don't need God. You can operate exactly like Sears & Roebuck or General Motors or IBM—but the blessings will all be gone."[70] In contrast to Pierce's characterization of World Vision's "slick, market-driven" fund-raising appeals, he offered "personal identification with individual human needs."[71] Pierce believed World Vision sacrificed its religious identity as it substituted faith in professionalization over prayer.

If World Vision also began to venture outside an exclusively evangelical orbit, Pierce returned to the fundamentalism and evangelicalism where he felt most comfortable.

While World Vision faced criticism among other NGOs for its past overlap between its evangelism and humanitarian work, Samaritan's Purse highlighted the indistinguishable overlap in their ministry as a positive. Among evangelicals, Pierce promoted his evangelist credentials as a badge of honor that contrasted Samaritan's Purse with others that appeared to water down their Christian identities in order to achieve greater success. In contrast to World Vision's "do-goodism," Pierce challenged Samaritan's Purse not to be ashamed to "fly the banner of Jesus Christ high." He had learned from World Vision that "who pays the piper, calls the tune" and forbade Samaritan's Purse to accept government aid.[72] Under Pierce, Samaritan's Purse grew modestly as a small evangelical missionary agency apart from other government and humanitarian organizations.

By 1975, Pierce was diagnosed with leukemia, but it did not keep him from continuing to scour the world for individual needs to meet. In between travels and treatments, he discovered a potential successor to mentor. Pierce's friend and fellow evangelist Billy Graham introduced Pierce to his son, Franklin. Franklin Graham's story resembled Pierce's. Having rebelled from the faith of his youth, Franklin had little interest in education or Christian gentility, but he shared Pierce's need for adventure. In 1975, Franklin Graham accompanied Pierce on an around-the-world tour designed to expose him to the world's spiritual and physical needs. The trip set Graham on a new course, eager to follow Pierce's design for Samaritan's Purse to meet individual, emergency missionary needs. In 1978, Pierce died, and, a year later, Franklin Graham followed in Pierce's footsteps as the twenty-eight-year-old president of Samaritan's Purse.[73]

Samaritan's Purse has grown under Graham into a sizable organization while adhering to Pierce's principles. Graham attributes his success to Pierce's "God room" principle. He is committed to Pierce's notion that God will always provide resources beyond his organization's capacities to plan and fund-raise. Like Pierce, Graham has also built Samaritan's Purse around his own personality, soliciting support through personal stories of individual and emergency needs encountered through his own danger-filled travels. Evangelism also remains central. As a crusade evangelist like both Pierce and his father, Billy, Franklin Graham says that his organization is "not just a Christian relief organization. We are an evangelistic organization." Responding to claims of proselytism, Graham declares, "I will take advantage of each and every opportunity to reach [people] with the gospel message that can save them from the flames of hell."[74] Like Pierce, who never shied away from preaching against the wickedness of all non-Christian, "pagan religions," Graham has made headlines for his attempts to work in Muslim countries after his public criticism of Islam.[75] The evangelical identity of Samaritan's Purse remains front and center in shaping its public persona.

Conclusion

Today, World Vision and Samaritan's Purse are both among the top ten largest INGOs in the United States. Bob Pierce planted both with the same religious identity, and both remain decidedly Christian organizations, but their relationships with their founder help illustrate their differences. Pierce lived in times of change—an evolving American evangelicalism, professionalization, transitions in Christian missions, and new relationships with humanitarian development agencies and government relations. Yet Pierce remained stubbornly consistent with his faith perspective, and his religious commitments forced him to draw lines he was unwilling to cross.

World Vision outgrew its founder. Established as an evangelical mission agency, it is now a Christian relief and development organization. As a respected industry leader, it is known as a savvy practitioner, relied upon by governments for its expertise and extensive delivery networks around the world. It remains Christian and, in many countries, strongly evangelical. It never hides its Christian identity, but it also markets itself as a uniformly respected global INGO.

As World Vision's own religious identity transformed, Pierce clung to his original vision and rooted Samaritan's Purse in the same evangelical soil where he felt most comfortable. Samaritan's Purse continues to walk in Pierce's footsteps. While it has pursued limited governmental funding and added community development to its list of activities, the bulk of its work still supports career and short-term missionaries, individual emergency relief, and evangelism. Samaritan's Purse remains tied to its evangelical base and promotes its work primarily through its religious identity. It is often not as readily received as a peer among other leading humanitarian organizations as is World Vision.

Some scholars have dismissed the significance of religious identity among INGOs and advocate a general homogenization of humanitarian language and practice. Others too eagerly tag all Christian agencies with the same label. Both generalizations overlook the different ways particular organizations' Christian identities shape their rhetoric, donor constituencies, and practice on the ground. In particular, the relationships of World Vision and Samaritan's Purse with their founder demonstrate how the tensions and evolutions within a specific religious identity play a pivotal role in shaping the history and development of religious philanthropy.

Notes

1. This question served as the last line of Pierce's first book on his travels in China. Ken Anderson and Bob Pierce, *This Way to the Harvest* (Grand Rapids: Zondervan, 1949).

2. For versions of the White Jade story, see Marilee Pierce Dunker, *Man of Vision: The Candid, Compelling Story of Bob and Lorraine Pierce, Founders of World Vision and Samaritan's Purse* (Waynesboro, Ga.: Authentic Media, 2005), 83–84; Franklin Graham and Jeanette Lockerbie, *Bob Pierce: This One Thing I Do*, 5th ed. (Waco, Tex.: Word, 1983), 74–75; Gary F. VanderPol, "The Least of These: American Evangelical Parachurch Missions to the Poor, 1947–2005" (PhD diss., Boston University School of Theology, 2010), 40; Bob Pierce, *Orphans of the Orient: Stories That Will Touch Your Heart* (Grand Rapids: Zondervan, 1964), 55–60; and Richard Gehman, *Let My Heart Be Broken . . . with the Things that Break the Heart of God* (Grand Rapids: Zondervan, 1960), 119.

3. By development, I am referring to the field of study and network of organizations that seek to work for long-lasting change in communities. What counts as development and the nature of the

process varies widely from building roads and hospitals to establishing locally based economic cooperatives. For an overview, see Gilbert Rist, The *History of Development: From Western Origins to Global Faith* (New York: Zed Books, 2008).

4. Rachel M. McCleary, *Global Compassion: Private Voluntary Organizations and U.S. Foreign Policy since 1939* (New York: Oxford University Press, 2009), 25–28. McCleary reports the ten largest INGOs from 1940 to 2005. Based on 2005 numbers, World Vision remains second while Samaritan's Purse is tenth. Both organizations' most recent annual reports are available from their respective websites: www.worldvision.org and www.samaritanspurse.org.

5. Currently, faith-based organizations make up one-third of all INGOs and one-half of total INGO revenue. See Rachel M. McCleary, "Private Voluntary Organizations Engaged in International Assistance, 1939–2004," *Nonprofit and Voluntary Sector Quarterly* 37, no. 3 (September 2008): 512–36. In 1946, the revenue shares of faith-based relief and development NGOs were 64 percent Jewish, 16 percent Catholic, 7 percent ecumenical Christian, 5 percent evangelical, 4 percent mainline Protestant, and 3 percent faith-founded Christian. In 2004, the percentages were almost reversed: 41 percent evangelical, 28 percent faith-founded, 13 percent Catholic, 7 percent Jewish, 6 percent ecumenical, and 4 percent mainline Protestant. Religious organizations dominated the INGO environment until the 1960s–1970s, when secular organizations rose to make up the vast majority of development aid. However, new religious INGOs, mostly from within the evangelical sector, have seen the most recent growth.

6. John Boli and George M. Thomas, "World Culture in the World Polity: A Century of International Non-Governmental Organization," *American Sociological Review* 62, no. 2 (1997): 171–90; Frank J. Lechner and John Boli, *World Culture: Origins and Consequences* (Malden, Mass.: Blackwell, 2005); and John Boli and David V. Brewington, "Religious Organizations," in *Religion, Globalization, and Culture,* ed. Peter Beyer and Lori G. Beaman (Boston: Leiden, 2007), 203–31.

7. Within the field of organizational studies, this general homogenization is called institutional isomorphism. See Paul J. Dimaggio and Walter W. Powell, "The Iron Cage Revisited: Institutional Isomorphism and Collective Rationality in Organizational Fields," in *The New Institutionalism in Organizational Analysis,* ed. Walter W. Powell and Paul J. DiMaggio (Chicago: University of Chicago Press, 1991), 1–40.

8. For Weber's collected writings on charisma and bureaucracy, see Max Weber, *Max Weber on Charisma and Institution Building: Selected Papers,* ed. with an introduction by S. N. Eisenstadt (Chicago: University of Chicago Press, 1968).

9. The World Bank may best define this approach of secular development's engagement with religion. See Katherine Marshall and Marisa Van Saanen, *Development and Faith: Where Mind, Heart, and Soul Work Together* (Washington, D.C.: World Bank, 2007); Katherine Marshall and Lucy Keough, *Finding Global Balance: Common Ground between the Worlds of Development and Faith* (Washington, D.C.: World Bank, 2005); and Scott M. Thomas, "Faith and Foreign Aid: How the World Bank Got Religion and Why It Matters," *Brandywine Review of Faith and International Affairs* (Fall 2004): 21–29.

10. For a critique of a world-culture view of religion, see McCleary, *Global Compassion;* Yujun Mei, "The Changing Discourse of International Humanitarian Charitable-Relief NGOs" (PhD diss., Arizona State University, 2003); and Rachel M. McCleary, "Taking God Overseas: Competition and Institutional Homogeneity among International Religious Private Voluntary Organizations," paper presented at the annual meeting of the International Studies Association, Montreal, Quebec, Canada, March 17, 2004.

11. While aspects of Pierce's story serve to substantiate Weber's thesis of an organization moving from charisma to bureaucracy, this remains only one aspect of the institutional stories of World Vision and Samaritan's Purse. The specifics of religious identity are also important. For another study of a religious organization, see Jerome P. Baggett, *Habitat for Humanity: Building Private Homes, Building Public Religion* (Philadelphia: Temple University Press, 2001).

12. Following George Marsden, I adopt a historical over theological definition of fundamentalists and evangelicals that portrays a developing American evangelicalism as a self-designated

transdenominational network of leaders, institutions, and publications composed mainly of theologically conservative Protestants who broke from separatist fundamentalism in the early 1950s. See George M. Marsden, "The Evangelical Denomination," in *Evangelicalism and Modern America,* ed. George M. Marsden (Grand Rapids: Eerdmans, 1984), vii–xix.

13. There are several biographical treatments of Pierce's life. I have drawn basic details from the following: Graham and Lockerbie, *Bob Pierce;* Dunker, *Man of Vision;* Norman Rohrer, *Open Arms* (Wheaton, Ill.: Tyndale House, 1987); Gehman, *Let My Heart Be Broken;* "Dr. Bob Pierce Biography," n.d., Folder 23, Box 6, Collection 506, Records of *Decision* Magazine, Archives of the Billy Graham Center, Wheaton, Illinois.

14. Joel Carpenter, *Revive Us Again: The Reawakening of American Fundamentalism* (New York: Oxford University Press, 1997).

15. Carl F. H. Henry, "The Uneasy Conscience of Modern Fundamentalism" (1947), in *Two Reformers of Fundamentalism, Harold John Ockenga and Carl F. H. Henry,* ed. Joel A. Carpenter (New York: Garland, 1988).

16. For the standard work on the rise of the "new evangelicalism," see George Marsden, *Reforming Fundamentalism: Fuller Seminary and the New Evangelicalism* (Grand Rapids: Eerdmans, 1987).

17. President Harry Truman lauded Youth for Christ's efforts. Newspaper magnate William Randolph Hurst also publicized Youth for Christ in his twenty-two papers. See "William Randolph Hearst's Editorial Endorsement of 'Youth for Christ,'" *United Evangelical Action* (July 16, 1945): 13.

18. Joel Carpenter, "Geared to the Times, but Anchored to the Rock," *Christianity Today* 29, no. 16 (November 8, 1985): 46.

19. Some cite the number of evangelical missionaries as doubling from 15,000 in 1951 to 27,000 by 1955. See Ted W. Engstrom, *Reflections on a Pilgrimage: Six Decades of Service* (Sisters, Ore.: Loyal, 1999), 53; and Joel A. Carpenter, "Youth for Christ and the New Evangelicals," in *Reckoning with the Past,* ed. D. G. Hart (Grand Rapids: Baker Books, 1995), 368.

20. Military and crusade language was common. Evangelists were "Christian commandos" with "arsenals" for worldwide evangelization. See Carpenter, *Revive Us Again,* 178–79; Richard V. Pierard, "Pax Americana and the Evangelical Missionary Advance," in *Earthen Vessels: American Evangelicals and Foreign Missions, 1880–1980,* ed. Joel A. Carpenter and Wilbert R. Shenk (Grand Rapids: Eerdmans, 1990), 155–79; and Merv Rosell, "God's Global 'Go!'" *Winona Echoes* 51 (1945): 260–65.

21. Graham and Lockerbie, *Bob Pierce,* 66; Dunker, *Man of Vision,* 73; "Dr. Bob Pierce Biography."

22. Ken Anderson, "Ambassador on Fire," *Youth for Christ Magazine,* June 1948, 16.

23. Billy Graham called him "one of America's leading missionary statesmen." See "Bob Pierce, 'This Is Your Life,'" *World Vision Magazine* (May 1961): 4; and John Robert Hamilton, "An Historical Study of Bob Pierce and World Vision's Development of the Evangelical Social Action Film" (PhD diss., University of Southern California, 1980), 20.

24. Dunker, *Man of Vision,* 97–100.

25. CARE was the only secular INGO breaking the top eight largest INGOs in 1950 and 1960. McCleary, *Global Compassion,* 25–28; J. Bruce Nichols, *The Uneasy Alliance: Religion, Refugee Work, and U.S. Foreign Policy* (New York: Oxford University Press, 1988), 10.

26. Hamilton, "An Historical Study of Bob Pierce," 97.

27. Christina Klein, *Cold War Orientalism: Asia in the Middlebrow Imagination, 1945–1961* (Berkeley: University of California Press, 2003), 5. Klein advocates a cultural integrationist outlook of Cold War ideology alongside political containment. Pierce's perspective demonstrates Klein's theory in the realm of evangelical missions and religious philanthropy.

28. Pierce continued publicly to refer to non-Christian religions as "pagan" throughout his career.

29. Carl F. H. Henry, *Confessions of a Theologian: An Autobiography* (Waco, Tex.: Word, 1986), 197.

30. McCleary, *Global Compassion,* 27–28. McCleary's numbers were recalculated into real 1960 dollars.

31. "Declaration of Internationalization," May 31, 1978, Central Records, World Vision International (WVI), Monrovia, California.

32. Specifically, Pierce borrowed the child sponsorship concept already being employed by China's Children's Fund (later renamed Christian Children's Fund). He hired Earl Raetz, who had worked for China's Children's Fund, to implement the sponsorship concept for World Vision in Korea.

33. World Vision introduced pastors' conferences by 1953 that annually gathered together thousands of pastors from numerous denominations for education and spiritual support. By 1957, World Vision defined its ministry through five key objectives: (1) stimulate public interest in missionary work; (2) conduct evangelistic campaigns; (3) hold conferences for native pastors; (4) promote and expand social welfare services; and (5) give emergency aid to churches, missions, hospitals, and others. Gehman, *Let My Heart Be Broken,* 172.

34. A leading film producer noted, "Nobody in his generation had the impact on behalf of mission on the domestic audience as Bob Pierce." During the 1950s–1960s, Pierce averaged more than one film per year. See Hamilton, "An Historical Study of Bob Pierce."

35. Pierce hired a Hollywood public relations firm for his own appearances. World Vision became increasingly well-known through the international tours of its Korean Orphan Choir beginning in 1961. The choir sang at churches and auditoriums as well as at Carnegie Hall, the White House, and before heads of state. The popular *This Is Your Life* show also featured Bob Pierce in 1961. Pierce appeared on the *Today* show in 1965 to promote his *Vietnam Profile* film.

36. The ICL was the forerunner to the Fellowship and National Prayer Breakfast movement. Richard Halverson, chair of World Vision's board and acting president in Pierce's absence, was also director of the ICL. See D. Michael Lindsay, "Is the National Prayer Breakfast Surrounded by a 'Christian Mafia'? Religious Publicity and Secrecy within the Corridors of Power," *Journal of the American Academy of Religion* 74, no. 2 (June 1, 2006): 390–419; D. Michael Lindsay, "Organizational Liminality and Inter- stitial Creativity: The Fellowship of Power," *Social Forces* 89, no. 1 (2010): 163–84; and Jeff Sharlet, *The Family: The Secret Fundamentalism at the Heart of American Power* (New York: HarperCollins, 2008).

37. In 1960, Catholic Relief Services received 61.6 percent of their funding from federal sources; Church World Service received 55.2 percent; CARE received 67.8 percent; and Lutheran World Relief received 57.4 percent. McCleary, *Global Compassion,* 27–28.

38. Gehman, *Let My Heart Be Broken,* 171.

39. Franklin Graham, *Rebel with a Cause* (Nashville: Thomas Nelson, 1995), 141. On faith missions, see Michael S. Hamilton, "More Money, More Ministry: The Financing of American Evangelicalism since 1945," in *More Money, More Ministry: Money and Evangelicals in Recent North American History,* ed. Larry Eskridge and Mark A. Noll (Grand Rapids: Eerdmans, 2000), 104–106; and Dana Robert, *Occupy until I Come: A. T. Pierson and the Evangelization of the World* (Grand Rapids: Eerdmans, 2003).

40. Pierce's daughter, Marilee Pierce Dunker, wrote a candid biography of her parents, *Man of Vision, Woman of Prayer* (Nashville: Thomas Nelson, 1980), that provides insight into the toll Pierce's personality took on himself as well as on friends and family. The book was reissued in 1984 and 2005 (bibliographic information for the 2005 edition is cited in note 2 above and is the edition cited through- out the notes). Dunker, *Man of Vision.*

41. Clive Christie, *The Quiet American and The Ugly American: Western Literary Perspectives on Indo-China in a Decade of Transition, 1950–1960,* Occasional paper no. 10 (Canterbury: University of Kent at Canterbury, Centre of East Asian Studies, 1989), 38; William J. Lederer and Eugene Burdick, *The Ugly American* (New York: Norton, 1958).

42. Bob Pierce, "We Need More 'Ugly' Americans," *Washington Post and Times Herald,* April 12, 1959.

43. Privileges included no income tax, reduced shipping and postage rates, and admittance to the commissary.

44. McCleary, *Global Compassion,* 83–84.

45. See Engstrom, *Reflections on a Pilgrimage*, 123. In the early 1970s, fiscal accountability became a huge issue for religious nonprofits. World Vision partnered with the Billy Graham Evangelistic Association to form the Council for Financial Accountability, made up of many evangelical nonprofits seeking to self-regulate their fund-raising efforts. Engstrom also wrote countless books on Christian leadership; for example, see *The Art of Management for Christian Leaders* (Waco, Tex.: Word Books, 1976).

46. VanderPol, "The Least of These," 85–86; Hamilton, "More Money, More Ministry," 107.

47. MARC introduced the concept of "unreached people groups" to evangelical missiology. Ted W. Engstrom, "The Use of Technology: A Vital Tool That Will Help," in *One Race, One Gospel, One Task*, 2 vols., ed. Carl F. H. Henry and W. Stanley Mooneyham (Minneapolis: World Wide, 1967), 1:315–16; Edward R. Dayton, "Computerize Evangelism," *World Vision Magazine* (March 1966): 4–5; David Lundquist, "Missions Need R and D," *World Vision Magazine* (October 1966): 18–19; Edward R. Dayton, "Research, A Key to Renewal," *Journal of the American Scientific Affiliation* 21 (March 1969): 15–17.

48. Pierce first partnered with the U.S. government in 1959 in "Operation Handclasp," using empty bins on navy ships to transport World Vision food aid. Much of World Vision's early official relationship with USAID was in offset for shipping commodities. Beginning in 1962, World Vision established World Vision Relief Organization (WVRO) to distinguish its evangelistic from social welfare work to meet separation of church and state restrictions. WVRO remained a subsidiary of World Vision until court precedent after the 1997 Charitable Choice Act under George W. Bush made the strict separation unnecessary. VanderPol, "The Least of These," 85; Rohrer, *Open Arms*, 139; Linda D. Smith, "An Awakening of Conscience: The Changing Response of American Evangelicals toward World Poverty" (PhD diss., American University, 1986), 289.

49. World Vision Board minutes, July 16, 1965, WVI Central Records. Pierce reports Secretary of State Dean Rusk wired officials in Vietnam requesting that Pierce be given the best possible treatment and whatever resources he needed.

50. Dunker, *Man of Vision*, 155–71; Graeme Irvine, *Best Things in the Worst Times: An Insider's View of World Vision* (Wilsonville, Ore.: BookPartners, 1996), 21–24.

51. World Vision Board minutes, December 9, 1965, and June 12–14, 1966, WVI Central Records.

52. Bob Pierce, *Big Day at Da Me* (Waco Tex.: Word Books, 1968), 11; Hamilton, "An Historical Study of Bob Pierce," 154–58; *Vietnam Profile*, David Wisner, 1965 (World Vision U.S. Archives, Federal Way, WA); "Vietnam Profile, Souvenir Booklet," WVI Central Records.

53. Pierce, *Big Day at Da Me*; Pierce, *Vietnam Profile*, 1967.

54. For the political reaction of INGOs to U.S. policy in Vietnam and Southeast Asia, see Scott Flipse, "To Save 'Free Vietnam' and Lose Our Souls: The Missionary Impulse, Voluntary Agencies, and Protestant Dissent against the War, 1965–1971," in *The Foreign Missionary Enterprise at Home*, ed. Grant Wacker and Daniel A. Bays (Tuscaloosa: University of Alabama Press, 2003), 206–22; and Nichols, *The Uneasy Alliance*. Also see articles in *Peace and Change* 27, no. 2 (April 2002).

55. Andrew LeRoy Pratt, "Religious Faith and Civil Religion: Evangelical Responses to the Vietnam War, 1964–1973" (PhD diss., Southern Baptist Theological Seminary, 1988).

56. Examples of evangelical conversations on missions include the Congress on the Church's Worldwide Mission (Wheaton, Illinois, 1966), the World Congress on Evangelism (Berlin, 1966), and, later, the First International Congress on World Evangelization (Lausanne, 1974).

57. "Total Evangelism Appeal Letter," March 1965, acting president, Richard Halverson, Folder 37, Box 21, Collection 165, Records of the Evangelical Fellowship of Missions Agencies (EFMA), Archives of the Billy Graham Center, Wheaton, Illinois; Graham and Lockerbie, *Bob Pierce*; Dunker, *Man of Vision*; Rohrer, *Open Arms*; Gehman, *Let My Heart Be Broken*; "Dr. Bob Pierce Biography."

58. Pierce, *Big Day at Da Me*, 28.

59. Irvine, *Best Things in the Worst Times*, 22.

60. Ken Waters, "How World Vision Rose from Obscurity to Prominence: Television Fundraising, 1972–1982," *American Journalism* 15, no. 4 (1998): 69.

61. Ibid., 70. See descriptions of World Vision's 1975 telethon, *One to One,* in Hamilton, "An Historical Study of Bob Pierce," 205.

62. W. Stanley Mooneyham, "The Churches and Development: Caring Can't Wait," *International Review of Mission* 69 (January 1980): 56.

63. World Vision U.S. employees are still asked to affirm the Confession of Faith adopted by the National Association of Evangelicals in 1942, but they may choose to affirm the Apostles' or Nicene creeds. This is not, however, always uniformly practiced or enforced. In other countries where World Vision operates, religious discrimination is illegal. In countries where there is no local Christian community, such as predominantly Muslim countries, World Vision hires local Muslims to provide relief services. See "The Christian Witness Commission Final Report," September 1995, WVI Central Records; and Alan Whaites, "Pursuing Partnership: World Vision and the Ideology of Development—A Case Study," *Development in Practice* 9, no. 4 (August 1999): 414.

64. The agenda of the 1982 World Vision National Directors' Conference was taken over by global South leaders who felt Western management did not understand their perspectives.

65. It was a growing global evangelicalism, rather than secular development, that convinced World Vision of the need for organizational change. At the 1974 Lausanne First International Congress on World Evangelization, new and persuasive voices from Two-Thirds World evangelicals preached of the necessity for both evangelism and social concern without the dichotomies framed by Western Christians. Through the congress, World Vision leaders found themselves more closely aligned with the evangelicals of the global South rather than with many American evangelicals. "Report of the Internationalization Study Committee," presented April 21, 1976, by Graeme Irvine at the World Vision Combined Boards in Honolulu, Hawaii, Central Records, WVI, Monrovia, California; Irvine, *Best Things in the Worst Times,* 78; author's interviews with Bill Kliewer and Sam Kamaleson.

66. Dunker, *Man of Vision,* 193–94.

67. Graham and Lockerbie, *Bob Pierce,* 77.

68. Graham, *Rebel with a Cause,* 140, 161.

69. Lee Grant, "He Only Wants to Save the World," *Los Angeles Times,* January 22, 1975, G1, G6.

70. Graham and Lockerbie, *Bob Pierce,* 53.

71. Bob Pierce, *Samaritan's Diary,* 1973, vol. 1, Folder 4, Box 1, Collection 593, Records of Lillian Dickson, Archives of the Billy Graham Center, Wheaton, Illinois.

72. Graham, *Rebel with a Cause,* 149; Graham and Lockerbie, *Bob Pierce,* 83. After the promotion of funding for faith-based non-profits spearheaded through the presidency of George W. Bush, Samaritan's Purse now does accept limited government funding.

73. Graham, *Rebel with a Cause,* 165; Graham and Lockerbie, *Bob Pierce,* 81–85.

74. Graham, *Rebel with a Cause,* 187.

75. Graham most notably referred to Islam as "a very evil and wicked religion." Michael Wilson, "Evangelist Says Muslims Haven't Adequately Apologized for Sept. 11 Attacks," *New York Times,* August 15, 2002.

5 Catholic Charities, Religion, and Philanthropy

Fred Kammer, S.J.

THIS ESSAY FOCUSES on Catholic Charities in the United States—what it does, how it is funded, and how it faces the tensions of philanthropy and Catholic identity. In the Catholic Charities world, the framework for this consideration is captured in a single word: pluralism. This essay explains the network's understanding of pluralism, how the faith-based debates of the past two decades did or did not affect Catholic Charities, and, using "the pluralism diamond," the tensions experienced by a religiously affiliated social service network, the ways to maintain balance and identity amid those tensions, and the rationale for religiously affiliated social service agencies to partner with government, the largest funder of social services in the country.

Part 1: An Overview of Catholic Charities in the United States

It may be helpful at first to understand that the Catholic Charities USA network is not a single national organization with local branches like the Boy Scouts of America, the Salvation Army, or the Red Cross. Because the Catholic Church is structured in individual dioceses and because of the grassroots histories of these ministries, the Catholic Charities agencies are largely "homegrown." (Dioceses are administrative divisions of the Roman Catholic Church that are generally based upon geographical areas as large as a single state [for example, Idaho or Wyoming] or as "small" as a large metropolitan area [such as Boston or Washington, D.C.].[1]) Many agencies are organized as a single not-for-profit corporation within a single diocese—for example, Catholic Community Services of Baton Rouge. They also may have different names, such as "Catholic Charities," "Catholic Social Services," or "Catholic Family Services."

In many dioceses, however, there are multiple affiliated organizations under the heading of a Catholic Charities office or secretariat. In some, there exist separate institutions—for example, an individual home for the elderly ("St. Christopher's Residence") or a housing complex ("Hope Homes")—created as separate not-for-profit corporations for legal, financial, and funding purposes. In other dioceses serving large geographical areas, there may be individual county organizations that are separately incorporated to serve local populations, such as Catholic Social Services of Monroe County, one of several branch agencies of Catholic Charities in the Archdiocese of Detroit. In still other dioceses, the separate agencies may be specialty organizations serving particular people in need—for example, a housing corporation, a counseling agency, or an organization providing legal services for immigration and naturalization. To make it even more confusing, some dioceses, such as Youngstown, combine geographical agencies and specialty organizations under one organizational umbrella.[2] Finally, in a few rare situations, a single Catholic Charities agency may operate in more than one diocese, usually because of a specialty service—for example, a food-buying cooperative or a statewide or regional contract to deliver certain services.

Such organizational diversity often reflects a sense of subsidiarity within the diocese. However, all of the diverse agencies are in some way subject to coordination or supervision by the diocesan Catholic Charities agency and/or the diocesan bishop, as is the case in a diocese with a single agency.

> While separately incorporated, Catholic Charities retains a public identity with the Church for religious reasons not only rooted in its origin, but also integral to its continuing identity and mission. Its religious integrity requires a formal connectedness to the diocese through corporate structures that meet the requirements of the law of the Church (canon law) and the state law governing the corporation, as well as federal and state laws that may regulate some funding programs.[3]

Separately incorporated organizations can also be a challenge to the diocese in terms of keeping a strong sense of identification with the diocese and coordination among the agencies.[4]

Whom Do Catholic Charities Serve?

But what do these organizations do and whom do they serve? For an overview, we turn to the 174-page *Catholic Charities USA 2009 Annual Survey Final Report,* prepared by the Center for Applied Research in the Apostolate (CARA) at Georgetown University.[5] This was the latest published report at the time of writing and is fairly representative of services and trends over recent years. The survey reports that, in 2009, "2,391 local Catholic Charities agencies and affiliates provided services to 9,164,981 unduplicated clients."[6] An "unduplicated client" is a single person. He or she may receive multiple services; for example, a person with mental health problems may be counseled as well as receive assistance with a medical bill and even housing in a shelter for the homeless. (Statistics on services provided in the pages that follow report on the services provided by Catholic Charities agencies, although in some cases two or more services may be received by a single person.) The annual survey is itself a challenge for the statisticians because statistics have to be collected from a number of organizations and their staffs across the country, often working in multiple affiliated agencies within a single reporting diocese.[7]

Who were these nine million people served by Catholic Charities in 2009? As the survey emphasizes, "Children under age 18 and seniors age 65 and over comprise 42 percent of unduplicated clients served by Catholic Charities member agencies and affiliates."[8] Of all those served, 2,720,814 (30 percent) were children under eighteen years of age; 4,472,568 (49 percent) were adults eighteen to sixty-four years of age; and 1,132,708 (12 percent) were sixty-five years and older. An additional 838,891 (9 percent) were not classified by age. In terms of socioeconomic characteristics, CARA reports that a total of 58 percent of the persons served by Catholic Charities had family incomes below the federal poverty line ($22,050 for a family of four). This economic concentration reflects most people's perception that Catholic Charities serve the poor and needy, but the data also indicates that Catholic Charities serve many others in the community as well.

What Services Do Catholic Charities Provide?

What services do these nine million people receive from Catholic Charities? First and foremost, it is food. Using the figures for *services* provided in a year (totaling 14,975,726 client services provided, where one client may be "duplicated" in the sense of receiving more than one service) and the categories provided by CARA, table 5.1 shows what client services Catholic Charities provided in 2009.[9]

SERVICES THAT PROVIDE FOOD

Because *food services* are those most received by people from Catholic Charities, it may be good to look more closely at those numbers. Approximately half of those services was in "prepared food services," meaning congregate dining facilities (1,609,935), soup kitchens (1,484,735), and home-delivered meals (264,731). The other half was in "food distribution services," which included food banks and pantries (3,281,135) and other food services (575,843) such as food co-ops and food vouchers.[10]

Table 5.1. Services provided by Catholic Charities agencies, 2009

Service Types	Number	Percent
Services that provide food	7,216,379	48%
Services that build strong communities	3,956,234	27%
Other basic needs services	1,933,799	13%
Services that strengthen families	1,064,913	7%
Housing-related services	497,271	3%
Disaster services	99,665	1%
Programs for special populations	207,465	1%
Total client services provided	14,975,726	100%

SERVICES THAT BUILD STRONG COMMUNITIES

While the meaning of food services might be clear to most Americans, the need for the vast array of *services that build strong communities* reflects the many community problems that are often invisible to the ordinary person unaffected by them. Fifty-one percent of these services in 2009 (1,999,189) addressed the need for social support by frail and vulnerable people. Key among these were elders and children. For seniors, 163 reporting agencies provided services such as counseling, case management, transportation, services for the homebound, caregiver support, respite care, chore services, employment services, homemaker services, senior companion programs, home repairs, retired senior volunteer programs, foster grandparent programs, adult day care, legal services, guardianships for seniors, assisted living, bereavement support, and senior centers.[11] For children, agencies indicated an array of programs and services for children of various age groups, including child day-care services (57 agencies, programs, or offices), mostly in center settings but also in family-based settings; transportation services (18 agencies); respite care for children (17 agencies); and support services for non-parent relatives raising children (112 agencies).[12] Additional services to children came in enrolling 18,246 children in Children's Health Insurance Program (CHIP), Medicaid, and/or other health insurance programs.[13]

In addition to care for children and elders, these community-building services included education and enrichment (730,645 people served), socialization and neighborhood services (490,850 served), services to at-risk folks (430,263), and health-related services (305,287).[14]

OTHER BASIC NEEDS SERVICES

Under the heading of *other basic needs services,* CARA reported on assistance with clothing (604,873 persons), utilities (332,815), finances (234,292), prescriptions (50,566), and other basic needs (711,253).[15] The total of persons served was 1,933,799, fully 13 percent of the services of Catholic Charities in 2009. At the neighborhood, local office, and agency level, these needs—together with food—are often considered to be the focus of "emergency assistance" workers. When destitute families come to many offices or programs, they need "all of the above." Emergency assistance workers usually have small funds for assistance, food or transportation vouchers, and a list of telephone numbers of other churches and social agencies that can be called to cobble together $25, $50, $100, or $400 for a utility bill, a rent deposit, a uniform for work, or shoes for school, just enough to help this or that individual or family to make it to another day.

SERVICES THAT STRENGTHEN FAMILIES

Catholic social teaching views the family as the most basic and important of social units in society. If families in great numbers are unhealthy, then an entire society is unhealthy. Recognizing this reality, Catholic Charities agencies focus a number of programs and

Table 5.2. Services that strengthen families by Catholic Charities agencies, 2009

Service Types	Persons	Percent
Counseling and mental health services	419,222	39%
Immigration services	319,952	30%
Refugee services	100,465	10%
Pregnancy services	93,977	9%
Addiction services	87,315	8%
Adoption services	43,982	4%
Total services to strengthen families	1,064,913	100%

services on the family, in addition to many of those already described as community focused. In 2009, staff and volunteers provided *services that strengthen families* to 1,064,913 persons (see table 5.2).[16]

It is important to note that many of these programs require the intensive services of professionals such as psychologists, social workers, attorneys, addiction specialists, translators, and a wide variety of counselors with differing specialties. Again, no one agency offers all of these services, but the focus on families is central to the mission of Catholic Charities agencies.

HOUSING-RELATED SERVICES

In the larger category of *housing-related services,* Catholic Charities agencies in 2009 served 497,732 clients, down 17 percent from the 598,953 clients reported in 2008. Services reported under the heading of housing include temporary shelter for 144,671 clients (42 percent), housing services for 205,262 persons (34 percent), supervised living services for 64,789 persons (12 percent), permanent housing for 60,196 clients (9 percent), and transitional housing for 22,814 persons (3 percent). The people served by this array of programs included intact families, elderly and disabled persons, parents and children fleeing abuse, homeless individuals and families, persons with mental health and addiction problems, persons with developmental disabilities, ex-offenders, runaway youth, and young adults transitioning from foster care to more independent living.[17]

DISASTER SERVICES

Disaster services, like disasters themselves, are often seasonal and localized. In 2009, Catholic Charities agencies reported serving 99,665 clients, down from the post-Katrina, Rita, and other storm-driven highs: 420,422 clients in 2007 and 567,334 persons served in 2006. Of those served, 45,591 were children or adolescents, 45,034 adults, and

7,097 were senior citizens (3,943 persons were not age-specified in reports).[18] The nature of the services often depended on the kind of disaster involved, its duration, the services provided by other local and regional and national agencies, and the resources of the church and local community. As a leading representative of the Salvation Army said at a meeting that we both attended in the early 1990s, "No disaster is like any other disaster."

PROGRAMS FOR SPECIAL POPULATIONS

The CARA report also specifies that 207,465 other people in *special populations* received services from Catholic Charities agencies in 2009. Among these groups were victims of crimes, women who have had abortions, prisoners and ex-offenders, families of prisoners, persons with disabilities, migrant workers, victims of international and domestic trafficking, veterans, gang members, undocumented persons, and military personnel.[19]

Who Does the Work of Catholic Charities?

The CARA survey for 2009 indicates that agencies reported the involvement of 337,527 people in their programs and services: 66,067 people were paid staff; 6,702 were board members; and 264,758 were volunteers. This last number can fluctuate easily depending on the number and kinds of programs using volunteers, the economy, disaster work, and other factors. In terms of paid staff in 2009, 68 percent worked full-time, and 32 percent held part-time positions on staff; 54 percent of all staff worked at the program level, while four in ten worked as administrative support staff, clerical workers, and other support staff. Those working at the program level included professionals, paraprofessionals, consultants, contractors, and program supervisors. Only 7 percent of staff worked at the executive or director level. The gender breakdown of paid staff was 72 percent female and 28 percent male, although the executive level was 51 percent female and 49 percent male. Staff were 52 percent white, 29 percent black or African American, 15 percent Hispanic or Latino, 4 percent Asian, Native Hawaiian, or Pacific Islanders, and 0.5 percent Native American or Alaskan Native.[20] As discussed above, their areas of specialization and expertise varied as much as the wide range of services delivered by agencies.

Board members tended to be male (60 percent) and predominantly white (83 percent), while females (40 percent) and persons of color (6 percent black, 9 percent Hispanic, 1 percent Asian, and 0.5 percent Native American)[21] were underrepresented in terms of the people served by Catholic Charities or the composition of the Catholic and general population of this country. Their roles also may have varied depending on the kind of board on which they served, whether as corporate board members, advisory board members, or on specialty corporation boards such as those focused on housing or immigration services. Regardless, board members have serious responsibilities for understanding the Catholic character of their agencies and promoting their identity in the complex reality of today's agencies.

Who Pays for the Work of Catholic Charities?

The total income reported in the CARA survey for 2009 was $4,270,309,450. This $4.3 billion included cash revenue for Catholic Charities, reflecting the diversity of the programs offered and the communities within which the agencies worked (see figure 5.1): approximately 67 percent of total income came from state, local, and federal governments; 11 percent from community support, including corporate, individual, and foundation funding; 11 percent from program fees charged to those who could afford to pay for services, often on a sliding scale; 3 percent from investments, business, and other income such as bequests, capital campaigns, gains on sale of property, membership dues, rental income, sales of assets, and thrift shop revenues; 3 percent from diocesan and church support; and 2 percent from United Way and the Combined Federal Campaign (CFC). Add to this the $128 million (3 percent) of in-kind contributions, including in-kind salaries, contributed supplies, equipment, space, and other goods and services, for total income in 2009.[22]

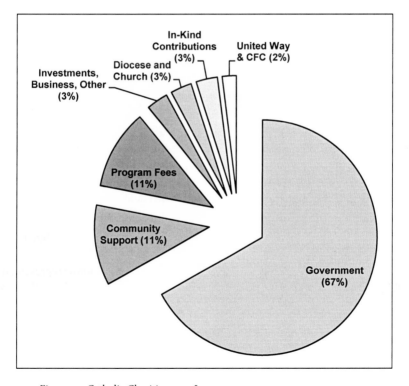

Figure 5.1. Catholic Charities 2009 Income

Of the funds received by Catholic Charities agencies from the federal, state, and local governments, CARA asked the agencies to report these funds in six important areas of governmental and human service activity: health and human services (86 percent); agriculture (6 percent); housing and urban development (6 percent); labor (1 percent); Federal Emergency Management Agency (FEMA) (1 percent); justice (0.4 percent); and the Veterans Administration (VA) (0.2 percent).[23] Because the amount for health and human services ($1,681,896,905) was by far the bulk of any government funding, it might be good to note CARA's clarification:

> A quarter (26 percent) of Health and Human Services funding went to programs to help children and families—almost $450 million in government revenue supported those programs. Medicaid, Medicare, and programs for older Americans and for refugee resettlement together received close to $690 million in government revenues.[24]

The programs to help children and families included foster care and residential care for children, independent living programs, child welfare programs, runaway youth services, Head Start, child day care, family support and reunification, social and community services, developmental disabilities programs, and services for those receiving Temporary Assistance for Needy Families (TANF).

In most of the government-funded programs, individual agencies would engage in contracts with the respective branch of the government at the local or state level to provide services to a specific population or populations in a certain geographical area. Catholic Charities and many other voluntary organizations engage in these "purchase of service" contracts as a way to bring the resources of the local organizations—skills, commitment, organizational capacity, community base and credibility, volunteers, matching funds, and supervision—to the service of the wider community in ways requested and funded by elected officials to meet community, family, and individual needs. Often there are competitive preliminaries in government contracting processes, and the large and varied scope of services provided by Catholic Charities in partnership with various governments reflects the credibility and proven services of many local agencies and their leadership in the fields of human and social services, counseling, housing, and disaster relief.

Expenses for the year 2009 for Catholic Charities agencies and affiliates totaled $4,275,186,136, of which approximately 60 percent ($2,583,281,443) was expended for salaries, wages, benefits, and payroll taxes. This seems normal for nonprofit social service organizations where the greatest investment is in the people who make the services happen. Seven percent of expenditures went to direct cash assistance provided to or for clients ($276,700,214), often in the form of vouchers for food or bus tokens, payments to landlords or utility companies, direct payments to health care providers or for medicine, or other third-party payments. In my experience, it is rare for Catholic Charities agencies to disburse money directly to clients. Almost 90 percent of total expenditures were on the programs that provide services to the clients of Catholic Charities. As CARA notes, "Less than 10 percent of expenditures were on management and general expenses, and about 2 percent of total expenses went to fundraising."[25]

Part 2: Pluralism: From Jefferson to Obama

In 1803, Louisiana became part of the United States of America when Thomas Jefferson purchased much of the Mississippi River valley from Napoleon Bonaparte. The Ursuline Sisters in New Orleans were concerned about whether they would be allowed to continue their ministries when New Orleans was no longer part of a Catholic country. So, as Americans are free to do, they wrote to President Jefferson. His handwritten letter in response, dated May 15, 1804, is in the archives of the New Orleans Ursuline community. It reads as follows:

> I have received, holy sisters, the letter you have written me wherein you express anxiety for the property vested in your institution by the former governments of Louisiana. The principles of the constitution and government of the United States are a sure guarantee to you that it will be preserved to you sacred and inviolate, and that your institution will be permitted to govern itself according to its own voluntary rules, without interference from the civil authority. Whatever diversity or shade may appear in the religious opinions of our fellow citizens, the charitable objects of your institution cannot be indifferent to any; and its furtherance of the wholesome purposes of society by training its younger members in the way they should go, cannot fail to ensure it the patronage of the government it is under. Be assured it will meet all the protection which my office can give it. I salute you, holy sisters, with friendship and respect. [Signed TH. JEFFERSON][26]

Thus began the complex and generally positive relationship of Catholic Charities, education, and health care with the government of the United States and, subsequently, various state and local governments. It brought together the constitutional protection of religion ("free exercise"), the voluntary sector of this society, and the desire of government to promote the common good through a variety of means, including religiously inspired services to the population. As we will see, this is an area of extreme complexity that can generate strong tensions among well-meaning people.

On February 5, 2009, President Barack Obama signed an executive order to create a revamped White House Office of Faith-Based and Neighborhood Partnerships. This order expanded the "initiative started by the Bush administration that provides government support—and financing—to religious and charitable organizations that deliver social services."[27] A news article went on to report on one major unresolved question from the Bush program, namely, whether religious groups that receive federal money for social services can hire only those who are members of their denomination. It indicated as well that there are other controversies associated with this program, namely, whether funded churches or groups can proselytize those they serve, whether they can discriminate among those to be served on the basis of religion, and whether religious groups outside the mainstream, such as the Church of Scientology, might participate in government funding for social services. Thus, what may have seemed simple in the time of Thomas Jefferson has become far more complicated in the days of George W. Bush and Barack Obama, made more controversial by the availability of public dollars to support such services and the political hype of these "initiatives" by various public officials (although no significant new dollars were appropriated for these purposes during the two terms of the Bush administration or the first part of the Obama administration).

On November 17, 2010, President Obama issued an executive order entitled "Fundamental Principles and Policymaking Criteria for Partnerships with Faith-Based and Other Neighborhood Organizations," amending a 2002 executive order of President Bush. The new order set out certain fundamental principles for contracts with and federal grants to such organizations, including: (a) competition on an equal footing; (b) no discrimination against program beneficiaries on the basis of religious belief; (c) compliance with the Establishment and Free Exercise Clauses of the First Amendment; (d) separation in time and location of explicitly religious activities of organizations from programs and services that are government funded and only voluntary participation in religious activities by social program beneficiaries; (e) protection of religious character, independence, autonomy, name, and symbols of the organization and its premises; (f) protection of the right to select board members on a religious basis; and (g) protection of religious references in mission statements, charter, and other governing documents. Beneficiaries were also entitled to be referred to other service agencies if they objected to the religious character of the funded organization. The executive order drew a swift editorial from the *New York Times* complaining that the order failed to "draw a firm line barring employment discrimination on the basis of religion."[28]

These issues in the Obama executive order and in the continuing debates over the faith-based initiatives are not new in the world of Catholic Charities. Agency leaders discuss them generally under the heading of "pluralism."[29] The reheated debates that greeted President Bush's faith-based initiatives and those of the Obama administration may be important for the nation, but, for Catholic Charities USA leaders across the nation, they can be very frustrating. This is because so much history and so much of the social services reality and experience in this country often is unknown or ignored in the public debates.

For purposes of the current discussion, it is important to note that, in addition to welcoming the Ursuline Sisters to New Orleans, the colony also provided financial support to the work of the sisters because it was seen as serving the whole community. In the letter that Sister Therese of St. Francis Xavier first wrote to President Jefferson on behalf of the Ursulines, she pleaded that their ministries were "for the public good" and that their institution was both "useful" and "necessary." This snatch of history suggests that public-private partnerships are not new in this country and that we might learn much from the many years and experiences of the past.

Since the late 1800s, the partnership that religious social service providers and other organizations have developed with cities, counties, states, and the federal government involve regular contracting to care for vulnerable infants, protect children from abusive family situations, operate group homes for severely disabled adults, resettle refugees, provide training for the unemployed, and house elderly residents. Governments are more likely to contract out social services to religious and other agencies that specialize in such services than to provide direct social services themselves. (This is similar to the building of government ships and airplanes, done by major corporations, or medical research that is funded by government at university medical schools.) In addition, in the social arena, governments largely retain to themselves the direct functions of income support programs such as Social Security, unemployment compensation, Temporary Assistance to Needy Families (TANF), and Supplemental Security Income (SSI). They also determine eligibility for income programs and benefits such as Supplemental Nutrition Assistance Program (SNAP) (food stamps), Medicaid, and Medicare. On a number of occasions, when social service arrangements between religious providers and governments have been challenged, the U.S. Supreme Court has sanctioned such social service contracts, distinguishing such programs from its much more restrictive rulings on public aid to religious elementary and secondary education.

With this historical preface, we can now turn to the current debate over faith-based social initiatives. Since the welfare reform debate during the mid-1990s, our politics have seemed almost silent about the needs of families who are poor and vulnerable. They figured little in the 2000 and 2004 presidential campaigns and debates; and, in 2008, concerns about poor families were smothered in the debate over the Iraq war, the general economic downturn, and what candidates would do for middle America. When President Bush first urged congregations to take a more active role in meeting their communities' social needs, that call was consistent with the call of the U.S. bishops to Catholic parishes in the two pastoral letters of the 1990s: *Communities of Salt and Light* on the parish's social mission and *Called to Global Solidarity* on parish responsibility for suffering people worldwide.[30] Catholic Charities agencies welcomed the concern of the administration for mobilizing congregations because much more local action certainly was needed. What is called "parish social ministry" already had been an important emphasis in Catholic Charities for three decades.

Catholic Charities agencies also had another, equally important role through which they served as instruments of community service for Catholic dioceses. In this capacity, they had cared for cocaine-addicted infants, provided foster homes for abused children, staffed group homes for adult persons with mental disabilities, built housing for the elderly, fed hungry families, sheltered abused wives and children, welcomed refugees and immigrants, and provided job training to welfare recipients. In this gospel-inspired capacity, they worked in active concert with parishes and with local, state, and federal governments that contracted with them for these services to people of all faiths and none.

Some in the recent faith-based debate have expressed fears about unseemly competition among churches. This seems strange to Catholic Charities agencies, which often have effective collaborations with Lutheran Services in America, the Salvation Army,

Volunteers of America, members of the United Jewish Federation, and other faith-based organizations. It is in these areas of social services and advocacy for justice and peace that the most effective forms of ecumenism occur.

What advantages might come from this twenty-first-century emphasis at the federal level on the importance of faith-inspired social services? How might such partnerships be improved? When President Bush pledged to simplify bureaucratic requirements and establish a level playing field for religiously inspired and other service providers, Catholic Charities applauded this intention. Government bureaucrats sometimes overreached and, in so doing, threatened the organizational integrity of agencies. The poor and vulnerable deserve the best qualified and most effective services. This is why Catholic Charities support efforts to credential licensed professionals, screen out volunteers who may be dangerous to children, and accredit agencies for services. In the view of Catholic Charities leaders, agencies not only can but also should be both mission driven and competent. Moreover, to promote more effective partnerships, governments should pay their social service partners in a timely and adequate fashion. When they do not, agencies often have to borrow to meet payroll and pay other expenses, incurring interest charges that are usually not reimbursed by public authorities. Government also should eliminate unfair advantages of for-profit corporations now invading the world of social services with a thirst for margins of profit that may jeopardize the well-being of abused children and the frail elderly.

In the Catholic community, our practice has generally been to establish separate organizations to serve those who are poor and vulnerable. Incorporating such programs separately from local parishes and dioceses has many advantages, including economies of scale, targeting of fiscal and personnel resources, and the ability to hire professional staff and qualify for accreditation. Entering directly into a government service contract would subject a parish or local congregation to a host of new rules, including opening up its budgets to government audits. For most local churches, it is more practical to create or collaborate with a separate nonprofit organization to handle administrative headaches. This might also obviate some of the concerns of opponents of faith-based initiatives about direct assistance to churches and of some churches about becoming "entangled" with government.

Before a new administration goes too far down the road of some new promotion of so-called faith-based initiatives, however, there are caution signs to note along the way. Reports in the *National Congregations Study* conducted by university researchers in the late 1990s and again between 2006 and 2007 are the most telling. What they reveal, in part, is the distinction between what volunteers in church congregations do in terms of the kinds of services that they render and what church-sponsored social services agencies such as Catholic Charities do. That distinction should add more reality to public policy debates on government initiatives in this area. The comprehensive 1998 *National Congregations Study* of 1,236 churches was led by Professor Mark Chaves, then of the University of Arizona and now at Duke University.

The first significant finding of the 1998 study was that large congregations, African American congregations, and Catholic and theologically liberal and moderate Protestant congregations were most likely to avail themselves of the provisions of "charitable choice," part of the welfare reform legislation that allowed states to contract directly with church congregations to deliver social services. Those least likely to apply for government funds were congregations described by their leaders as theologically and politically conservative. This first finding contrasted sharply with the national political debate, where those who most advocated for charitable choice provisions were political and religious conservatives and those most opposed were political and religious liberals.

The second significant finding was that churches were more likely to engage in activities that address the immediate needs of individuals for food, clothing, and shelter than in projects that require sustained involvement to meet longer-term goals. In other words, the kinds of services most needed by people moving from welfare to work—job training, transportation, child care—were very seldom conducted by churches. This second finding is related to the work of volunteers and was supported by the experience of Catholic Charities nationwide, where volunteer numbers had increased substantially precisely as emergency services such as food and shelter programs had increased markedly. The survey of congregations also indicated that the total number of volunteers provided by individual congregations remained small. They were most likely to be involved in areas such as food and housing, where organizations were able to take advantage of congregations' capacity to mobilize relatively small numbers of volunteers to carry out well-defined tasks.[31]

Even more caution now should follow from the findings of the *National Congregations Study—Wave II*. It reports from the second phase of the study, this time of 1,506 congregations. The key finding of this 2006–2007 study is that, even six or seven years "after the Bush administration's faith-based initiative, *there is no increase* since 1998 in congregations' involvement in social services, receipt of public funds for their social services work, or collaboration with government."[32] Other changes in church congregations nationwide were reported in the survey, but no change was reported in this key area, where so much public policy debate and time had been expended over the previous nearly twenty years.

If that is the case, how had we arrived at this 2009 heralding of the faith-based initiative that, in fact, has produced little effect? To understand, we have to return to the welfare reform debate of the mid-1990s and persistent and even strident messages of the proponents of charitable choice and other provisions of that legislation. They had argued that private religious providers were better than public providers, so government programs for the poor should be reduced. In making this argument, proponents had continued trying to separate church and government in ways that were not true to history or to the present realities of social services. For example, one U.S. senator observed to me, "The church social services have millions of volunteers, but few people ever volunteer at the welfare or social security office." To this I responded there was a broad middle ground, where agencies like Catholic Charities or Lutheran Social Ministries use government dollars for programs in which there are thousands of volunteers as well. This middle ground was an uncomfortable truth for those trying to demonize government and glorify church programs.

Later, when Catholic Charities USA and other major religious social services providers opposed the logic of dividing church and government in this way—and the resulting draconian cuts in government social services and family support programs—the same people then argued that government money corrupts the private religious provider, who is restricted in terms of proselytism and thus denies to the poor the essentially religious component of needed personal change that could only come in a church-based program. Therefore, it was argued, government should cut back on supporting welfare and social services programs for the needy (in effect, including the work of religiously sponsored social services) and let the churches pick up the slack with tax-exempt contributions, an army of volunteers, and muscular spiritual reform for welfare-dependent families. The White House faith-based office was an outgrowth of this thinking that, with much fanfare and small financial investments, local congregations would transform their communities and the poor. According to the *National Congregations Study* above, it does not appear that such has occurred or was even possible.

It should be clear at this point that the debate over government funding and encouragement of "faith-based initiatives" needs to make distinct what seems to have eluded those who see the world only in terms of the church-government "either/or." First, there are social services agencies that are sponsored by religious bodies—Catholic Charities, Lutheran Social Services, Jewish charities, etc.—that have a long-standing relationship to government, and that association has given rise to the current partnerships that generally have the following key indicators: service to people in need without regard to their religion; refusal to proselytize the poor in serving them; religious and ethical values to which the agency is committed and which guide its identity, purposes, and means; hiring of staff and recruitment of board members who respect and are committed to the agency's mission and identity, even if they do not belong to the sponsoring church; the possible retention of certain positions within the organization for co-religionists, such as the chief executive officer, the mission officer, and, in Catholic Charities, the director of parish social ministry; fiscal and service accountability of the agency to the funding partners; and some formal affiliation with the sponsoring church. These characteristics seem to have weathered decades of testing in various forms and appear to validate these partnerships from both sides (church and state), allowing both government funding and tax exemptions. These relationships are not, however, without problems, as we discuss in part 3.

Second, there is the basically new proposal of the past decade or so to fund churches or congregations directly by government to deliver social services. This proposal, to whatever extent implemented, has continued to raise a number of religious and legal questions: whether hiring of all staff can be restricted to co-religionists;

whether proselytizing is allowed and, in the context of the welfare reform debate, necessary to "cure" the poor; whether certain religions will be "tainted" by government money or government relations; whether to allow government to regulate the practices of churches such as service quality, finance, and hiring; and whether to restrict social services only to those of the same religion. These arrangements continue to be highly debated, are questionable at best within the constitutional framework that has evolved over the past century, and, as we have seen from the *National Congregations Study,* have had little impact.

The initiative—proposed as the cure for poverty and dependence—received major impetus from the proponents of the "welfare reform" of the 1990s and was implemented in part in the Bush administration's White House office. One might well conclude, however, that it was not only badly conceived but also not needed, doubtfully legal, and has not taken root in American social services or in American churches.

Part 3: The Pluralism of Catholic Charities

In the wake of the confusing history and dubious state of the faith-based initiatives of the past decade or two, it would be good to look more carefully at the complex and nuanced position of Catholic Charities on pluralism—as articulated and practiced in various ways across the country. Before doing so, I would like to restate my own understanding of what makes Catholic Charities *Catholic.* In the face of those who do not understand our service to other-than-Catholics, our partnership with governments, the diversity of our own staffs and boards, or the seemingly "secular" nature of many of our services, it became important, in the 1990s, to reaffirm our Catholic character in terms drawn deeply from the Judeo-Christian Scriptures, the history of the mission of Catholic Charities, authoritative documents of the Catholic Church, and the experiences of Catholic Charities agencies across the country. Based on these multiple sources, there are ten ways that Catholic Charities are Catholic:

1. This ministry is rooted in the Scriptures.
2. This ministry has been an integral part of the Catholic Church for two thousand years.
3. Catholic Charities promotes the sanctity of human life and the dignity of the human person.
4. Catholic Charities is authorized to exercise its ministry by the diocesan bishop.
5. Catholic Charities respects the religious beliefs of those they serve.
6. Catholic Charities recognizes that some services require attention to the physical, mental, and *spiritual* needs of those they serve.
7. Catholic Charities has a special relationship to the Catholic diocese and to Catholic parishes.
8. Catholic Charities works in active partnership with other religiously sponsored charities and with the civic community.

9. Catholic Charities supports an active public-private partnership with government at all levels.
10. Catholic Charities blends advocacy for those in need and public education about social justice with service to individuals, families, and communities.[33]

To return to our more pointed discussion of pluralism, it is important to note that, in the discussion above of the 2009 survey by CARA, the areas of government contracts for services and the amounts of funding involved were only briefly described. The actual survey data are broken down into subcategories, such as twenty-five separate categories of funding from health and human services programs ranging from Medicaid and Medicare to child day care, mental health services, and Hurricane Katrina relief programs. Suffice it to say, there are literally thousands of separate agreements between Catholic Charities agencies and some branch and level of government to provide services to people in need in this country, and they involve hundreds of millions of dollars of program services. This has prompted a long history within the Catholic Charities network of focusing on the meaning of pluralism in U.S. social services and, specifically, pluralism as a characteristic of the Catholicity of contemporary Catholic Charities agencies. How do agencies view and maintain their Catholic identity within these realities?

The most participative and formal Catholic Charities statement on pluralism is entitled simply "Catholic Charities and Pluralism." This 1987 policy statement was developed in draft by a task force of members, discussed in regional meetings around the country, and then, after debate and amendments, approved by the membership congress at its meeting in San Antonio. The statement reads as follows:

Pluralism in this paper means that state or conditions of affairs in our country in which a variety of religious traditions live and work under a constitutional, democratic government which recognizes persons' rights to religious freedom and freedom of conscience.

1. *Catholic Charities agencies and institutions are voluntary associations* which incorporate a religious identity and, as such, are concrete dynamic expressions of the human and constitutionally protected rights of freedom of religion and association.
2. *When viewed theologically,* Catholic Charities agencies and institutions can be considered to both transcend and enhance the interest of the state to the extent that they are grounded in and embody religious meaning and values.
3. *Catholic Charities agencies and institutions have a prophetic, critical role* to play in drawing from their value system to participate in education and public debate about social issues.
4. *Catholic Charities agencies and institutions enhance genuine pluralism* by enabling choice, promoting action in society, and by joining with other religious bodies and social agencies in ongoing dialogue that fosters individual freedom and liberty, and to discern, call attention to, and oppose the causes of oppression.

5. *As advocates for and contributors to the common good,* Catholic Charities agencies, as well as other voluntary social agencies which make similar contributions, deserve not only acceptance but support which should not be conditioned on requirements that weaken agency identity and integrity.

6. *The state, as the political entity formally responsible for the common good,* may appropriately require accountability of Catholic Charities and other voluntary agencies for standards of service and expenditures of public monies.[34]

Thus, the statement combines positions on constitutionality within the framework of the United States (freedom of religion and association, pluralism, and free speech) with those drawn from Catholic social teaching and theology (the common good, justice, advocacy, and subsidiarity).

There are five key assertions in the policy statement: (1) Catholic Charities agencies are an expression of First Amendment rights of freedom of religion and association; (2) in theological terms, Catholic Charities agencies are essentially more valuable ("transcend"[35]), in a way, than the political entities that fund and regulate them because Catholic Charities agencies express and embody religious beliefs and values; (3) in keeping with the principle of subsidiarity and U.S. pluralism, Catholic Charities agencies and services enrich the world of social welfare by providing variety and freedom of choice in society; (4) because Catholic Charities agencies embody constitutional rights, enrich social welfare, and contribute to the common good, government should not only support their work but also try not to undermine their identity and integrity by *intrusive* funding or regulatory requirements; and (5) Catholic Charities agencies acknowledge that they must be held accountable for money received from government and the services that they contract to deliver to people in need.[36]

At the time of the development of the policy statement, I was asked to make a presentation on pluralism at a meeting of Catholic Charities representatives from the mid-South region. From that initial presentation in 1987 and discussions at the Catholic Charities USA annual Leadership Institute between 1992 and 2001, I tried to capture the reality of pluralism within Catholic Charities, given the tensions that arise from the combination of democratic and religious values, the diversity of staff and persons served, the pressures in American political life, the variety of funding sources, the regulatory and ethical requirements, and the demands of different constituencies. (See figure 5.2.) I first used the image of a "diamond"[37]; because of its durability and beauty, it still depicts very aptly the array of forces, factors, and opportunities of Catholic Charities agencies. Light shining through a diamond also reflects and is refracted in many ways.

In trying to conceptualize key areas of stress associated with pluralism, the diamond identifies certain institutional and other relationships—*stakeholders,* we might say—that create the pluralism within a Catholic Charities agency but that also present problems. Three points on the diamond represent funding constituencies: the church (dioceses and the Catholic faithful), the civic community (United Way, foundations, corporations, and private donors), and government at various levels. The right side of

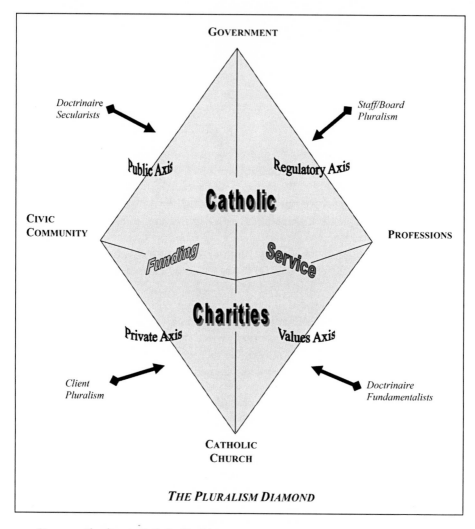

Figure 5.2. Pluralism in Catholic Charities

the diamond mirrors the left and represents major influences on the shape of services provided by agencies: who, what, how, when, where, and why. The three points of influence are:

1. The Catholic Church, with its values, principles, norms, and compassion drawn from Scripture, theology, Catholic social teaching, and Catholic Christian spirituality that inspired the very creation of these agencies and that sustains them today;

2. The legal and regulatory framework and specific requirements imposed by government in enabling legislation, regulations, and contractual provisions that attach to specific funding as well as its general constitutional and legal framework; and
3. The ethics and skills of the professions (social workers, therapists, attorneys, accountants, fund-raisers, public relations specialists, etc.) represented in the staffs and services, which often are standards expected and monitored by the civic community, funding sources of all kinds, individual donors, and accrediting bodies.

The Catholic Charities agency is at the center of these forces and is influenced by each of them in different ways. It is the pressure of these diverse forces, like the Earth's pressure on carbon, that creates the hardened and beautiful diamond that is Catholic Charities in this country. The challenge—no small feat of strength, balance, or even grace—is to keep them all in proper proportion so the diamond is not split or crushed.

Outside the diamond, I have identified four key sources of tension in maintaining this balance. They exist because of the multiple constituencies and funding sources of Catholic Charities—church, government, civic community (including the poor), and the professions. First, in the upper left are what the 1987 pluralism task force called *doctrinaire secularists*. These are the folks pushing on the "public axis" (government and civil society) who, in pursuit of extreme forms of church-state separation, urge curtailing government funding to sectarian agencies, tying the advocacy arm of tax-exempt groups, trying to eliminate competition with business by nonprofits, or imposing controversial values or practices that conflict with the religious values of the agencies (for example, insisting on abortion referrals, adoptions by gay couples, reports of undocumented clients to civil authorities, or mandatory staff health insurance coverage for contraception).

In the lower right corner, pressing on the "values axis" where Catholic Charities blend elements drawn from the Catholic Church and the professions of staff, are those I call the *doctrinaire fundamentalists*. Here are both Catholics and other faithful who have a very narrow view of religion and its role in public life. From this outside pressure point, state licensing and professional ethics are challenged in the name of religious freedom and values, such as objections to requiring licensing of counselors or handicapped accessibility of buildings. Some Catholics insist on only their own narrow interpretation of what Catholics and Catholic Charities should do about war or abortion in the public sector, that all adopted babies should have Catholic parents, or that collaboration with "suspect" religious or secular groups should be avoided.

In the lower left-hand corner is the pressure on the "private axis" that comes from *client pluralism*. Catholic Charities and church leadership actively promote the service of all in need in the community, and this openness usually is required by government and civic funders as well. Here, the problems come when a client wants an abortion referral or contraception information, insists on seeing only a Catholic counselor, demands as a Catholic to be moved to the top of the adoption waiting list ahead of non-Catholics, or expects free service regardless of the sliding scale designed to give some recognition to the priority concern for the poor in Catholic social thought.

The fourth stress point of the diamond is *staff and board pluralism* in the upper right of the diamond along the "regulatory axis." Moved by nondiscrimination requirements of government and civic funders, the need for professional staff to meet often highly specialized service requirements, the recognition of the richness that an ecumenical staff brings to service delivery, and the decline in the number of priests and religious in Catholic Charities agencies, staffs have become immensely varied in terms of religious affiliation (or none).[38] In addition, prompted by funding sources, practical ecumenism, and the need to involve the wider community and persons of varying skills and backgrounds in policy making and fund-raising, many agencies have expanded board membership beyond the Catholic community. This is true of corporate boards, and, where the corporate board members remain the bishop and a few others, it is the case of advisory boards that often exercise genuine policy leadership.

This staff and board pluralism can strain the ability to agree on agency goals and priorities or ethical norms for professional and other services, to project a consistent image in the midst of the civic community's pluralism, and even to coalesce within the agency around a coherent mission and identity. This can make Catholic Charities vulnerable to critics in the civic community and even those within the Catholic community who do not understand the complexity of Catholic mission and identity. Ultimately, it could threaten the moral and financial support of the agency.

While each constituency and funding source brings its own strengths and support to Catholic Charities, individually or in combination, they can present challenges to the identity and survivability of the agency. What does an agency need to do, then, to maintain its balance and sustain the beauty and strength of the diamond? A number of concrete steps are necessary, which essentially protect and enhance the ten ways that agencies are Catholic.[39]

1. Catholic Charities must identify the agency and its mission as both Catholic and an expression of the social mission of the Catholic Church, an embodiment of the servant model of church, explicitly authorized by the local diocesan bishop, and actively linked to Catholic parishes and the larger Catholic community. Clarity about mission and identity gives the agency a strong foundation.

2. Agencies should adopt and adapt as appropriate the *Catholic Charities USA Code of Ethics* and educate all board members, staff, and volunteers on its substance, relevance, and everyday requirements.

3. Catholic Charities must respect the pluralism of all clients based in their natural rights, dignity, and freedom. They must serve all clients without regard to their religious affiliation but within the limited means so often available to the agency and the priorities arising out of its mission and identity.

4. Agencies must deliver quality services and, where appropriate, seek the licensing and accreditation that ensure that quality reaches clients, collaborators, and the entire community.

5. Catholic Charities should hire staff and develop boards that understand and are committed to the mission of the agency and will act in accord with the church's basic values and principles as applicable to the agency. This "hiring and recruiting for mission" must respect the religious diversity of staff and board within the limitations of these values and principles.

6. Agencies should strengthen the identity of staff and boards by purposeful exploration of agency identity and mission, by improving their knowledge and skills, and by values clarification. They should promote a spirituality of professional service by providing opportunities to staff and board to explore their mission, to raise consciousness as to the service of others by the people of God, and to unite work with prayer. Again, these practices must be offered in ways respectful of staff religious diversity.

7. Management must work with the agency board and staff to engage them regularly in processes that ensure organizational integrity, renewal, and development regarding mission, strategic planning, quality improvement, regulatory compliance, fiscal and program audits, transparency practices, and staff and volunteer development.[40]

8. Catholic Charities should maintain an active political responsibility, in collaboration with the diocese, including advocacy on social issues, pluralism, and human life and dignity.

9. Agencies should maintain the well-earned place of Catholic Charities agencies in the public sector, delivering quality family and social services and resisting every effort to dilute their identities for the sake of securing or maintaining public or other funding.

10. Catholic Charities should continue and enhance collaboration with government, civic partners, and even those whose views are antithetical to those of the agency on one or another social or family issue. They should respect the shared values of other religious groups by ecumenical convening and collaboration in action within the scope of their common values.

11. Boards and management must provide fiscal accountability to governmental and other funders and regulatory and contract compliance with requirements that do not unduly intrude upon their protected freedoms and their underlying mission and values.

These expectations and requirements are not new in the world of Catholic Charities. They are the lessons of decades of experience and found in the practices of those agencies that are able to hold together their various stakeholders in ways that advance the mission of Catholic Charities and serve the many people within their communities.

Part 4: Why Partner with Government?

Although Catholic Charities and other religiously sponsored nonprofits have worked out their partnership arrangements with government over much of the past century, we can see from the preceding section that it is not without a lot of care and effort on the part of agency boards, management, and staff and not without occasional misunderstanding and conflict. Why not eliminate the governmental partners and simplify the work of being a Catholic Charities agency?

In June 1997, I was with the Volunteers of America (VOA) at their national meeting. Like Catholic Charities, VOA local agencies have a high percentage of government contracts for funds to support a variety of their programs. As a religious organization that spun off from the Salvation Army in the early part of the twentieth century, VOA makes no apology for their partnerships with government. As Catholic Charities has done, they affirm the positive values of their public-private partnership, as shown in various materials that I received in connection with this meeting:

> Many Volunteers of America services receive some local, state and federal government support. Enhancing this long-standing partnership with the citizen, we also engage the American spirit of giving through foundations, corporations, churches and individual donors, and the work of thousands of dedicated volunteers. The result is an efficient and accountable organization. More than 85% of combined Volunteers of America revenues go directly to program services.

VOA's description of a "long-standing partnership with the citizen" is very striking. Decisions about government programs for the poor and vulnerable are how elected officials choose to meet the needs of citizens with the taxes paid by citizens and in programs often adopted at the request of citizens. Rather than a negative, VOA in effect begins with this positive consideration. To go back to the "ten ways that Catholic Charities are Catholic," the one point in my experience that is most surprising, even to Catholics, is number nine: *Catholic Charities support an active public-private partnership with government at all levels.* It could also be the most controversial. In my years at Catholic Charities USA, I found that this fact was unknown to most people, a practical mystery to liberals, and a sometimes scandal to conservatives. The partnership positioned Catholic Charities in a middle place between those who would have social services delivered solely by government or entirely secular organizations and those who eschew any relationship with government and any role of government in delivering needed social services or care of the poor. This partnership between Catholic Charities and government is hardly new in this country and at least 1,500 years old in other parts of the world.

This brings us to why Catholic Charities agencies do and *should* enter into such partnerships with local, state, and federal governments. Even this discussion, however, must be seen in light of the responsibility of all the community to care for those in need in their midst. In their 1999 statement *In All Things Charity: A Pastoral Challenge for the New Millennium,* U.S. Catholic bishops posed the question, "Who can and should respond to the call for charity and justice?" In their answer, they specifically mention every baptized person, families, parishes, religious congregations, lay associations, dioceses, and the public, private, and voluntary sectors of society. Meeting the needs of the poor and vulnerable is everybody's business, and everyone's contribution is needed today in a country where tens of millions of people still live in poverty.[41]

Government has a moral responsibility for justice in society in Catholic social teaching. Pope Benedict emphasized this in his first encyclical letter when he wrote, "It is true that the pursuit of justice must be a fundamental norm of the State and that the aim of a just social order is to guarantee to each person, according to the principle of subsidiarity, his share of the community's goods."[42] Further, "Justice is both the aim and the intrinsic criterion of all politics. Politics is more than a mere mechanism for defining the rules of public life: its origin and its goal are found in justice, which by its very nature has to do with ethics. The State must inevitably face the question of how justice can be achieved here and now."[43]

The U.S. bishops explained this responsibility earlier in their 1999 pastoral letter on charity:

> Our Catholic tradition teaches that the moral function of government is to protect human rights and secure basic justice for all members of the commonwealth. Society as a whole and in all its subsidiary parts is responsible for building up the common good and for responding to the needs of the poor and vulnerable. But government is responsible for guaranteeing that the minimum conditions for social activity, including both human rights and justice, are met.[44]

The bishops described particular government policies within its moral responsibility, including the provision of certain services to ensure basic human needs.

> How society responds to the needs of the poor through its public policies serves as the litmus test for whether it conforms to the demands of justice and charity. The Church has long supported minimum wage and fair labor standards as essential for the protection of workers. For those who cannot find fair wages or cannot work due to age, disability, parental responsibilities, or another cause, the economic safety net must be ensured by government insurance and income support systems. "The programs that make up this system should serve the needs of the poor in a manner that respects their dignity and provides adequate support."[45]

This provision of social welfare programs received attention from the Second Vatican Council, which the bishops also cited in their pastoral letter.

> Catholic social teaching assigns a positive role for government in social welfare. Thus the Fathers of the Second Vatican Council declared that "the growing complexity of modern situations makes it necessary for public authority to intervene more frequently in social, cultural and economic matters in order to achieve conditions more favorable to the free and effective pursuit by citizens and groups of the advancement of people's total well-being." As a result of the Great Depression, which lasted from 1929 to 1941, it became evident to people of the United States that only the government could develop resources to ensure regular income support for aged, disabled, or otherwise needy families. It has accomplished this by establishing such vehicles as

Social Security; retirement, disability, and survivors' programs; unemployment compensation; workers' compensation; food stamps; and dependent children programs. No private charity has the resources, for example, to provide steady monthly support to families without adequate income. These beliefs and principles, however, have come under attack during the latter part of the twentieth century as a negative attitude developed with regard to the responsibility of government to develop the policies and programs that make it possible for all people to fulfill their basic human needs.[46]

The bishops' discussion balances a variety of roles: all in society have a responsibility for those in need; government has a special responsibility to ensure human rights and basic justice; and, in fulfilling its role, modern government has to provide basic income and social services to those who cannot work or have special needs.

Does government have to be the provider of all social services to people in need? Not at all. As we already have seen, in the United States, a partnership has evolved in which government decides to fund a service needed by the elderly, abused children, the homeless, or people with disabilities; then it contracts with a nonprofit organization to provide those services. As the bishops described this, "For at least a century, religious and community-based nonprofit organizations have been providing social services under contracts with governments at all levels. This system of joint responsibility has served children and families, communities, and society very well."[47]

Two concrete examples may help to explain the complementarity of government and social service agencies. Nowhere is this more evident than in the child welfare system, where government exercises its legal powers to remove abused children from their homes and supports them financially. Then, government entrusts many of these abused children to the care of private agencies in a variety of group homes, foster care placements, and institutions. While religious agencies with public funds do not use them to proselytize, they do, in fact, attend to the full person: physical, emotional, intellectual, and spiritual. Similarly, when refugees come to the United States fleeing war and persecution, the government admits them to the country and provides basic funds for core resettlement services and even time-limited welfare support. Yet it is church volunteers recruited by religious social services providers who sponsor the refugees, offering friendship and teaching them about U.S. customs. Volunteers and staff provide intense social and personal support in the critical first months of resettlement.

With this framework in mind, why would Catholic Charities choose to be one of those nonprofit agencies that agrees to participate with government in meeting the social service needs of the poor and vulnerable? Why not leave this to other groups? There are a number of compelling reasons.

First, government partnerships strengthen Catholic Charities' gospel-based mission of diakonia (service). Put very simply, the mission of Catholic Charities begins in service to people in need, and these partnerships make it possible for agencies to carry out that mission more effectively and widely. As Pope Benedict emphasized, this diakonia lies at the heart of the identity of the church; without it, the church is not true to its inner nature and its mission in the world. Whether the means are surplus government grain in the fifth century, good will donations in the "poor box" in the parish, or contemporary partnerships with a city or state, service to the needy is an intrinsic part of the Catholic Church. It is who we are and who we are called to be.

Second, government partnerships greatly expand the ability of Catholic Charities to bring quality care and compassionate service to people in need. Partnerships with public authorities multiply church and community resources many times over, allowing agencies to bring their expertise, commitment to quality, and gospel-based compassion to millions more people and in a greater variety of programs and services than would be available otherwise. They help as well to strengthen agency infrastructure, which in turn facilitates broader services to communities. The ability to use public funds, however, is often dependent on the religious and other human and financial resources of the agencies. These resources initially create the organizations, staff and fund their core competencies, establish their capacity to partner with governments, and often provide a financial "match" of some sort required by the public partner.

Third, government partnerships support the public sector's responsibility to serve the common good and protect the most vulnerable in society. In Catholic social teaching, the common good represents "the sum total of social conditions which allow people, either as groups or as individuals, to reach their fulfillment more fully and more easily."[48] While the common good is everyone's responsibility, these partnerships allow Catholic Charities specifically to assist public bodies in their special responsibilities for its promotion and for the care of the poor and vulnerable.

Fourth, government partnerships promote the Catholic principle of subsidiarity by having the actual delivery of services, even those which government must fund, performed by religious and other nonprofit community-based organizations. As the U.S. bishops had indicated in their pastoral on charity, there are some things best done by government, such as the determination of eligibility for benefits and direct assistance payments. But, in the area of social services to the poor and vulnerable and in service to American pluralism, government's responsibilities can and should be served in a variety of ways and by a number of providers who bring a wealth of trained staff, volunteers, private funds, and dedicated commitment to their part of this partnership. The bishops put it this way: "This pluralism has been an essential characteristic of twentieth-century social service delivery in the United States. Pluralism in public programs is strengthened and made more genuine when individuals can choose to receive social services through a variety of providers, including religiously affiliated social services organizations."[49] The availability of a plethora of organizations to partner with government is a richness developed in U.S. communities across the country, and it allows government to bring services to people in need through local and familiar outlets. The Salvation Army, Lutheran Services, Jewish Federation, Volunteers of America, YMCA, Catholic Charities, senior and community centers, and hundreds of other organizations are a richness not found in comparable number and scope in other countries. By working together, government and its partners ensure pluralism, consumer choice, and community responsiveness in the delivery of greatly needed services to our most vulnerable citizens—whether funded from city hall, the state capitol, or Washington.

Fifth, government partnerships bring the Catholic Church into sectors of society where it may not normally be present, enhancing its reputation for good among the general population and enabling it to reach populations it might not otherwise touch. Being able to provide housing to the elderly, resettlement services to refugees, and care for persons with disabilities allows the Catholic Church, through Catholic Charities, to be present to people with whom it may have only occasional or no contact otherwise. This is an enormous source of credibility for the gospel and for the Catholic community, creating immense good will in many communities.

Sixth, government partnerships enable the church to exercise faith-based influence on a major sector of civil society—as we can do in education and health care—whose roots are actually in the church. Because the Catholic Church sponsors the largest voluntary social services, education, and health care networks of institutions in the United States, it is able to bring gospel-based values and experience to these critically important fields of human endeavor so central to the common good of any society. These three sets of professions and institutions, however secular they may seem, all have their roots in the ministries of the Catholic Church. In the world of social services and social welfare, the very size and scope of the Catholic Charities network give it the opportunity to bring its values, ethics, and passions into debates over the shape of social services and the professions associated with them. Combined with the social work schools in Catholic universities, this network has an enormous influence on social work practice and social institutions. This is especially important as a growing number of for-profit corporations move into the field of human services and as the strictures of budget cuts and managed care threaten the quality of care in the interest of the bottom line.

Seventh, government partnerships give Catholic Charities both familiarity with the workings of publicly funded services and a set of practical relationships with policy makers from which to advocate for more effective social policies and programs. In other words, Catholic Charities gain "credibility." Providing assistance to nine million people in a year is an incredible experience to bring to the national debate about the common good and how to care for the poor and vulnerable. Even more particularly, by actually operating programs and providing services that elected officials have decided are needed by the public, Catholic Charities can work with these same officials to try to ensure that programs are as effective as possible in meeting those needs. This advocacy takes the form of legislative testimony, regulatory advocacy, working on government commissions, participating in research, or informal communications with elected or appointed officials. Through dialogue and work with public officials, Catholic Charities and others in the voluntary sector are able to bring innovative programs, initially funded by other sources, to the attention of policy makers as models for future legislative or administrative initiatives.

Eighth, government partnerships are effective "good news"—immensely good people in faith-based organizations reaching out to the least of these. This partnering with cities, states, and the national government is effective charity, an immense treasure of the church and something of which all Catholics—liberal and conservative, Republican and Democrat and Independent—can be proud. Enormous human, financial, and spiritual resources are brought together in the service of those most in need in U.S. society. In addition, the hands-on work of Catholic Charities, done together with an array of public and private partners, puts flesh on the bones of the church's teaching about the just and caring society. As Pope John Paul II put it, "Today more than ever, the Church is aware that her social message will gain credibility more immediately from the *witness of actions* than as a result of its internal logic and consistency."[50]

Conclusion

Pluralism, as we have seen, is both an opportunity and a challenge for Catholic Charities. "Getting it right" has taken almost a century, but it remains a constant task at which the leaders and staff of agencies must carefully work. The opportunities of weaving together so many stakeholders and so rich a variety of resources should not be taken lightly, nor should they be easily dismissed by outside commentators unfamiliar with the realities and complexities of contemporary social welfare in this country.

Notes

This essay is adapted and updated from chapters 2, 3, and 7 of *Faith. Works. Wonders.—An Insider's Guide to Catholic Charities* (Eugene, Ore.: Pickwick, 2009). Used by permission of Wipf and Stock Publishers.

1. A diocese generally is headed by a bishop or archbishop who may have assistant bishops to help with the administrative and pastoral responsibilities of the bishop. The diocese, in turn, is organized into parishes headed by a pastor or administrator. Often, when Catholics speak of "local churches," the reference is to a diocese as opposed to the universal Catholic Church. A parish tends to be more neighborhood-based in the urban areas of heavily Catholic cities and more geographically spread in rural areas, sometimes covering one or more counties. Speaking of "grassroots" Catholic activities refers to the work done in a particular church parish or even in a neighborhood center or service center within a larger parish.

2. See, for example, the organizational structure of the diocese of Youngstown. Brian R. Corbin, "Catholic Identity and Institutional Practice: A Case Study of Catholic Charities of Youngstown, OH," *Charities USA* 31, no. 2 (2004): 11–14.

3. Melanie DiPietro, "Organizational Overview," in *Who Do You Say We Are? Perspectives on Catholic Identity in Catholic Charities,* ed. Jo-Ann Leitch (Alexandria, Va.: Catholic Charities USA, 1997), 28.

4. See Corbin, "Catholic Identity and Institutional Practice."

5. Mary L. Gautier and Melissa A. Cidade, *Catholic Charities 2009 Annual Survey Final Report* (Washington, D.C.: CARA, 2010). CARA (Center for Applied Research in the Apostolate, a research center affiliated with Georgetown University) began this annual survey work for Catholic Charities USA in December 2002.

6. Ibid., 3.

7. CARA mailed the twenty-page 2009 *Annual Survey* in late December 2009 to 171 executive directors for completion online. Between January and June 2010, a total of 140 agencies and affiliates participated in the 2009 survey, a response rate of 82 percent. Because of variations in agency data collection methods, CARA advises that trend analysis should be made with care. Ibid., 1–2.

8. Ibid., 3 (emphasis in original).

9. Ibid., 16.

10. Ibid., 18–19.

11. Ibid., 21.

12. Ibid., 22.

13. Ibid., 23.

14. Ibid., 16.

15. Ibid., 16, 31.

16. Ibid., 32. Details are set out at 33–37.

17. Ibid., 38–42.

18. Ibid., 43 and in earlier CARA survey reports.

19. Ibid., 16, 44.

20. Ibid., 150–52.

21. Ibid., 155.

22. Ibid., 5–6.

23. Ibid., 11.

24. Ibid., 12.

25. Ibid., 9–10.

26. Michael D. Place, "The Ursulines' Legacy: A History of 'Doing What Needs to Be Done,'" *Charities USA* 29, no. 2 (2002): 16–18.

27. Jeff Zeleny and Laurie Goodstein, "White House Faith Office to Expand," *New York Times*, January 5, 2009. The White House also announced that there would be a twenty-five-member advisory council to the office and that the president of Catholic Charities USA (Larry Snyder) would be a member.

28. "A Flawed Faith-Based Fix," editorial in the *New York Times*, November 22, 2010. The editorial complained that a 2007 Justice Department memo "dubiously concluded that the government cannot order religious groups not to discriminate as a condition of federal funding" and that that memo "should have been withdrawn long ago" by the Obama administration.

29. I have written on these themes a number of times over two decades and am drawing on these writings for parts of this essay. See, for example, "Pluralism," *Charities USA* 14, no. 7 (1987): 23–27; "The Pluralism Diamond," *Social Thought* 14, no. 2 (1988): 23–36; "Churches and Government" (April 24, 1996), "Churches and Social Services" (May 17, 2000), and "Faith and Fiction" (July 11, 2001) in my regular column in the *Catholic Commentator*, diocese of Baton Rouge newspaper; and "Public-Religious Partnerships," *America* 184, no. 11 (April 2, 2001): 6–10.

30. National Conference of Catholic Bishops, *Communities of Salt and Light: Reflections on the Social Mission of the Parish* (1993) and *Called to Global Solidarity* (1998).

31. Mark A. Chaves, *National Congregations Study*, 1998 (Ann Arbor: Inter-University Consortium for Political and Social Research, 2002). The study was sponsored by the National Opinion Research Center.

32. Mark Chaves and Shawna Anderson, "Continuity and Change in American Congregations: Introducing the Second Wave of National Congregations Study," *Sociology of Religion* 69, no. 4 (2008): 420 (emphasis added).

33. This part is adapted and updated from my article, "10 Ways Catholic Charities Are Catholic," *Charities USA* 25, no. 1 (1998): 1–4.

34. "Catholic Charities and Pluralism," 1987 Policy Statement of Catholic Charities USA, *Charities USA* 14, no. 9 (1987): 27 (emphasis in original).

35. The earlier draft debated in regional meetings read, "of a higher order."

36. Adapted from Kammer, "The Pluralism Diamond," 24.

37. Ibid., 32.

38. In my experience as a local director at Catholic Community Services in Baton Rouge, our other-than-Catholic staff were among the most loyal to the agency and its mission, often sharing deep values and religious commitments in their work for the agency and those it served.

39. These are adapted from Kammer, "The Pluralism Diamond," 34–36. See also Charles J. Fahey, "The 'Catholic' in Catholic Charities," in *Who Do You Say We Are?* 19–23 on "essential elements."

40. Catholic Charities USA, *Code of Ethics* (Alexandria, Va.: Catholic Charities USA, 2007), 10.

41. United States Catholic Conference, *In All Things Charity: A Pastoral Challenge for the New Millennium* (Washington, D.C.: U.S. Catholic Conference, 1999), 19–33.

42. Pope Benedict XVI, *God Is Love: Deus Caritas Est* (San Francisco: Ignatius Press, 2006), 62.

43. Ibid., 66.

44. USCC, *In All Things Charity,* 38.

45. Ibid., quoting *Economic Justice for All,* no. 210.

46. Ibid., 38–39, citing *Gaudium et Spes,* no. 75.

47. Ibid., 42.

48. Pontifical Council for Justice and Peace, *Compendium of the Social Doctrine of the Church* (Vatican City: Libreria Editrice Vaticana, 2004, distributed by Washington, D.C.: U.S. Conference of Catholic Bishops, 2004), 72, quoting *Gaudium et Spes,* no. 26.

49. USCC, *In All Things Charity,* 39.

50. Pope John Paul II, *Centesimus Annus* (1991), no. 57.

6 "Intelligent Leadership in the Cause of Racial Brotherhood"

Quakers, Social Science, and the American Friends Service Committee's Interwar Racial Activism

Allan W. Austin

RECALLING THE EARLY years of the American Friends Service Committee (AFSC), Rufus Jones wrote that he and the organization's first members, "conscious of a divine leading," had gone to work "aware, even if only dimly, that we were 'fellow-laborers with God' in the rugged furrows of the somewhat brambly fields of the world."[1] Jones's remark reveals a fundamental characteristic of Quaker religious identity: a belief in "the duty of Friends to live their faith and in so doing make the world a better place."[2] The many Quaker books of discipline today with "faith and practice" in their titles bear clear witness to this enduring foundational tenet of Quaker identity. The 1997 edition of Philadelphia Yearly Meeting's *Faith and Practice,* for example, connects belief and activism in Friends' testimonies, which it describes as "expressions of lives turned toward the Light, outward expressions reflective of the inward experience of divine leading."[3]

By the 1920s, Friendly testimonies once again pointed to the need to engage racial intolerance. Despite a historical Quaker pride in their efforts to end slavery, the early twentieth century saw "Quaker interest in racial justice [reach] a nadir."[4] This reality, amid the resurgent nativism and revived Ku Klux Klan of the 1920s, prompted the AFSC to undertake interracial activism. "If the Service Committee could send hundreds of workers abroad and spend millions of dollars giving relief to French, Germans, Russians, Poles, Austrians, and the Albanians," Mary Hoxie Jones asked, "why could it not spend some money and thought on a subject nearer home, the relations between the colored and white race?"[5]

The earliest AFSC responses to such queries emerged from the "inner conscientiousness" of individual Quakers, each motivated by a Friendly belief in the Inner Light.[6] The conviction that all human beings were potentially good led Friends to believe that every individual could be reformed (and even, perhaps, perfected), encouraging these early activists to understand racism as an individual problem best approached by engineering contacts between carefully selected groups to remove prejudice from individuals who suffered from misunderstanding and ignorance. While the earliest attempts to connect faith and practice in this way proved short lived, these efforts established the foundation on which AFSC interracial activism would build.

As the AFSC's program expanded in the 1930s, its leaders engaged social scientists and their ideas at the AFSC-sponsored Institute of Race Relations. There, Quakers came into contact with new, secular ideas about race, responded to them, and, ultimately, made social science meaningful for themselves in a religious context. The scholars reinforced the Friendly faith in reforming individuals by emphasizing that "human nature is plastic and subject to control," an explicitly environmental understanding of culture that paralleled Friendly ideas about the Inner Light and human perfectibility. But the scholars also pushed Quakers to see issues deeper than just flawed individuals and, thus, to see the need to revise the practice of their faith to include the reform of society as well.[7] Confronting tensions within both the Religious Society of Friends and American society,[8] these Quaker activists came to understand new imperatives of their lived faith as they attempted to put their ideals into action by providing "intelligent leadership in the cause of racial brotherhood."[9]

Early AFSC Interracial Activism

Created in 1917 to work with conscientious objectors during the Great War, the AFSC quickly expanded its service work in Europe and the United States after the war.[9] In 1924, Chairman Rufus Jones urged the AFSC to take up even more "tasks lying clearly at our door—God-given tasks which *we* can do better than anybody else." Among the new challenges that Jones wanted the AFSC to tackle was helping to build "better interracial relationship[s] . . . by quietly forming new contacts, bringing people together in friendly groups and practicing the spirit and ideals of our way of life."[10] Jones's interest in interracial problems reflected a growing concern among Quakers about race relations in the United States, and the AFSC created an Interracial Section (working along with Foreign Service, Peace, and Home Service sections) to "apply the Friendly principle of brotherhood [to race relations]."[11] Given a broad mandate to undertake "something along interracial, inter-class, and international lines," the Interracial Section decided, in early 1925, to work to bring about "a better understanding between the races in our own country and abroad."[12] A small start to solving a complex problem, the Interracial Section connected faith and practice in its interracial activism.

As it went to work, the Interracial Section had to cope with more than just the racist attitudes of American society; it also had to negotiate racism among Friends. A 1928 survey titled "Friends and Race Relations" summed up a long list of problems.[13] An uncompromising look at Quakers and race, this report identified a passive racism embodied in a "lack of interest in the Negro" as well as an "unwillingness or inability to discuss race relations and race contacts calmly, with openness of mind." It also noted an active racism reflected by educational and religious segregation.

Amid a broad program of interracial work in this vexed context, three projects stand out in terms of the time and effort invested by the Interracial Section as it worked to turn faith into practice. Although limited by monetary constraints, these programs all grew out of the Quaker belief in the Inner Light, described by historian Thomas Hamm as "the idea that all human beings are potentially good and can be appealed to in terms of that good, because they have something of the divine in them."[14] Believing in the efficacy of developing a broader understanding of other cultures to combat individual prejudice, the Interracial Section pursued projects that carefully engineered social interactions between different groups to increase dialogue and cross-cultural understanding.

The first project brought three Japanese college students to the United States to bridge international misunderstandings by interacting with people both on and off campus. The AFSC was especially pleased with student Yasushi Hasegawa, believing that "his speaking and visiting has done a very great deal to interpret Japanese life to America. [He] has quite fulfilled the purpose of the committee in bringing over these Japanese [students], which was to bring to the American people a better conception of the life and thought of the Japanese people."[15] As the AFSC explained, before "coming to America [Hasegawa] rather questioned the sincerity of Americans. However, he feels that he has met with true sincerity since he has been here."[16] "I have behaved in America," Hasegawa wrote in expressing his high hopes, "just as I behaved among my folks in Japan. . . . I think that what I have done either in Japan or America is trifling; but I hope the loving peaceful spirit I have been trying my best to exhibit may have by the grace of God [made] some friends on this side of the Pacific as well as on the other shore."[17]

Pleased with this program, the Interracial Section wanted to interpret African American life and culture to white Americans, hiring Crystal Bird, a young black woman, to "do the same type of thing that Mr. Hasegawa did last year, [providing] a splendid means for breaking down prejudice and for building up a constructive understanding on the part of our Friends' communities toward the colored race."[18] Bird shared the committee's general outlook on interracial relations, and the AFSC reported that she saw "her work [as] lifting aside the curtain which separates the white people from the colored people, and presenting to the white people the humanness of colored people. She trusts that wherever she goes, she can bring an understanding of the colored people that will lead to a greater knowledge of their problems, their difficulties, and their progress."[19] In speaking to an estimated 50,000 people, Bird combined "the presentation of accurate information in speeches and the singing of the spirituals. Many people have been reached through the message of music, who perhaps otherwise could not have been touched." Her speeches analyzed prejudice and highlighted "the contributions of the Negro race."[20]

While the Japanese students and Bird had delivered the AFSC's message to white audiences, the Interracial Section also experimented with bringing a white audience to the African American community in Philadelphia with its sponsorship of "tours of understanding" designed to teach whites about "Negro life and culture."[21] The first tour occurred in late 1926, when fifteen Friends and their five black guides observed a "careful, detailed schedule" capped by a performance in a private home by the well-known singer Marian Anderson. The section's report on the first tour of understanding noted that "all who were present on the trip have spoken very highly of the thoroughly interesting experience which they have enjoyed."[22] A second tour of understanding in early 1927 emphasized the key lessons that the AFSC hoped to teach, noting the benefits of interracial connections and stressing that "only by seeing and talking and feeling with these [blacks], our fellow citizens, can one receive the deep stimulus that such a trip gives one." AFSC reports went to great lengths in demonstrating that African Americans could achieve—and, in many cases, had already achieved—all that whites had accomplished, describing efficient, "scientific," and successful businesses and schools. Participants once again praised the tour, and the AFSC's report noted that the evening concluded "with a mingling of humbleness, happiness and a hope and belief in the value [of] sharing, which would leave us never the same, but further along the same path of life we are all doing."[23]

AFSC staffers praised these initial efforts to connect faith and practice in building an interracial brotherhood that helped individuals better understand prejudice and discrimination. Despite these positive feelings, however, the Interracial Section had exhausted its momentum by 1929. Its goals had proved elusive from the start, in part because Friends struggled with racism—both overt in cases of segregation and prejudice as well as subtle in a too-common tone of paternalism and condescension—and economic problems that limited both the vision and the efforts of the AFSC. But the demise of the Interracial Section did not signal the end of AFSC activism because the organization had already crafted plans for the American Interracial Peace Committee (AIPC), an even more ambitious effort to conquer racism and war simultaneously. Despite real enthusiasm for this effort to translate faith into practice, however, familiar problems led executive secretary Alice Dunbar-Nelson to sum up its results pessimistically in 1931, describing four fruitless years of "hammering on cold iron."[24]

AIPC leaders drew up an ambitious agenda for the new organization, describing a "joint effort of representative American Negroes working in close cooperation with the [AFSC] to develop and promote the active support of the Negroes of America in the cause of peace in this and every other land." The AIPC, leaders Leslie Pickney Hill and Helen Bryan explained, hoped to build an educational campaign for both blacks and whites that demonstrated key linkages between race and peace. The AIPC leaders, continuing to stress the Interracial Section's intuitive belief in the importance of modeling interracial contacts to overcome prejudice, hoped that including blacks in their peace efforts would "promote understanding, goodwill, and cooperation between the races in America." Presenting the accomplishments and contributions of African Americans to the nation and the world, much like earlier Interracial Section programs, would also "serve the cause of reconciliation and peace."[25]

Despite—or, perhaps, because of—its great ambitions, the American Interracial Peace Committee survived only four years. Financial problems exacerbated by the Great Depression constantly limited AIPC efforts. As Dunbar-Nelson observed as the AFSC slashed funding repeatedly, these cuts made her "committee a mere fund raising affair, with the secretary raising money to pay her salary to raise more money—with no opportunity for expansion, putting over a program, or a policy." This would, she warned, eventually reduce the AIPC to "a rather ridiculous and sordid affair."[26] After the AIPC's demise, AFSC general secretary Clarence Pickett emphasized that financial limitations had determined the decision to lay down the organization; as he regretfully explained, the interracial agency had "depended almost entirely on [the AFSC] for subsidy." When the latter could no longer afford the subsidy, the former could no longer afford to continue its work.[27] Hill agreed that the AIPC had failed to overcome the "worldwide depression [that] bore down most heavily and disastrously everywhere upon the classes represented by the disadvantaged American Negro."[28]

Personality clashes—often centered on Dunbar-Nelson—further hindered AIPC work, adding to its financial problems. While Dunbar-Nelson's assertive personality generated some conflict, her vexed position as an African American resulted in condescending and even insulting relationships with some Quakers. When race problems were brought to the AFSC, for example, its leaders often called on Dunbar-Nelson for help, even if these issues did not fall within the purview of her committee's work; her race alone (among an otherwise largely white organization) made her the ideal candidate to help with all "race" issues. Dunbar-Nelson had uneven—and sometimes hostile—relationships with most of her co-workers. Critical of a perceived series of snubs by leading Quakers within the AFSC, Dunbar-Nelson confided in her diary, "However I have no quarrel with the Quakerfolk. I can watch them and weigh them and feel superior to them." She was, as she put it plainly, "*not* impressed."[29] Just "tired of the whole damn mess" by the time her job officially ended, Dunbar-Nelson wrote, "These damn Quakers make me tired . . . , begrudg[ing as they do] spending 2,000 dollars for work among 12,000,000 Negroes!"[30]

In addition to monetary and personnel issues, the AIPC also confronted racism among the Religious Society of Friends. At work, for example, Dunbar-Nelson experienced a dismal encounter with a "little Quaker lady from the Swarthmore meeting" who visited the AIPC and "added considerably to the gayety of nations by her stringent objections to the Negro in general and Negroes in Quaker meetings in particular." Dunbar-Nelson described the visitor's "bitter" complaints that the Quaker tried to cover with the excuse that she "'had colored servants, etc., etc.' We all had a good laugh after she had gone. If she had known I was colored she would have died."[31] Despite Dunbar-Nelson's attempt to shrug this incident off, it revealed a key obstacle to AIPC work: belief in the Inner Light might encourage action (on the part of individual Friends), but the need for consensus often led to inaction (on the part of corporate bodies of worship, which recalcitrant individuals could immobilize).[32] This tension had been prevalent in

American Quakers' race work since at least antebellum efforts at abolition. The historical clash between what historian Ryan P. Jordan has described as "the lay person's conscience on the one hand and the need for sectarian coherence on the other" proved a formidable obstacle.[33]

Hill's report as the AIPC folded suggested the sometimes problematic relationship between Quakers and African Americans. While he praised Friends for their belief "in the brotherhood of men" and their willingness to work *with* (and not just *for*) African Americans, he was disappointed in how quickly whites, and especially Friends, had lost interest in the project. Hill observed that whites had increasingly come to see interracial activism as "unpopular" and offering "little glamour or romance." Instead of remaining steadfastly committed to the cause, he concluded, "Even among Quakers we have to observe a steady widening outreach of interest and activity away from the Black Man."[34] Given these realities, the AIPC could not continue.

The AFSC Considers Social Science: The Institute of Race Relations, 1933–1934

But even as the AIPC collapsed, individuals were pushing the AFSC in new directions. The momentum generated by these concerned activists ultimately helped Service Committee workers to see broader implications of practicing their Quaker faith. In fall 1932, Helen Bryan, an interracial activist who had connections with Philadelphia-area Quaker Meetings and the AFSC, "called together a group of people in [her] apartment . . . to analyze . . . the work which [they had] attempted to do up to date, and then asked for definite suggestions of work that the [Race Relations] Committee [of the Philadelphia Yearly Meetings] might plan to carry on in the future." After reflecting on past work and sharing time for prayer, Crystal Bird Fauset, another veteran of early AFSC activism, "hesitatingly" shared an idea "precious to her" that she had been nurturing for some time, suggesting the creation of an integrated school for "studying together under the best teachers that could be secured, and in the light of the best scientific knowledge that could be gathered . . . conflicts between races, and ways of preventing such conflicts."[35]

Acting on Fauset's leading and taking advantage of increasing collaboration between Philadelphia Friends and the AFSC, Bryan pressed the Quaker service organization to take up this project. Aware of Friends' complicated relationships with race, she understood the need to proceed cautiously, observing that "each one must be led along this line of thought with the utmost care." Convinced of the proposed school's "most significant potentialities," Bryan planned to move as slowly as necessary with Friends and their organizations, knowing the necessity of allowing "the Quaker mind . . . to readjust to this new conception of the place that our Committee might [occupy] in the developing field of race relations."[36]

Moved by Fauset's idea and Bryan's enthusiasm for it, AFSC leaders agreed to cooperate in supporting the Institute of Race Relations, an annual conference starting in 1933 (and continuing, with interruptions, to 1941). The Institute, a monthlong enterprise, drew well-known scholars of the "culture-and-personality" school, a "loose network" of academics who "explicitly rejected biological theories of race and investigated instead how different 'cultures' produced diverse patterns of human behavior."[37] Contact with these scholars encouraged some Friends to explore the intellectual scaffolding—both secular and religious—that underlay their earlier interracial efforts. While these contacts would confirm old AFSC interracial methods rooted in a belief in the Inner Light, new and broader understandings of race issues slowly but decisively convinced Quakers that their religious faith demanded a new practice of interracial activism, aimed at the reform of society as well as the individual.

Bryan's pitch for this new approach to race activism arrived at an opportune time. The Interracial Section and the AIPC had failed to create sustained programs, but AFSC members remained interested in such work. Bryan's proposal offered these Friends the opportunity to continue this work while reconsidering their activism in light of current social science scholarship. Having a decade's worth of experiential knowledge, AFSC members now investigated cutting-edge scholarship to see what it might add to their efforts to generate sustainable activism. Along the way, unexpected changes occurred in their understanding of Friendly identity and activism.

As planning for the Institute of Race Relations moved ahead under the auspices of the Race Relations Committee of the Philadelphia Yearly Meetings, sociologist Charles S. Johnson, closely connected to the culture-and-personality school that advocated "social engineering" to build egalitarianism, stepped in to lead its planning. He viewed the multiracial United States as "an excellent laboratory" to test theories of environmental determinism that were replacing older arguments that race determined culture. The project would be helped along, he noted, by a fortunate "combination of circumstances which means that the most outstanding men in the social field are very often most liberal men in race relations. This is true of our best sociologists and anthropologists,— Boaz [sic], Herskovitz [sic], Park, Ross, Donald Young, [and] Kimball Young."[38]

At the initial organizational meeting for the Institute, AFSC executive secretary Clarence Pickett began the proceedings by noting "the long standing interest of the Society of Friends in interracial work, and more recently of the interest of the Committee of Race Relations in modern techniques and the findings of science in the field of race relations."[39] Pickett's introduction blended Quaker history and modern social science nicely; the conversation that followed, however, suggested the trajectory of the Institute in its early years in focusing on secular ideas about race work, devoting little time to the connections between Quaker principles and the Institute's work.

Indeed, the participants who followed Pickett focused almost exclusively on social science to the detriment of Quaker faith and practice. Bruno Lasker, for example, noted how the proposed Institute's systematic analysis of race relations would connect "practitioner and scholar" in adopting "a thoroughly realistic approach." Otto Klineberg, a key scholar in the culture-and-personality school, reinforced Lasker's academic orientation, calling for a "scientific" and "purely realistic approach" that would destroy racial myths.

Franz Boas, a founder of the environmental school of thought, reinforced the message in emphasizing the need to overcome the emotional baggage of race issues.[40]

Despite the scholars' clearly secular emphasis, Quakers hoped to use the Institute to connect contemporary social science to their interracial activism. Friends envisioned "a center where, with an interracial faculty and an interracial student body, persons may study the techniques of interracial relationships and programs and may have access to scientific information regarding the background and environmental factors of certain racial groups."[41] Importantly, this description emphasized intergroup interactions, a long-held approach of the AFSC and Quakers involved in race work but now explicitly connected to social science. In addition, the Institute, in building on current scientific understandings of the world, would study the importance of environment, a small start on the part of Quakers to making environmental determinism meaningful for their work.

Quakers struggled, however, to include religious ideas in the Institute's curriculum. Promotional materials for the first Institute of Race Relations emphasized social planning, and not religion, as the best approach to race problems. One pamphlet, for example, explained that this project had "grown out of the realization that there is need of a more direct, scientific approach to interracial situations which are increasing in complexity throughout the world." A broadly scientific approach to interracial relations, Institute planners hoped, would result in a new set of "techniques [with] a background of fact and impartial analysis" developed under the guidance of "the foremost thinkers."[42]

The secular orientation prevailed as the first Institute of Race Relations opened in 1933 and faculty presented biological racism as outdated and unfounded, pointing out that the "more race is analyzed the more difficult it becomes to define it scientifically. [If] you analyze it sufficiently you analyze it out of existence." Thus, race was a social construct: "It is important to keep in mind in dealing with race, the distinction between biological and social phenomenon. . . . The real definition of race rests less upon biological differentiation than upon the cultural and social significance given to them."[43]

The secular understanding that "human nature is plastic and subject to control"—a concept consonant with the Inner Light's faith in human progress—led the faculty to suggest, echoing AFSC race work in the 1920s, that the study of prejudice and other racial groups presented the best solution, breaking down "provincialism" and exposing how "misleading myths [and] rationalizations" kept African Americans subordinated. Building on new scholarship, faculty taught that "scattered recent studies . . . are beginning to reveal . . . highly sophisticated and efficient African cultures [that had] both affected and in turn [been] affected [by] the culture of The New World." An appreciation of African accomplishments, both in Africa and the United States, much like the AFSC had argued since the 1920s, would improve interracial relations. In this way, positive changes could be engineered as Americans managed "a mosaic of racial fragments." As a result, the faculty concluded, "the new concept of social planning, which our present economic disorganization has made imperative, permits a deliberate and dispassionate social strategy founded upon a sounder knowledge of the cultural environment, which determines the social behavior of all individuals and groups."[44]

Such a substantial set of problems, the faculty agreed, could only be addressed through "realism," "science," and social engineering. The curriculum thus reflected the scholars' doubts about the efficacy of religious organizations in racial reform. Churches, they argued, became increasingly political and conservative once established, often reinforcing traditional racial attitudes. While Quakers had linked their faith to their interracial work, the first Institute of Race Relations clearly eschewed religion in favor of science.

During the first Institute, controversy arose at Friends' schools. Max Yergan spoke at the Institute, but, when he tried to enroll his two sons at Westtown (a Friends' school founded in 1799), it caused "a tremendous disturbance." Despite lobbying from AFSC members Ray Newton and Clarence Pickett to accept Yergan's children, the school flatly refused.[45] Swarthmore College (founded in 1864 by a committee of Friends) made a decision that fall to deny admission to a black student, reinforcing the reality that Friends remained deeply divided on race. Despite President Frank Aydelotte's promise that African American students would be considered for admission by the college in the future, Pickett explained, the incident revealed that Friends, "like others, are divided among themselves. There is a great deal of interest in promoting better interracial relations among a great many of the leading Friends, but on the other hand you have individuals who have interracial prejudices."[46]

As the Philadelphia Yearly Meetings' Committee on Race Relations planned the second Institute of Race Relations, it opened conversations with the AFSC about establishing a closer working relationship.[47] These talks did not bear immediate fruit, and the 1934 Institute followed the program of its predecessor "in broad outline," continuing to stress the application of "a tested scientific approach to the universal problem of race conflict."[48] Continuing to stress science and environmental determinism, the 1934 Institute of Race Relations also slighted organized religion as a solution to race problems. Although Quaker Henry Cadbury taught a history of Friends and race at the Institute, the curriculum only glanced at the Religious Society of Friends. Most discussion about religion continued to emphasize the conservative orientation of most established churches. At best, Johnson concluded, "The church plays a curious and sometime contradictory role in social and racial relations."[49]

The continuing secular emphasis in 1934 pushed participants, including some Friends, to begin to see a broader problem that suggested the need for new methods of practicing their faith. Johnson, for example, reported disagreements between participants over what goals to establish and how best to pursue them. One group, he explained, saw a dysfunctional economy that created uncorrectable "social [and] economic abuses"; it wanted to completely "change the system . . . by any tactics deemed effective." Another group agreed on the need for substantive change but preferred gradually modifying the present system "through rational planning and experimentation." A third group thought education and the adaptation of social philosophies could fix society. Whatever the solution, Johnson warned against paternalistic efforts to help African Americans, hoping that future efforts would be "more cooperative."[50]

Quakers, beginning a sustained effort to make the Institute more meaningful for themselves, praised the 1934 gathering but, seemingly sensing a lack of practical application for Friends at the first two gatherings, noted that action must follow. In this way, Friends wrestled for control of the Institute by insisting that it must help to connect faith and practice. Arthur James, for example, appreciated the "scientific approach" that emphasized environmental determinism, but he argued "that scientific findings are of little avail except as acted upon. . . . We must be down on the road having sympathetic human contacts rather than looking at the problems from an intellectual balcony." Frank Watson reinforced this point, warning that, while Friends had held "an historical testimony on Slavery, an issue that is dead, we do not have a testimony on today's problem of Segregation."[51]

While pleased with the success of the 1934 venture, Race Relations Committee members had financial worries that led them to ask the AFSC for increased cooperation. Cadbury argued that the AFSC ought to take over this effort, suggesting that, under the "stronger auspices" of the organization, Quakers could work to "mutual advantage" to advance the Religious Society of Friends "in the field of race in which Friends need to think and act on a reconsidered basis."[52] Pickett agreed with Cadbury's call for new interracial practices, acknowledging "a good deal of latent interest in the field of race relations," and the Peace Section of the AFSC assumed control of the Institute of Race Relations.[53]

The AFSC Adapts Social Science: The Institute of Race Relations, 1935

As the AFSC assumed responsibility for the Institute of Race Relations in early 1935, its new role portended significant changes that would include a more "religious" focus as well as a broader view of race problems.[54] Most important, the enhanced role of the AFSC and, as a consequence, Quakers at the Institute started to shift the curricular focus away from its secular emphases. As Friends began to advocate the study of nonviolence at the summer school, for example, they recognized the need to broaden the course of study, and the 1935 agenda included a much heavier emphasis on economics as well. In addition, Quakers also became more interested in translating what had been taught into Friendly activism as they began more systematically to reconnect faith and practice.

Continued divisions among Friends concerning race accompanied this renewed Quaker interest in race relations, however, and these internal obstacles to activism became clear at a gathering held in January. Described by the *Friends Intelligencer* as "a challenging conference on Friends' attitudes in regards to race relations," the meeting drew a large crowd "with various shades of opinion" to the Cherry Street Meeting House.[55] The gathering suggested a revived concern in connecting Quaker faith to racial activism that would inform the way that Quaker planners and participants shaped and responded to the 1935 Institute of Race Relations.

Dr. Frank Watson of Haverford College spoke first and searchingly questioned Quakers' "convictions regarding Race in the light of Christianity." He suggested that Friends ought to be "a little further to the left in [their] thinking on the subject of race relations." Urging Friends not to confuse problems of crime, health, or poverty with race, Watson highlighted the importance of religious activism and asked how Quakers might better harmonize their actions with their religious convictions, pointedly wondering, "Are we failing to realize that of God in every man?"[56]

Dr. Henry J. Cadbury of Harvard spoke in the evening and delivered an even more searching critique of Quakers accompanied by a strong call to action. Cadbury tried to convince Friends to stop resting on the laurels of long-ago abolitionists, arguing that past successes meant little in a present in which African Americans were excluded from Swarthmore College and many Friends schools. "It makes little difference in our Society," he warned, "that at other times in our history we were distinctive. In fact, we are going backward. We are less generous, less liberal and less prepared to grant equality to the Negro than we used to be. We are indifferent and are ignorant of some of the facts that would make indifference less possible." As a result, he concluded, there was at present "no distinctive Quaker position [on race]."[57]

Having presented the magnitude of the problem, Cadbury hoped to reignite Friendly activism by drawing on approaches pioneered earlier by the Interracial Section and the AIPC. Cadbury suggested that Quakers share information about racial problems in the United States and the rest of the world as well as about black achievements. While doing so, he warned, emphasizing the necessity of faith-inspired action, race work should be undertaken in concert with "the Friendly spirit." In addition, he urged "more intimate association with Negroes, but we need to have the right technique. Meet your first Negro not as a Negro but as someone interested in something else— the intellectual approach." Ultimately, Cadbury explained, "There is a white problem in America—not a Negro problem."[58]

The conversation that followed Cadbury's presentation focused on the persistent problem of segregation among Friends, who clearly remained divided on racial issues. When one attendee raised the issue of all-white Meetings, noting that many Quakers argued that blacks "are so emotional they would not like Quaker meeting anyhow," Cadbury pointed out that Quakers had been making this argument since the last century. Supporting Cadbury, another participant argued that segregation was incompatible with Quakerism. While the discussion did not cover much new ground, the idea upon which it was based—that "Quakers should continually evolve our testimony as the needs demand"—suggested Friendly interest in shaping an evolving religious identity as they developed new strategies of race activism that would strongly influence the 1935 Institute of Race Relations.[59]

Quakers, indeed, immediately affected the curriculum of the 1935 Institute. The committee formed to oversee the AFSC's work with the Institute, weighted with Friends, actively planned the curriculum, relying less on Johnson to develop classes and instead presenting him with a course of study in April, with Bryan noting a willingness "to modify the names of the courses so that they shall more neatly conform to [Johnson's] phraseology" but not much more.[60] The new course of study emphasized concrete action (as opposed to abstract theory) as Friends began more consciously to incorporate their ideals into the Institute of Race Relations. Ray Newton of the Peace Section, for instance, pressed Johnson to include the study of "eliminating interracial injustice through nonviolent means." Willing to balance the inclusion of Quaker ideals with other secular theories, the final schedule leaned heavily in its final week on nonviolence.[61] While the 1935 Institute did not abandon theory, it emphasized linking Quaker faith and practice, and Bryan hoped that the Institute might help Friends coordinate their activism into "a constructive, unified piece of work which would be of prophetic value."[62]

The 1935 Institute generated new excitement among some Quakers. In part, this resulted from the broader—and even, at times, radical—ideas that had been presented, ranging from "respect for the personality of the racially different" to "establishing almost immediately a new social order based on use rather than profit." Supporters of the latter position at the Institute, including A. Phillip Randolph and Ira Reid, saw racism arising from "a faulty economic system" that made nonviolence nonviable. While participants could not agree on "any single method in their practical approach to the problem of race," many argued that religion, "based upon a conviction for equality and fraternity," should be at the forefront of attempts at racial change. In addition, the attendees concurred on the importance of education, believing that many people, including Friends, were inactive on race issues because they were uninformed.[63]

Quakers saw real value in the 1935 Institute for themselves, drawing on social science to reinforce the earlier efforts of the Interracial Section and the AIPC while also acknowledging a newly understood need to reform society as well as the individual. Alfred H. Cope, secretary of the AFSC branch in Chicago, wrote a detailed report, "Techniques for Tolerance," from a Quaker's perspective that highlighted key outcomes of the Institute for Friends. Beginning with the assumption that "prejudice is acquired and not inherent" and should be overcome "by integration and by pacific means," Cope stressed environmental causes of race conflict. As a result, he favored education and awareness as part of an "indirect approach" that would "not arouse the race question by discussing it too publicly." He also suggested that presenting "some prominent Negro, Jew, or Oriental in a community where such an individual may be positively appreciated, will have the greatest weight in the long run." Noting that educational work might start in Friends schools, Cope obliquely acknowledged ongoing problems by euphemistically suggesting the need for expanded work there.[64]

Cope ended his report with a radical call verging on a Friendly revolution that grew from his new understanding of a broader problem that required revised applications of the Friendly faith to the world. "It must be recognized," Cope wrote, "that prejudice is an outgrowth of the presence of different conflicting groups, many of them economic, [and] that the removal of economic conflicts will in large part remove racial conflicts."

Since this was true, he continued, Friends "must not merely battle within an existing social order to bring a better understanding, [but] must seek to modify that social order to a cooperative system, based upon the respect for individuals and their differences, and seek a social order which must be operated for use and not for profit if we are to eliminate the type of conflicts which make the race issue so difficult." Urging the recognition that prejudice made a cooperative system impossible, Cope hoped that Quakers would work "to dispel ignorance and activate a sufficient group of people so that arguments for racial equality may be not merely correct, but also potent enough to make a general impact." As he concluded,

> In regard to the correlation between interracial cooperation and economic change, it is interesting to realize the real contribution of the Society of Friends toward such a step. One of the outstanding leaders known to the Society of Friends has said that he agreed with Lenin that capitalism is unavoidably greedy and destructive to mankind. He has gone on to say that because capitalism by nature chooses the methods of violence it is not necessary that it shall be overthrown by violence. Thus at a time of interracial conflict the Society of Friends may at once attempt to dodge the easy expedient of palliatives, and at the same time attempt to inject every possible amount of pacifism and reason into the Race problem.

While more radical than many Quakers, Cope's report suggested how the pressures of the Great Depression and the social science emphasis of the Institutes moved some to consider broader definitions of and solutions to race issues.[65]

The Committee on Race Relations issued a report, "Quaker Experience with Questions of Race," that reinforced many of Cope's conclusions and presented the need to adapt Quaker practices of their faith to changing circumstances. It began with an extensive overview of Quaker history, emphasizing that "the founders of Quakerism affirmed definitely the religious equality of all races. The early Friends believed that God was the Father of all men [and] that he 'made of one blood all nations for to dwell upon the face of the earth', and [that] the light which lightens every man was in the heathen races of Europe, Asia and America." As Friends first came in contact with "alien races" in America, they had "accepted not only Indians but negroes as objects of divine redemption." While the use of "objects" denied the agency of those who needed Friendly guidance, the report praised the Quakers' "just, humane, and pacific Indian policy" as well as Friends' translation of "religious ideals into the terms of democracy, economic justice and universal liberty" in their crusade against slavery. But, it warned, while abolitionist Friends represented "one of the most illuminating historical illustrations of Quaker testimony," the record since had been decidedly mixed. "Where fearless but humble conscientiousness had free play," it read, "the Society of Friends made a significant contribution to this cause of righteousness, but where blind acceptance of the status quo or of the traditional fathers prevailed, and where self-interest, sloth, pious aloofness from great public issues, or self-centered concern for the reputation of the Society in petty matters was manifest, there Quakerism fell short of its high calling."[66]

media

Moving to current issues, the report stressed that abolitionism had not ended race conflict. While Friends had focused on education during Reconstruction, economic issues had been neglected. Calling for an honest appraisal of Quaker shortcomings, the report urged that "nothing less than the renewal of the radical democracy of early Quakerism is likely to bring present day Quakerism into worthy succession to the precedents of our fathers." Advocating pricking the conscience of Friends to rally them, the report called for Quakers "to identify ourselves with the oppressed." Acknowledging that the "new injustice [is] more subtle than formal slavery," the report believed that the Quaker past could inspire an evolving commitment to contemporary race issues: "The Quaker testimony on race is not a fixed or static thing, neither is it an abstract theory. It is a growing and continuing application of fundamental principles to the changing circumstances of a changing world." Arguing that "race divisions represent a focal point on which many of the Quaker testimonies converge" and connecting race to international tensions, the report ended with a clear call to activism and leadership. "With so many of our own principles at stake and realizing the danger to all mankind which the continuance of interracial hostility threatens," the report concluded, "it behooves the Society of Friends to prepare itself for intelligent leadership in the cause of racial brotherhood." Such leadership, the report implied, could build on techniques pioneered for Quakers by the Interracial Section and the AIPC but would need to continue adapting the practice of their faith to meet the challenges of a rapidly changing world.[67]

The Demise of the Institute of Race Relations, 1936–1941

While the 1935 Institute of Race Relations offered much for Quakers to build on and future gatherings continued to highlight the key messages that had been honed by the first three meetings, the Institute faced decline in the following years. Financial problems, a constant concern, became even more acute. In addition, divisions and continuing racism among Friends further hindered AFSC efforts. Finally, attempts to reenergize the project by changing the location and offering college credit for its students failed to draw more students while increasingly pulling the Institute of Race Relations further from Quaker control. The Institute of Race Relations met for the last time in 1941, overtaken by internal problems and a world at war.

The 1936 Institute broke even financially, if barely, as instructors, drawing connections between race and peace work, continued to stress intergroup contact and cooperation, which were given new urgency by the looming global conflict. Faced with developing worldwide crises, the AFSC redoubled its focus on engineering positive intercultural exchanges. "In this world of prejudices and intolerance," the AFSC explained in presenting the school as a technique in interracialism itself, "it is extremely difficult to know persons of other races. . . . But one of the most valuable factors in the Institute is the fact that for three weeks individuals of differing races may live, think, work, plan together for the ultimate good of the races concerned and in that process may come to know, respect and admire the individuals of the various races."[68]

Faculty at the 1936 Institute of Race Relations also built on previous curricula in continuing to emphasize economics and activism.[69] As the faculty continued to link environmental determinism with economics, the 1936 Institute required students to tackle "practical projects."[70] Among these projects—which included creating a course of study for worker education, studying discrimination in higher education to develop techniques to counter it, and working on plans to contest discrimination in states without civil rights bills—some students arranged materials "which would be peculiarly useful to Friends groups," a clear indication of the desire to use the Institute to link Quakers' faith and practice. Bryan praised the hands-on projects for contributing to one of the most effective Institutes yet, and Quaker students also saw real value in their participation. As one student explained in urging Friends to attend future Institutes, Quaker activism "in the field of race relations [is] still largely traditional and therefore considerably out of touch with radically changing situations." If Friends were to act, she continued, interracial activism could "be intelligently redirected only by first-hand knowledge of what beside philanthropic efforts, is most needed to ease racial tensions in the United States. . . . Only responsible and clear-headed colored leaders can provide such knowledge." Thus, Friends needed to widen "their intellectual horizons, bounded before by familiarity chiefly with their own social and family intimates."[71] Similarly, the pamphlet *Race and Its Relations to Members of the Religious Society of Friends* urged Quakers to educate themselves and then develop Meeting projects to address racial issues.[72]

As the 1937 Institute approached, Quakers were once again reminded of the imposing obstacles to interracial activism that remained. Most notably, controversy erupted when Media Friends School in Pennsylvania enrolled a black student in its nursery program. Four students were withdrawn immediately, and the parents of thirty-five others threatened not to return the following year, once again exposing deep divisions among Quakers on the issue of race.[73]

The Institute of Race Relations experienced important changes in 1937 as it moved to Cheyney State Teachers College. More important than the move, the publicity materials, reflecting a continued desire to link faith and practice, described "a definite emphasis on the religious approach to race" that organizers hoped would "secure the attendance of a larger proportion of Friends" and provide continued attention to shaping a curriculum "that would have a greater practical emphasis."[74] Jointly sponsored by the AFSC, which provided financial support, and the Committee on Race Relations, which organized the event, the 1937 Institute was staffed by a faculty that included fewer academics than in previous years.[75]

As talks about reviving an AFSC race relations agency began,[76] the AFSC moved ahead with sponsoring the 1938 Institute of Race Relations, which had yet another new home, this time at New York University, where it carried college credit for the first time.[77] These innovations did not stabilize the program, however. Instead, financial problems torpedoed plans for the Institute of Race Relations in 1939, although NYU's School of Education did offer some classes that summer. Unable to raise sufficient funds for 1939, the AFSC looked into the possibility of holding an abbreviated Institute in 1940. Despite a drastically reduced budget, however, the project was not revived in 1940, either. The Institute of Race Relations did resurface in 1941, but with mixed results from the Quakers' perspective. Held at Westtown School for three weeks in July under the leadership of Otto Klineberg of Columbia University and Alberta Morris of the Committee on Race Relations, the program ran a deficit of about $200, and some concerns arose about the secular nature of the program. One Quaker student summarized the worries bluntly, writing that the "Institute was not run according to Friendly principles." As a result of this (as well as the fact that Klineberg brought a number of outspoken Columbia students with him), "discussions were rigidly controlled by the dictates from [Klineberg] rather than by the wishes of the group."[78]

Conclusion

Despite their disappointments with the 1941 Institute, Friends hoped to run the Institute of Race Relations again in 1942, but the Japanese attack on Pearl Harbor on December 7, 1941, scotched these plans. The entry of the United States into World War II immediately and dramatically changed AFSC work, and both its members and local Friends now saw little chance of supporting an Institute in 1942. As Alberta Morris reported to Pickett on December 17, "The relative importance of an Institute in 1942, with the uncertainties which the last ten days have presented, [was] seriously discussed by the Committee." Given the new and daunting workload members foresaw, sponsoring the Institute in 1942 would be "impossible."[79] The Institute of Race Relations as a Quaker enterprise had ended.[80]

The Institute had provided Friends with an invaluable opportunity, however, to evaluate and refine their interracial theories and techniques while considering what modern social science might contribute to Quaker faith and practice. In this way, Quakers had confronted a rapidly changing world both by looking to the lessons of the past and by embracing new outlooks for the future. In looking backward, Friends involved with the Institutes of Race Relations found much in the social science of the day that fit comfortably with the theological foundations of their earlier activism. Theories of environmental determinism effectively supported the Quaker assumption that all human beings were capable of reform and progress. In this way, the theories of the "culture-and-personality" scholars comfortably reinforced past Friendly tactics that had emphasized carefully engineering intergroup and intercultural exchanges.

While much at the Institutes of Race Relations had reinforced old Quaker ideas and methods, however, the faculty's heavy emphasis on economics had pushed at least some Friends to conceive a broader problem. In this way, Quaker activists found themselves as much shaped by the culture as shaping it with their reform efforts. No longer did they simply assume that the root of racial difficulties rested only with racist individuals; now, instead, at least some Quakers saw systemic problems that required more sweeping change. While AFSC workers still saw the need to change individuals to achieve real reform, their new efforts at race relations would include projects designed to change society as well.

Quakers and members of the AFSC thus found themselves at a crossroads as conflict engulfed the globe, uncertain of which direction to take but forced nonetheless to connect their faith and practice in new ways. As they did so, the lessons of the past and the new ideas for the future held out possibilities. Emerging from the Institutes of Race Relations with new and broader understandings of the implications of putting their faith into practice in order to provide "intelligent leadership in the cause of racial brotherhood," AFSC workers took new directions during and especially after World War II, focusing on efforts to reform discriminatory practices in housing, education, and employment. Faced with a new and confusing world, Quakers would rely on the lessons of the 1920s and 1930s as they moved forward—with an evolving sense of the meaning of Quaker faith and practice—to meet the challenges of the wartime present.

Notes

From *Quaker Brotherhood: Interracial Activism and The American Friends Service Committee, 1917–1950.* Copyright 2012 by the Board of Trustees of the University of Illinois. Used with permission of the University of Illinois Press. The chapter title is from "Quaker Experience with Questions of Race," 1935, Arch Street, 1921–1929, Philadelphia Yearly Meeting (hereafter referred to as PYM) Committee on Race Relations, Box 1, Friends Historical Library, Swarthmore, Pennsylvania (hereafter referred to as FHL). I would like to thank Patrick Hamilton, Justin Nordstrom, Becky Steinberger, and members of the symposium for commenting on earlier drafts of this work.

1. Quoted in Mary Hoxie Jones, *Swords into Ploughshares: An Account of the American Friends Service Committee, 1917–1937* (Westport, Conn.: Greenwood Press, 1937), vii–viii.

2. Thomas D. Hamm, *The Quakers in America* (New York: Columbia University Press, 2003), 157.

3. Philadelphia Yearly Meeting of the Religious Society of Friends, *Faith and Practice: A Book of Christian Discipline* (Philadelphia: Philadelphia Yearly Meeting, 1997), 67. The 1997 edition later uses the quote by Jones (although misattributed) that begins this essay (150). For examples of various books of discipline, see Hamm, *The Quakers in America*, 264–65.

4. Hamm, *The Quakers in America*, 169–71.

5. Jones, *Swords into Plowshares*, 168.

6. Henry J. Cadbury, "Quaker Service and Social Change," *AFSC Bulletin*, April 1948, AFSC Serials, 1947–49, American Friends Service Committee Archives, Philadelphia, Pennsylvania (hereafter referred to as AFSCA).

7. Summary of Course of Lectures at the Institute of Race Relations, 1933, AFSC Interracial: Institute of Race Relations, 1933, AFSCA; Joanne Meyerowitz, "'How Common Culture Shapes the Separate Lives': Sexuality, Race, and Mid-Twentieth-Century Social Constructionist Thought," *Journal of American History*, 96, no. 4 (March 2010): 1059.

8. This give-and-take between the AFSC and American society and culture is not uncommon in the experience of many philanthropies. As Lawrence J. Friedman argues, "Individual charitable impulses are shaped by organizational stimulants and constraints," resulting in "complex and variable philanthropic weaves." This chapter also demonstrates how cultural and intellectual forces worked in conjunction with AFSC concerns to shape a changing understanding of the world in which Friends

worked. See Lawrence J. Friedman, "Philanthropy in America: Historicism and Its Discontents," in *Charity, Philanthropy, and Civility in American History*, ed. Lawrence J. Friedman and Mark D. McGarvie (New York: Cambridge University Press, 2003), 2–3.

9. For a history of the earliest years of the AFSC, see J. William Frost, "'Our Deeds Carry Our Message': The Early History of the American Friends Service Committee," *Quaker History* 81, no. 1 (Spring 1992): 1–51.

10. Untitled, n.d., AFSC Conferences, 1924, AFSCA; Extracts of Minutes sent to Executive Board and Committee on Reorganization, n.d., AFSC Executive Board, 1924, AFSCA; Frost, "'Our Deeds Carry Our Message,'"43.

11. Minutes of a Meeting of the AFSC, May 28, 1925, AFSC Minutes: General Meeting, 1925, AFSCA; Frost, "'Our Deeds Carry Our Message,'" 43. For a more detailed history of the Interracial Section, see Allan W. Austin, "'Let's Do Away with Walls!': The American Friends Service Committee's Interracial Section and the 1920s United States," *Quaker History* 98, no. 1 (Spring 2009): 1–34.

12. Special Meeting of Executive Board of AFSC, October 22, 1924, AFSC Minutes: Executive Board, 1924, AFSCA; Minutes of Interracial Committee, April 23, 1925, AFSC Minutes: Interracial Committee, 1925, AFSCA.

13. For the discussion that follows, see "Friends and Race Relations," 1928, AFSC: Interracial Section (general), 1928, AFSCA. For a fuller exploration of racial problems, see Austin, "'Let's Do Away with Walls!'"

14. Hamm, *The Quakers in America*, 200–201.

15. Minutes of Interracial Committee, February 3, 1927, AFSC Minutes: Interracial Committee, 1927, AFSCA.

16. Minutes of Interracial Committee, March 3, 1927, AFSC Minutes: Interracial Committee, 1927, AFSCA.

17. Yasushi Hasegawa to Wilbur K. Thomas, June 18, 1927, General Files, 1927, Interracial Publications, Interracial Section, Japanese Student, Hasegawa, AFSCA.

18. Minutes of Interracial Committee, July 7, 1927, AFSC Minutes: Interracial Committee, 1927, AFSCA.

19. Minutes of Interracial Committee, October 6, 1927, AFSC Minutes: Interracial Committee, 1927, AFSCA; Minutes of Special Meeting of Interracial Committee, July 21, 1927, AFSC Minutes: Interracial Committee, 1927, AFSCA.

20. Minutes of Interracial Committee, June 7, 1928, AFSC Minutes: Interracial Committee, 1928, AFSCA.

21. Minutes of Interracial Committee, October 7, 1926, AFSC Minutes: Interracial Committee, 1926, AFSCA; Forrester B. Washington to Margaret Jones, November 2, 1926, General Files, 1926, Home Service Publications, AFSC, Interracial Section, General, 1926, AFSCA.

22. Minutes of Interracial Committee, December 2, 1926, AFSC Minutes: Interracial Committee, 1926, AFSCA; Margaret E. Jones to Forrester B. Washington, November 26, 1926, General Files, 1926, Home Service Publications, AFSC, Interracial Section, General, 1926, AFSCA.

23. "A Tour of Understanding," n.d., General Files, 1927, Interracial Publicity, AFSC, Interracial Section, Tour of Understanding, 1927, AFSCA; "Second Tour of Understanding," March 17, 1927, General Files, 1927, Interracial Publicity, AFSC, Interracial Section, Tour of Understanding, 1927, AFSCA.

24. Gloria T. Hull, editor, *Give Us Each Day: The Diary of Alice Dunbar-Nelson* (New York: W. W. Norton, 1986), 316–17.

25. Minutes of Interracial Peace Committee, May 19, 1927, AFSC Minutes: Interracial Peace Committee, 1927, AFSCA.

26. Alice Dunbar-Nelson to C. E. Pickett, February 15, 1930, AFSC Peace Section: Interracial Peace Committee, 1930, AFSCA; Minutes of Peace Section, February 26, 1930, AFSC Minutes: Peace Section, 1930, AFSCA.

27. C. E. Pickett to R. A. Flynn, editor and publisher, *National Negro Voice,* May 10, 1932, AFSC Interracial: General, 1932, AFSCA; Minutes of the AFSC, January 22, 1931, AFSC Minutes: General Meeting, 1931, AFSCA; Hull, *Give Us Each Day,* 420; Minutes of the Board of Directors, April 8, 1931, AFSC Minutes: Executive Board, 1931, AFSC Minutes of Board of Directors, October 5, 1932, AFSC Minutes: Board of Directors, 1932, AFSCA.

28. Leslie P. Hill to AFSC, March 25, 1931, AFSC Peace: AIPC, 1931, AFSCA. For the discussion that follows, see Leslie P. Hill to AFSC, March 25, 1931, AFSC Peace: AIPC, 1931, AFSCA; "Report of Activities of the American Interracial Peace Committee," June 1, 1928–March 15, 1931, n.d., AFSC Peace: AIPC, 1931, AFSCA.

29. Minutes of AFSC, May 24, 1928, AFSC Minutes: General Meeting, 1928, AFSCA; Hull, *Give Us Each Day,* 238, 252, 267.

30. Hull, *Give Us Each Day,* 391–92, 394–96, 407, 413, 417, 419; Minutes of Peace Section, January 28, 1931, AFSC Minutes: Peace Section, 1931, AFSCA.

31. Hull, *Give Us Each Day,* 258.

32. "Some Reflections of the Race Relations Conference," *Friends Intelligencer,* January 21, 1932, 351–52.

33. Ryan P. Jordan, *Slavery and the Meetinghouse: The Quakers and the Abolitionist Dilemma, 1820–1865* (Bloomington: Indiana University Press, 2007), 2.

34. Leslie P. Hill to AFSC, March 25, 1931, AFSC Peace: AIPC, 1931, AFSCA.

35. Helen Bryan to Thomas Jessie Jones, December 15, 1932, AFSC Interracial: Institute of Race Relations, 1933, AFSCA; Ethel Potts, "The Growth of an Idea," n.d., Projects: Institute of Race Relations, 1932–1941, Box 9, FHL.

36. Helen Bryan to Crystal Bird Fauset, September 29, 1932, Projects: Institute of Race Relations, 1932–1941, Box 9, FHL.

37. Meyerowitz, "'Common Culture," 1057.

38. Notes Regarding the Summer School on Race Relations, December 6, 1932, Projects: Institute of Race Relations, 1932–1941, Box 9, FHL; Meyerowitz, "'Common Culture," 1059–62.

39. Summary Minutes of March 25, 1933, Meeting to Consider an Institute of Race Relations, April 8, 1933, AFSC Interracial: Institute of Race Relations, 1933, AFSCA. For planning, see also Notes on Proposed Summer School, n.d., Projects: Institute of Race Relations, 1932–1941, Box 9, FHL; Helen Bryan and Crystal Fauset to Dr. Howard Odum, March 9, 1933, Projects: Institute of Race Relations, 1932–1941, Box 9, FHL; Minutes of the Organization Meeting of the Institute of Race Relations, March 25, 1933, Projects: Institute on Race Relations, 1932–1941, PYM Race Relations Committee, Box 9, FHL; Persons Who Attended the Meeting Regarding the Institute of Race Relations, March 25, 1933, Projects: Institute of Race Relations, 1932–1941, Box 9, FHL.

40. Summary Minutes of March 25, 1933, Meeting to Consider an Institute of Race Relations; Minutes of the Organization Meeting of the Institute of Race Relations, March 25, 1933.

41. For quote and the discussion that follows, see Suggestions for a Summer School in Race Relations, 1933, AFSC Interracial: Institute of Race Relations, 1933, AFSCA.

42. Institute of Race Relations Program, July 1–30, 1933, Projects: Institute of Race Relations, 1932–1941, Box 9, FHL. A faculty and class list can also be found in List of Instructors and Classes, 1933, AFSC Interracial: Institute of Race Relations, 1933, AFSCA. For the lecture series, see *The Institute of Race Relations Evening Lecture Series* pamphlet, 1933, AFSC Interracial: Institute of Race Relations, 1933, AFSCA.

43. Summary of Course of Lectures at the Institute of Race Relations, 1933, AFSC Interracial: Institute of Race Relations, AFSCA.

44. Ibid.

45. C. E. Pickett to Margaret E. Parker, Friends Africa Mission, Kenya, July 31, 1933, AFSC Interracial: Institute of Race Relations, 1933, AFSCA; C. E. Pickett to Helen Bryan, July 17, 1933, AFSC Interracial,

1933, AFSCA; Ray Newton to Wilmer Young, Westtown School, April 27, 1933, AFSC Interracial, 1933, AFSCA; James F. Walker, principal, Westtown School, to Max Yergan, n.d., AFSC Interracial, 1933, AFSCA; C. E. Pickett to Margaret E. Parker, Friends Africa Mission, Kenya, July 31, 1933, AFSC Interracial: Institute of Race Relations, 1933, AFSCA.

46. Ray Newton to Enoc P. Waters, Jr., Journal and Guide, November 1, 1933, AFSC Interracial, 1933, AFSCA; Donna McDaniel and Vanessa Julye, *Fit for Freedom, Not for Friendship: Quakers, African Americans, and the Myth of Racial Justice* (Philadelphia: Quaker Press of Friends General Conference, 2009), 343–45.

47. C. E. Pickett to Helen Bryan, September 2, 1933, AFSC Interracial, 1933, AFSCA.

48. Institute of Race Relations, July 1–28, 1934, AFSC: Interracial, Swarthmore Institute, 1934, AFSCA.

49. Course Summary, 1934 Institute of Race Relations (hereafter referred to as IRR), AFSC: Interracial, Swarthmore Institute, 1934, AFSCA; Course Syllabus, 1934 IRR, AFSC: Interracial, Swarthmore Institute, 1934, AFSCA.

50. Course Summary, 1934 IRR.

51. Minutes, Committee on Race Relations, November 20, 1934, 1929–1936, PYM Committee on Race Relations, Box 2, FHL.

52. Henry J. Cadbury to C. E. Pickett, October 1, 1934, AFSC: Interracial, Swarthmore Institute, 1934, AFSCA; Minutes, Committee on Race Relations, May 17, 1934, 1929–1936, PYM Committee on Race Relations, Box 2, FHL; C. E. Pickett to Charles S. Johnson, September 26, 1934, AFSC: Interracial, Swarthmore Institute, 1934, AFSCA; Henry J. Cadbury to C. E. Pickett, October 1, 1934.

53. C. E. Pickett to Charles S. Johnson, March 2, 1935, AFSC Conferences: Swarthmore Institute of Race Relations, 1935, AFSCA.

54. In doing so, these Quakers drew on the early history of sociology in the United States, which had blended Christianity and social science. See Susan E. Henking, "Sociological Christianity and Christian Sociology: The Paradox of Early American Sociology," *Religion and American Culture: A Journal of Interpretation* 3, no. 1 (Winter 1993): 49–67.

55. "Race Relations Conference," *Friends Intelligencer,* January 19, 1935, 44, available at AFSC Conferences: Swarthmore Institute of Race Relations, 1935, AFSCA.

56. Conference on Quakers and Race Relations, n.d., Projects: Conferences, 1928–1969, Box 6, FHL; "Race Relations Conference," *Friends Intelligencer,* 44.

57. Conference on Quakers and Race Relations, n.d., Projects: Conferences, 1928–1969, Box 6, FHL; "Race Relations Conference," *Friends Intelligencer,* 44.

58. Conference on Quakers and Race Relations, n.d., Projects: Conferences, 1928–1969, Box 6, FHL; "Race Relations Conference," *Friends Intelligencer,* 44.

59. Conference on Quakers and Race Relations, n.d., Projects: Conferences, 1928–1969, Box 6, FHL; "Race Relations Conference," *Friends Intelligencer,* 44. The willingness of at least some AFSC leaders and workers to evolve demonstrates some degree of "self-criticism" among those in the organization. While such reflection did not eliminate paternalism and other problems entirely, it did, at times, ameliorate what Friedman describes as the occasional philanthropic "disposition to impose their vision on others." See Friedman, "Philanthropy in America," 9.

60. Helen R. Bryan to Charles S. Johnson, February 8, 1935, Projects: Institute of Race Relations, 1934–1941, Box 9, FHL; Ray Newton to L. Hollingsworth Wood, March 7, 1935, AFSC Conferences: Swarthmore Institute of Race Relations, 1935, AFSCA. See also, Helen R. Bryan to Charles S. Johnson, March 29, 1935, Projects: Institute of Race Relations, 1934–1941, Box 9, FHL; Helen R. Bryan to Charles S. Johnson, April 10, 1935, Projects: Institute of Race Relations, 1934–1941, Box 9, FHL; Ray Newton to Committee on Race Relations, May 23, 1935, AFSC Conferences: Swarthmore Institute on Race Relations, 1935, AFSCA; Helen R. Bryan to Charles S. Johnson, February 18, 1935, Projects: Institute of Race Relations, 1934–1941, Box 9, FHL; Minutes of Committee on Race Relations, February 19, 1935, PYM

Committee on Race Relations, 1929–1936, PYM Committee on Race Relations, Box 2, FHL; Helen R. Bryan to Charles S. Johnson, April 17, 1935, Projects: Institute of Race Relations, 1934–1941, Box 9, FHL.

61. Evening Lecture Series, 1935 Institute of Race Relations, n.d., AFSC Conferences: Swarthmore Institute of Race Relations, 1935, AFSCA; Ray Newton to Charles S. Johnson, March 18, 1935, AFSC Conferences: Swarthmore Institute of Race Relations, 1935, AFSCA; Minutes of the Committee to Plan for the Institute of Race Relations, March 15, 1935, AFSC Conferences: Swarthmore Institute of Race Relations, 1935, AFSCA; Schedule of topics, n.d., July 1935, AFSC Conferences: Swarthmore Institute of Race Relations, 1935, AFSCA.

62. Helen R. Bryan to Charles S. Johnson, February 14, 1935, Projects: Institute of Race Relations, 1934–1941, Box 9, FHL.

63. Untitled, n.d., AFSC Conferences: Swarthmore Institute of Race Relations, 1935, AFSCA.

64. Alfred H. Cope, "Techniques for Tolerance," July 1935, AFSC Conferences: Swarthmore Institute of Race Relations, 1935, AFSCA.

65. Ibid.

66. "Quaker Experience with Questions of Race," 1935, Arch Street, 1921–1929, PYM Committee on Race Relations, Box 1, FHL.

67. Ibid.

68. Institute of Race Relations, n.d., Conference: IRR, 1936, AFSCA.

69. Ibid. For the discussion that follows, see Summary of Lectures at the 1936 IRR, n.d., Conference: IRR, 1936, AFSCA; Misc. Lecture Notes from 1936 IRR, n.d., Conference: IRR, 1936, AFSCA.

70. Data on the Institute of Race Relations, July 5–25, 1936, Conference: IRR, 1936, AFSCA.

71. Statements from Some of the Friends Attending the 1936 Institute of Race Relations, March 1937, Conference: IRR, 1936, AFSCA; Minutes of Race Relations Committee, September 22, 1936, 1936–1943, PYM Committee on Race Relations, Box 2, FHL; Facts Regarding the Daily Schedule of the IRR, n.d., Conference: IRR, 1936, AFSCA.

72. *Race and Its Relations to Members of the Religious Society of Friends,* n.d., Conference: IRR, 1936, AFSCA.

73. See Committee on Race Relations Minutes, May 18, 1937, 1936–1943, PYM Committee on Race Relations, Box 2, FHL; Untitled, December 1937, Projects: Friends Schools and Colleges, 1937–1945, PYM Race Relations Committee, Box 8, FHL; Form letter, n.d., Projects: Friends Schools and Colleges, 1937–1945, PYM Race Relations Committee, Box 8, FHL; Lillian B. Farnsworth to Dorothy Biddle James, March 2, 1937, Projects: Friends Schools and Colleges, 1937–1945, PYM Race Relations Committee, Box 8, FHL; Account of Friends School Incident, 1937, Projects: Friends Schools and Colleges, 1937–1945, PYM Race Relations Committee, Box 8, FHL; Request for an Opinion—Please Reply, n.d., Projects: Friends Schools and Colleges, 1937–1945, PYM Race Relations Committee, Box 8, FHL; Virginia Mullinger, Office Secretary, Memo, March 14, 1928, Projects: Friends Schools and Colleges, 1937–1945, PYM Race Relations Committee, Box 8, FHL.

74. Untitled Grant Application, 1937, AFSC Conferences: Institute of Race Relations, 1937, AFSCA; Committee on Race Relations Minutes, February 16, 1937, 1936–1943, PYM Committee on Race Relations, Box 2, FHL; Evening Lecture Series of the 1937 Institute of Race Relations, 1937, AFSC Conferences: Institute of Race Relations, 1937, AFSCA; "Practical Steps in Race Relations," n.d., AFSC Conferences: Institute of Race Relations, 1938, AFSCA.

75. Minutes of Committee on Race Relations, April 20, 1937, PYM Committee on Race Relations, 1936–1943, PYM Committee on Race Relations, Box 2, FHL; Institute of Race Relations, July 5–24, 1937, AFSC Committees: Race Relations, 1937, AFSC Conferences: Institute of Race Relations, 1937, AFSCA; Certain Facts Regarding the Institute of Race Relations from 1933 to 1937, AFSC Conferences: Institute of Race Relations, 1937, AFSCA.

76. Margaret E. Jones to C. E. Pickett, October 27, 1937, AFSC Committees: Race Relations, 1937, AFSCA; L. Hollingsworth Wood to C. E. Pickett, October 28, 1937, AFSC Committees: Race Relations,

1937, AFSCA; General File, AFSC Committees: Race Relations, 1937, AFSCA; C. E. Pickett to Robert C. Jones, November 16, 1937, AFSC Committees: Race Relations, 1937, AFSCA; C. E. Pickett to Frank D. Watson, Margaret M. Cary, Howard H. Brinton, Henry J. Cadbury, and J. Barnard Walton, December 23, 1937, AFSC Committees: Race Relations, 1937, AFSCA.

77. Helen R. Bryan Form Letter, n.d., AFSC Conferences: Institute of Race Relations, 1938, AFSCA; Form Letter, Helen R. Bryan to Members of Former Institutes of Race Relations, April 15, 1938, AFSC Conferences: Institute of Race Relations, 1938, AFSCA; Minutes of Committee on Race Relations, February 15, 1938, 1936–1943, PYM Committee on Race Relations, Box 2, FHL; Institute of Race Relations, July 25–August 12, 1938, AFSC Conferences: Institute of Race Relations, 1938, AFSCA; Rachel Davis DuBois to Helen R. Bryan, March 22, 1938, AFSC Conferences: Institute of Race Relations, 1938, AFSCA.

78. David C. McClelland, "An Evaluation of the Institute of Race Relations and Minority Problems," July 6–26, 1941, AFSC Conferences: Institute of Race Relations, 1941, AFSCA; "Statement of the Institute of Race Relations," July 6–26, 1941, AFSC Conferences: Institute of Race Relations, 1941, AFSCA.

79. Alberta Morris to C. E. Pickett, December 17, 1941, AFSC Conferences: Institute of Race Relations, 1941, AFSCA.

80. The Institute was revived and became a program at Fisk University in 1944. See McDaniel and Julye, *Fit for Freedom,* 221–22.

7 Religious Philanthropies and Government Social Programs

Sheila S. Kennedy

GOVERNMENT AGENCIES HAVE partnered with a wide variety of religious philanthropies for many decades, and, for most of that time, those partnerships have garnered relatively little attention or comment. That state of affairs changed rather abruptly in 1996 with the passage of Section 104 of the Personal Responsibility and Work Opportunity Reconciliation Act of 1996 (PRWORA).[1]

PRWORA was the first of a series of legislative acts that are usually referred to collectively as "charitable choice" laws. They were promoted as efforts to encourage greater numbers of religious charities (euphemistically labeled "faith-based organizations"[2]) to work with agencies of government to provide social services to the needy. The original charitable choice measures were buried within the massive welfare reform bill signed into law by President Clinton; however, when George W. Bush was elected president in 2000, he unveiled (with a good deal of fanfare) a new "faith-based initiative," incorporating and building on charitable choice legislation. The initiative was frequently described as a centerpiece of the Bush administration's domestic policy.

The Bush faith-based initiative and the various pieces of legislation that preceded it triggered a number of policy debates and generated significant political opposition. Those policy debates revolved around several quite disparate concerns, most notably:

Religious liberty. It is fair to say that most critics of charitable choice laws and the Bush faith-based initiative focused upon the First Amendment issues involved. The Establishment Clause prohibits government from funding, endorsing, or sponsoring religious activities. The American electorate has never reached consensus on what constitutes endorsement or sponsorship—or, for that matter, what constitutes "religion." It should thus be no surprise that charitable choice legislation touched an already-inflamed civic nerve.

Welfare and poverty. The definition and design of social welfare programs, the reasons for poverty, and the definition of the "deserving poor" have been notably contentious issues in American policy debates for reasons deeply rooted in history and religious culture. Both welfare reform and charitable choice reinvigorated that debate and generated additional scholarship around the topic of poverty.

Contracting out. The practice of providing government services through third-party surrogates or intermediaries rather than through employees—often (incorrectly) called "privatization"—and the management challenges attendant to such delivery have been at the center of acrimonious scholarly and public debate for at least the past quarter-century.

Efficacy. Efforts to measure the effectiveness of various social programs encounter methodological difficulties and resource constraints that complicate (or preclude) program evaluation generally and social service delivery mechanisms particularly. In the absence of reliable empirical data, ideological convictions hold sway—thus, the often-repeated claim that faith-based organizations achieve better results at lower cost, a claim that has not been, and probably cannot be, empirically verified.

While the faith-based initiative implicated all of these hotly debated issues, religious organizations contemplating a relationship with government need most of all to understand the parameters of the first two issues—church-state relationships and Americans' deep, religiously rooted divisions over poverty and welfare.

Religious Liberty and the First Amendment

While the scope and effect of the First Amendment's religion clauses have always been a subject of debate (especially since passage of the Fourteenth Amendment and the application of those clauses to the states), many historians and legal scholars argue that they must be understood as a primary example of the Founders' emphasis upon limiting the power and jurisdiction of the state. In this view, the original purpose of the religion clauses was to remove matters of religious belief and practice from the cognizance of the state.[3] Whatever the Founders' actual intent, the Supreme Court's First Amendment jurisprudence over the years has vacillated between so-called strict separation and accommodation. Each shift of interpretation has been met with satisfaction by some factions and denunciation by others. To characterize these highly politicized interpretations of the religion clauses as "contested" would be a distinct understatement; partisans view each case not just as a resolution of the matter at hand but also as a harbinger of decisions to come. When faith-based initiatives were introduced into this highly charged political context, extravagant claims—pro and con—should have been predictable.

The contemporary application of the religion clauses rests upon an extensive jurisprudence. The genesis of much of that jurisprudence was a 1946 decision in which Justice Hugo Black summarized the Establishment Clause; in an eloquent paragraph that has since been cited in numerous cases, Black wrote:

> The Establishment Clause means at least this: Neither a state nor the Federal Government can set up a church. Neither can pass laws which aid one religion, aid all religions, or prefer one religion over another. Neither can force nor influence a person to go to or to remain away from church against his will or force him to profess a belief or disbelief in any religion. No person can be punished for entertaining or professing religious beliefs or disbeliefs, for church attendance or non-attendance. No tax in any amount, large or small, can be levied to support any religious activities or institutions, whatever they may be called, or whatever form they may adopt to teach or practice religion.[4]

In other words, what government cannot do is benefit or burden religion itself. The mere fact that tax dollars are paid to a religious organization is not equivalent to funding religion, and a contract with a government agency does not, without more, turn the contractor into an arm of the state for constitutional purposes. Government may constitutionally purchase services, including social services, from sectarian sources or enter into other partnerships that involve the transfer of tax dollars to such entities, so long as the funds support secular rather than religious activities. Problems arise only when government agencies contract with "pervasively sectarian" organizations or with organizations that ignore applicable First Amendment constraints.

"Pervasively sectarian" organizations are defined by the courts as those in which the religious elements are so fundamentally interwoven into every aspect of programming that it would be impossible to separate them for purposes of ensuring that support goes only to the permissible, secular activities. The question of constitutionality, however, does not end with the inquiry whether an institution is pervasively sectarian. As Lupu and Tuttle have written,

> The U.S. Supreme Court's current interpretation of the Establishment Clause bars government funding of a broader set of activities than that encompassed by the phrase "inherently religious activities" [the Bush administration's formulation for "pervasively sectarian"]. The Court's interpretation does prohibit direct government funding of activities that are "inherently religious, . . . such as religious worship, instruction or proselytization," but it also prohibits funding of any activity that has significant religious content, whether or not that activity is "inherently religious."[5]

First Amendment issues raised by faith-based contracting can be either administrative or substantive; that is, they can arise because of the way a program is administered or conducted or because the provisions of the law (or the nature of the program) are unconstitutional. The potential for religious bias in the bid process is one concern. Constitutional law professor Douglas Laycock has noted that "choosing someone to deliver social services is more complex than picking the low bidder on a pencil contract. How do you keep thousands of government employees, federal, state, and local, from discriminating on religious grounds when they award grants and contracts?"[6] The saliency of Laycock's concern was underscored by statements issued by Pat Robertson and others during the original debates over Section 104, warning the administration against contracts with the Nation of Islam or the Scientologists. As Richard Foltin of the American Jewish Committee noted well before the passage of charitable choice laws, "It seems almost inevitable that, whatever claims may be made that contracts will be allocated on the basis of merit, in any given community the religious groups most likely to receive funds will be those associated with 'mainstream' faiths. And, even if the contracts are allocated on a totally objective basis, there is likely to be sharp distrust and suspicion that this is not the case."[7] These warnings have proved prescient. Since 1996, a number of cases have been brought against government agencies, alleging preference for religious organizations. In some cases, the preference was quite explicit: In *American Jewish Congress v. Bernick,* the challenge was to a California "solicitation for proposals" that was by its terms limited to "faith-based organizations or their nonprofit affiliates"—the state had established a religious "set aside" program. California responded to the lawsuit by settling the case and discontinuing the program.[8]

There are also First Amendment issues involved in contract monitoring. The Free Exercise Clause protects religious organizations against unwarranted intrusion, and the Supreme Court has interpreted the Establishment Clause to prohibit excessive "entanglement" between government and sectarian organizations. What is "unwarranted" and what degree of supervision amounts to "entanglement" are subject to interpretation.

At the heart of all First Amendment concerns is the constitutional requirement that government funds support only secular activities. Consistent with that requirement (if somewhat underprotective of it), charitable choice laws prohibit use of tax dollars for proselytizing and further prohibit conditioning service delivery upon participation in religious activities. States, however, have limited managerial resources with which to monitor programmatic content for constitutional compliance. Middle managers hired to administer service contracts cannot be expected to recognize any but the most egregious First Amendment violations, and most have very limited time to devote to such issues. If a constitutional violation is alleged and proven, the state can be held liable (only the government can violate the Bill of Rights because the Bill of Rights is, essentially, a list of things that *government* is forbidden to do), but because the laws do not define "religious organizations" or "proselytization," state contract officers do not get much guidance on these matters. The Economic Success Clearinghouse (formerly known as the Welfare Information Network), a widely consulted Internet resource for government officials and others who deal with welfare issues, has noted that "dialogue and 'gut instinct' are guiding the implementation of the ban on proselytization when contracting with federal funds."[9]

Inadequate monitoring resulting either from a lack of resources or a lack of sufficient constitutional competence has been highlighted by several lawsuits. In one example, early in 2005, a federal judge blocked the Bush administration from providing future funding to an Arizona mentoring organization that injected religion into its programming. MentorKids USA used tax dollars to support worship and religious instruction; according to the *New York Times,* the program hired only Christians to work as mentors and required mentors to sign and adhere to a "Christian Statement of Faith" and code of conduct. In another case, a federal magistrate ruled a Montana faith-based rural health program unconstitutional based on its "overt religiosity" and commingling of faith and health services.[10]

The challenge faced by state program managers is to ensure constitutional compliance by religious contractors without engaging in undue interference with their operations—interference that might be deemed to be "entanglement" and, thus, a violation of those contractors' First Amendment rights. As the Reverend Castanon of the United

Methodist Church warned in testimony to the Senate Judiciary Committee on Faith-Based Solutions, "As long as government attempts to separate what is religious from secular in entities like churches, synagogues, mosques, etc., it risks becoming excessively entangled with religion, thus advancing it or hindering religion, both clear violations of the establishment clause."[11] Managing contracts and evaluating contractor performance without intruding upon the constitutional prerogatives of the religious organization involved can be especially difficult when the faith-based provider has chosen not to form a 501(c)(3) affiliate. Monitoring and evaluation of fiscal performance will require review of books and records, and program costs may not have been segregated from other financial information. Even if there is a separate entity, some inquiry into the finances of the religious organization may be necessary if, for example, a church, synagogue, or mosque is entitled under the contract to reimbursement of substantial in-kind support to the program. Analysis of the cost of providing services may include the value of volunteer time, use of church equipment and facilities, and similar accommodations. Valuing those accommodations may require more review than the faith-based organization feels is constitutionally appropriate.

Finally, there is the requirement that public administrators provide secular alternatives for program participants who do not want a faith-based provider. Even assuming that welfare recipients know they have a right to a secular provider and are willing and able to exercise that right, an assumption that may be unwarranted,[12] providing an alternative can be a challenge in rural areas. Even in urban areas, access to more than one or two providers is frequently inconvenient or impractical for welfare clients who must depend on public transportation.

Ensuring that administrative processes conform to constitutional requirements may be more complicated than lawmakers recognize, but it is certainly possible. Much more difficult issues arise when the social programs being funded are essentially religious in nature. When government is directly contracting with faith-based drug treatment providers or engaging in religiously infused prison counseling, there is an almost insurmountable constitutional barrier. The nature of the dilemma is illustrated by the testimony of numerous advocates of religious interventions: They are very clear that they believe the most effective way to help drug addicts or prisoners is through religious transformation—what President Bush called "the power of faith."[13] A quotation from Jack Cowley, national director of operations for the InnerChange Prison Fellowship Ministry, is illustrative. Cowley explained, "We see crime as a result of sin and therefore we know that a relationship with Christ can heal people."[14] Unlike social services such as job training and placement, day care, or medical assistance—services that can be delivered in a constitutionally appropriate manner—many drug and prison programs are not merely faith-based, they are faith-*infused*. It is not accidental that so many prison programs are called "ministries."

Programs like InnerChange, Teen Challenge, or House of Hope are centered on religious belief. Acceptance of Jesus *is* the program. Prison Fellowship Ministries, one

of the most prominent of the religious prison programs, argues that crime is fundamentally a moral and spiritual problem that requires a moral and spiritual solution and
goes on to state, "Offenders do not simply need rehabilitation; they require regeneration
of a sinful heart." Operation Starting Line, another faith-based prison program, urges
participants to "make the decision for Christ."[15]

Faith-based drug treatment programs are equally focused on spiritual transformation as a methodology. Perhaps the best-known exemplar of faith-based drug treatment
programs is Teen Challenge. Religious conversion is absolutely central to Teen Challenge, as the following information from its website illustrates: "The main focus of Teen
Challenge of Chattanooga, Inc. is that of being a spiritual growth center where biblical
principles are taught. 80% of the respondents credited developing a personal relationship with Jesus Christ as a major influence in helping them to stay off drugs." A review
of a study by Dr. Aaron Bicknese, also posted on the Teen Challenge webpage, contains
the following passage:

> Responses to survey questions by Teen Challenge graduates confirm that a commit-
> ment to Jesus Christ provided them with the moral willpower needed to overcome
> a wide range of serious addictions. . . . The study found that according to responses
> from graduates, the nature of the commitment to Jesus Christ was crucial; it was not
> enough to have a vague belief in a higher power, one must commit to the Christ of
> the Bible.[16]

Successful or not (Teen Challenge's success claims are vigorously disputed by academic
critics of the program), government funding for programs having religious transformation as their central goal is by definition funding for religion and, therefore, constitutionally impermissible. Other programs encompassed by the charitable choice initiatives
may create environments within which constitutional violations are more likely to
occur, but it is possible to conduct such programs in a constitutionally appropriate fashion. Funding for programs like Teen Challenge and Prison Fellowship Ministries, however, is clearly indistinguishable from funding *for* religion and—under decades of First
Amendment jurisprudence—constitutionally prohibited.

The prohibition on direct government funding need not be fatal to the participation
of all faith-intensive programs; there are alternatives to direct government contracts
with such agencies that would arguably be constitutionally permissible. In *Agostini v.
Felton,* the Court (quoting from *Witters v. Washington Department of Services for the
Blind*) explained that, in order to be constitutionally permissible, any public money ear-
marked for secular purposes that ultimately goes to pervasively religious institutions
must do so "only as a result of the genuinely independent and private choices of individuals." In 2002, the Supreme Court resolved a number of uncertainties about the use
of vouchers when it handed down its decision in *Zelman v. Simmons-Harris.* That case
arose out of a Cleveland, Ohio, school choice experiment. The Court ruled that voucher
programs passed constitutional muster *if*—and this is a critical *if* for charitable choice

programs—the beneficiaries are provided with a genuine, meaningful choice between religious and secular programs.[17]

A properly structured voucher program for social services allowing recipients to choose between religious and secular providers would be very likely to pass constitutional muster.[18] If public dollars have been allocated for a secular purpose (nursing home care or drug treatment, for example) and if there is a "genuinely independent and private" choice of service provider, then—just as there is no constitutionally persuasive reason to prevent an elderly person seeking nursing home care from spending her benefits in a nursing home run by her religious denomination—there should be no reason to prevent a drug-dependent teen from choosing to enroll at Teen Challenge. (This approach would not save most prison ministries, for obvious reasons.) As the Court struggles for neutrality in its application of the religion clauses and searches for a formulation that neither burdens nor benefits religious practice and belief, the exercise of intervening independent choice sufficient to insulate government from a charge of endorsement would seem to be the fairest way to achieve evenhandedness.

Of all the First Amendment questions raised by charitable choice and the faith-based initiative, the issue that has been most politically contentious was the law's explicit exemption of religious contractors from federal and state antidiscrimination laws. It has always been the case that religious organizations' free exercise rights entitle them to an exemption from civil rights laws to the extent that such laws conflict with their religious beliefs.[19] In most states, however, this exemption has never applied to programs funded by government contracts. Those states acknowledge that religious organizations have a First Amendment right to hire and fire people in a manner consistent with their religious principles when they are spending their own money; they draw the line when use of government dollars is involved. The argument is that religious organizations do not have to take government money, and, if they choose to do so, they should be held to the same rules that apply to other bidders. Proponents of greater faith-based participation in government programs believe this is discriminatory. They see the religious provider's freedom to select employees dedicated to their faith-based mission as critical to the protection of institutional integrity.[20]

Although the law on point remains scanty to nonexistent, the Supreme Court's unanimous 1973 decision in *Norwood v. Harrison* may offer guidance to religious organizations debating whether contracting with government will require a change in hiring practices. In *Norwood,* the Court considered the constitutionality of Mississippi's practice of "lending" school textbooks to private schools that practiced racial discrimination; it ruled that the Constitution bars action by the state that aids private discrimination. The Court held that it is "axiomatic that a state may not induce, encourage or promote private persons to accomplish what it is constitutionally forbidden to accomplish." Proponents of the charitable choice exemption dismiss *Norwood* because "eradication of racially segregated public schools is a duty of the state. . . . To permit faith-based organizations to staff on a religious basis undercuts no duty of the state to ensure that it refrain from religious discrimination."[21]

As Melissa Rogers has noted, however, it is more difficult to dismiss *Dodge v. Salvation Army,* decided in 1989. In that case,

> The only court to have squarely faced this issue so far ruled in an unreported decision that, when an employment position within the religious organization was funded "substantially, if not exclusively" by the government, allowing the [religious organization] to choose the person to fill or maintain the position based on religious preference clearly has the effect of advancing religion, and is unconstitutional.[22]

Given the paucity of precedent on this point, a 2010 settlement in *Lown v. Salvation Army* may suggest where the weight of legal opinion lies. The suit, filed in 2004, asserted that the Salvation Army—a longtime partner in government antipoverty programs—had "reinvigorated" the religious content of its programming and made unlawful changes to its employment practices. According to the plaintiffs, the newly revised Salvation Army employment forms ask applicants to list the last ten years of church affiliations; require that they waive confidentiality of private communications with clergy and authorize disclosure of those communications to the Salvation Army; and ask for explicit commitments to support the organization's religious mission and preach the gospel of Jesus Christ. The complaint also alleged that the work environment had become "religiously hostile" to employees who believe they are being asked to breach their professional obligations to teenagers at risk for HIV, sexually transmitted diseases, or pregnancy.[23] In February 2010, the government conceded the impropriety of funding employees subject to such terms and settled the case on terms demanded by the plaintiffs. Although settlements are not precedents, they do signal what lawyers on a case believe would be the likely outcome of litigation.

Poverty and Welfare Policy

A religious charity contemplating a partnership with government would be well advised to understand the contending influences on poverty policy and the theological and political roots of the very different perspectives they will encounter. Welfare policy disputes have an even longer pedigree than does the modern idea of religious liberty in a limited state. The origins of our contemporary debates over government-funded social welfare programs can be traced at least as far back as 1349, the year England enacted the Statute of Laborers. That act prohibited citizens from giving alms, or charity, to those who had the ability to work—that is, to "sturdy beggars."[24] This first attempt to deal with what we would later call welfare was not about providing assistance; it was about forcing people to work. Not until 1601, in the reign of Elizabeth I, would a tax be levied to provide material assistance to the poor. The Elizabethan Poor Law established three categories of needy people: children without parents (or, at least, without parents who could care for them adequately); the able-bodied; and the incapacitated, helpless, or "worthy" poor. Vagrants, or able-bodied persons who refused to work, could be "committed to a house of correction, whipped, branded, put in pillories and stoned, or even put to death."[25] Help—however meager—was limited to the deserving or "worthy" poor.

The Elizabethan Poor Law incorporated a moral and theological distinction between the "deserving" and "undeserving" poor that would eventually be carried to the British colonies and reproduced in the laws of virtually all American states. It was the model that settlers brought to the New World; it was the approach adopted by the original thirteen colonies, and, as people moved west, it was the approach incorporated in the Ordinance of 1787, which prescribed rules for governing the Northwest Territory. To a significant extent, the distinction between the deserving and undeserving poor, the "categorizing" of people needing assistance, and the emphasis upon work have remained the primary framework through which the general public and federal and state policy-makers view social welfare and poverty issues today.

This paradigm found considerable support in religion. The belief that poverty is evidence of divine disapproval—that virtue is rewarded by material success—was held in one form or another by a number of the early Protestants who settled the colonies; it is a theological perspective that has continued to influence American law and culture. It was not until the Great Depression that blaming the poor for their own poverty became a minority position, and American lawmakers widely acknowledged the need for some sort of social safety net. Even then, it would be a mistake to assume that the dislocations of the 1930s or the passage of New Deal legislation changed Americans' deeply rooted beliefs about poverty, welfare, or their own history of self-reliance. As social historian Stephanie Coontz has written, "Most Americans agree that prior to federal 'interference' in the 1930's, the self-reliant family was the standard social unit of our society. Dependencies used to be cared for within the 'natural family economy' and even today the healthiest families 'stand on their own two feet.'"[26]

Coontz and other scholars have demonstrated that this widely held belief in self-sufficiency is inconsistent with the reality of the American experience. Pioneer families owed their very existence to massive federal land grants and state economic investment in new lands. In the early twentieth century, western populations depended on government construction of dams and federally subsidized irrigation projects. During the Depression, government electrification projects and other government subsidies were critical to the survival of the family farm. In the 1950s, Coontz notes, suburban families were "more dependent on government handouts than any so-called 'underclass' in recent U.S. history,"[27] thanks to the GI Bill and the National Defense Education Act, which subsidized the educations of a whole generation, and to the Federal Housing Authority and the Veterans Administration, which allowed Americans to purchase homes with artificially low down-payments and subsidized interest rates. Meanwhile, billions of dollars of government-financed inventions, production processes, and research enabled businesses to flourish, and, by the 1970s, Social Security had virtually wiped out the historic tendency for the elderly to be the poorest sector of the population.

Of course, many, if not most, of these programs benefited the middle and upper classes rather than those in need. Even between 1965 and 1971, during the height of Great Society antipoverty initiatives, 75 percent of American social welfare dollars went to the nonpoor. Nevertheless, despite the lessons of the Depression and the documented, pervasive reliance of middle- and upper-income families on a wide variety of government assistance programs, acceptance of poor relief or welfare continues to be viewed by many Americans as an entirely different matter—as evidence of a moral or character deficit. Neither welfare reform nor charitable choice can be understood without recognizing both the persistence and widespread acceptance of that perspective and of the continuing vitality of religious doctrines that support and inform it. At the same time, opposition to those measures cannot be understood without recognition of equally significant, countervailing political and religious influences that have argued for social justice and greater governmental responsibility for the poor. As Mary Jo Bane and Brent Coffin eloquently remind us,

> Indeed, these great religious traditions differ in their beliefs about ultimate reality, their approaches to community, and the types of institutions they foster. Yet for all their enduring differences, these traditions share central commitments: to the equal worth and sacredness of all men and women; to recognizing our shared vulnerability as finite creatures; and to our common needs for nurture and support to achieve our potential as creative participants in family, community, and society. The Torah, Bible, and Koran especially stress that the covenant community requires of its members a special obligation to the poor and vulnerable; by their treatment, the character of the entire community is measured.[28]

While many religious communities believe that charitable works should be done through nongovernmental channels, many others have insisted that working for social justice and sharing responsibility for those less fortunate must be a shared obligation of religious communities and government institutions. As with so many other issues in a diverse society, there has been no one "religious" or "faith-based" approach to social welfare issues. While many religions can point to a long history of outreach to the needy, both the nature and the extent of those efforts have reflected significant differences rooted in both doctrine and history.

The religious roots of Americans' historic approach to the (ostensibly) secular issue of poverty give evidence of the continuing salience of a Calvinist worldview that has shaped a distinctively Protestant approach to charitable and voluntary activities.

> In the nineteenth century, Catholics and Protestants who may all have agreed with the abstract proposition that "true Christian stewards" would share their talents and material resources with others to benefit society nevertheless had quite different perspectives on the reasons for stewardship, and significantly different beliefs about what such stewardship entailed. Protestants generally believed that they would be saved

through faith, not works; accordingly, they tended to see acts of benevolence not as a way to earn salvation, but as a way to manifest the depth of their faith and to evidence their likely status as elect. Catholics, on the other hand, had been taught that salvation rested on good works as well as faith, and that charity was a religious duty incumbent upon all believers. For them, charitable works were a way to earn salvation, not evidence of its probability.[29]

The doctrine of original sin has also played a role in shaping cultural attitudes toward poverty. Together, these doctrines have encouraged a belief that the poor are suffering for a reason, and that assisting them—helping them escape poverty—would thwart God's will. As one historian has put it, "Poverty was not understood as a problem to be fixed. It was a spiritual condition. Work-houses weren't supposed to help children prepare for life; they were supposed to save souls."[30]

These attitudes were never universally held; they co-existed, however uneasily, with early evangelical beliefs about the importance of covenant and the duty citizens owe each other. Furthermore, as America experienced industrialization and other social changes giving rise to new problems, including increases in alcoholism and prostitution, many Protestant denominations recognized a moral imperative to act. These competing theological and economic positions would later harden into the opposition philosophies we now call social Darwinism and the social gospel. An understanding of those very different worldviews is critical to an understanding of contemporary arguments for and against charitable choice.

The two names most commonly associated with social Darwinism are Herbert Spencer and William Graham Sumner. Spencer was an early and enthusiastic supporter of Darwin, but he took it a step further; he adapted—or appropriated—Darwin's theory of natural selection to justify an economic position. As Spencer saw it,

> Blind to the fact that under the natural order of things society is constantly excreting its unhealthy, imbecile, slow, vacillating faithless members, these unthinking, though well-meaning, men advocate an interference which not only stops the purifying process, but even increases the vitiation—absolutely encourages the multiplication of the reckless and incompetent by offering them an unfailing provision, and discourages the multiplication of the competent and provident by heightening the difficulty of maintaining a family.

Similar sentiments led Americans like William Graham Sumner to dismiss any moral claim on society's resources by those less fortunate.

> But the weak who constantly arouse the pity of humanitarians and philanthropists are the shiftless, the imprudent, the negligent, the impractical, and the inefficient, or they are the idle, the intemperate, the extravagant, and the vicious. Now the troubles of these persons are constantly forced upon public attention, as if they and their interests deserved especial consideration, and a great portion of all organized and unorganized effort for the common welfare consists in attempts to relieve these classes of

people. . . . Now who is the Forgotten Man? He is the simple, honest laborer, ready to earn his living by productive work.[31]

While later social scientists would conclude that the biological theory of evolution cannot and should not provide a framework for social policy, evangelicals like William Jennings Bryan saw Spencer and Sumner's philosophy as the logical outgrowth of Darwinian biology and a refutation of the essential philosophy of Jesus's Sermon on the Mount. Bryan's rejection of the biological theory was largely motivated by his conviction that its grounding in natural selection would be used exactly as Sumner and Spencer were using it—to justify harsh and punitive social policies and to undercut the importance of government efforts to address systemic causes of poverty.

The social problems and misery accompanying the dislocations of industrialization evoked a very different response from clergymen like Washington Gladden and Walter Rauschenbusch. Rather than biblical justifications for poverty, they stressed the biblical injunction that made us our brother's keeper. They criticized excesses of capitalism and competition and worked to ameliorate the causes and effects of poverty. Their "social gospel" rejected the notion that the poor were solely responsible for their own misery, and they championed efforts by government to address the structural and systemic forces that prevented the poor from improving their lot. Rauschenbusch, in particular, was a pivotal figure in creating and promulgating the social gospel; his books—*Christianity and the Social Crisis* and *Christianizing the Social Order*—were broadly influential among mainstream Protestants and enunciated a philosophy that fit well with the missions of the numerous voluntary organizations being formed as a response to the social problems of the day. "Rauschenbusch despaired of individualized attempts at social service because they perpetuated the corrupt social system. Sin was both individual and corporate. Saving souls was important, but so was transforming the social order."[32]

Susan Curtis has described the social gospel as the religious expression of progressivism in the early twentieth century and as a departure from the nineteenth-century Protestant emphasis on individualism. "In place of unbridled competition, individual responsibility for success, and government policies of laissez faire, social gospelers proposed cooperation, social responsibility for justice, and an interventionist welfare state." The social gospel thus reflected a significant shift in Protestant theology. For those who accepted the social gospel, salvation became a communal obligation rather than an individual one. It required a concerted attack on the "poverty, vice and filth that prevented many Americans from staying on the road to redemption."[33]

The God of the social gospel was not the angry and judgmental God of the Puritans. This God was "immanent," a loving, parental deity who had endowed humanity with moral agency which was to be used to improve the world and make it suitable for God's kingdom. This view of God, and our relationship to God, produced a further shift away from concern with the afterlife and toward much more earthly concerns with the evils of poverty, depravity, and injustice. Those who believed in the social gospel rejected the view of the poor held by the social Darwinists; for many of them, their personal experiences and volunteer work had convinced them that individual efforts alone were insufficient to change the conditions of poverty. Accordingly, they de-emphasized individual salvation in favor of what might be called "social salvation" or social justice, and the importance of improving the lot of the communities they lived in. Perhaps the most significant element of the social gospel was its emphasis on the importance of institutional structures in thwarting or enabling individual efforts. In sharp distinction to the social Darwinists, adherents of the social gospel emphasized structural or systemic solutions over personal transformation and lobbied for communal and governmental solutions to social problems.

The theological and philosophical divide between those who adhere to the social gospel and those whose roots remain in social Darwinism continues to inform—and inflame—policy disputes over welfare policy in the twenty-first century. It would be misleading, however, to suggest that welfare policy disputes are simply contemporary manifestations of earlier theological debates. Charitable choice and the presidents' faith-based initiatives are part of a movement that can be broadly described (depending on the political viewpoint of the narrator) as either a backlash against, or a correction to, the creation of what has been called the "administrative state" during the latter half of the twentieth century. That changing governmental landscape was itself a response to rapid, dramatic changes in American society, especially the growth both of actual diversity and (thanks to communications technology) awareness of it. The rapidity of technological innovation, the increased mobility of populations, the nationalization and globalization of legal and economic systems, and the seemingly inexorable growth of government have all contributed to a sharpening of the tensions between America's historic individualism and the growing interdependence of its citizens—not to mention the historic religious debate about individual versus social and governmental responsibility.

To all of these changes we must add the weakening of Protestantism's hegemony over American culture. America has become steadily more diverse, and there are now many more religious voices offering solutions to the question, "What shall be done about the poor?" Catholicism teaches that salvation rests on good works as well as faith and that collective giving is preferable to individual charity because special spiritual benefits accrue to those who unite with fellow believers in acts of charity and social compassion. Catholic theology insists that the needs of the poor take priority among the church's good works, and that teaching has characterized Catholic charity. That same theology has motivated Catholic leaders to support governmental social welfare provision. Jews have never constituted more than a small percentage of the U.S. population, but Judaism has contributed disproportionately to the broader American culture, especially in the areas of philanthropy and social justice. *Tzedakah* requires that Jews give aid and assistance to the poor and elderly and that they support other worthy causes. In Judaism, the highest form of giving is that which enables a person to become self-sufficient. Thus, many of the earliest Jewish social service agencies offered language, financial, and job assistance so that immigrants would be able to provide for themselves and, in turn, offer assistance to other immigrants who arrived after them. (There was also a prudential motivation for concentrating early philanthropic efforts on needs within the Jewish community itself, growing out of culturally internalized lessons of Jewish history: If the Jews did not take care of their own poor and elderly, no one else would. And if the Jews were seen as a burden to others, if they were unable either to sustain themselves or to contribute to the larger society, they would suffer discrimination and possibly even expulsion.)

More recent waves of immigration have added other religious traditions—notably, Islamic and Asian—to the American philanthropic landscape, and the beliefs of those immigrants will undoubtedly continue to shape and reshape national attitudes about poverty, charity, and the obligation of the state, just as, throughout American history, religious beliefs have motivated charitable giving and prompted (sometimes radical) moral and political movements for social change and equal justice.[34]

Aside from the particulars of their charitable convictions, it is important to recognize how many of America's original religious settlers brought with them not only distinctive theological beliefs about poverty and misfortune but also their own historical reasons to distrust the power and motives of government. From the earliest days of the country, the "dissenting" churches that had come to America to find religious liberty were skeptical of governmental involvement with religion and fearful of state overreaching. From early settlers like the Baptists to later groups like the Jews, many of America's religious communities have been both insistent on the separation of church and state and fiercely protective of their religious autonomy. Those beliefs persist, and they continue to inform opposition to the acceptance of government dollars for faith-based social service programs even while many religiously affiliated programs, including many operated under the auspices of those same religious groups, have increasingly come to depend on those dollars.

The Lay of the Land: Implementing Charitable Choice

The religious beliefs and constitutional constraints described above have constituted the framework within which partnerships between religious charities and government agencies have operated. And they have operated for a very long time. Whatever else one might say about charitable choice and the faith-based initiative, the idea of partnerships between religious philanthropies and government was anything but new.

As we have seen, large-scale government efforts to combat poverty did not exist before the Depression; by that time, many religious organizations had been providing services to the indigent and the elderly for decades. Government partnerships with established charitable institutions that had been providing social welfare were thus inevitable and were—and have remained—largely uncontroversial. Most—although certainly not all—of the longtime religious social service providers are separately incorporated nonprofit charitable organizations such as Catholic Charities, Lutheran Social Services, and Jewish Family Services that offer both employment and assistance on a professional, nondiscriminatory basis. Often, too, the structures of government programs have operated to minimize concerns about church-state violations. In many cases, government funds follow the individuals entitled to the benefits involved. For example, Medicaid patients may choose a nursing home or hospital, which then receives payment from the government. While these and similar benefits are not generally referred to as vouchers, they are functionally indistinguishable from vouchers, and they have long been an accepted part of the social service landscape. Direct contracts and other collaborations between government units and pervasively sectarian organizations, including individual congregations, have been less common but far from unusual.

Government financial support for religiously affiliated organizations providing social services has, thus, been a long-standing feature of most public welfare programs. In a 1969 study of findings from a 1965 survey of 406 sectarian agencies in twenty-one states, Bernard J. Coughlin reported that 70 percent of them were involved in some type of purchase of service contract with the government. A 1982 study by F. Ellen Netting, focusing on government funding of Protestant social service agencies in one midwestern city, found that some agencies received between 60 and 80 percent of their support from the government and that approximately half of their combined budgets were government financed. As far back as 1994, government funding accounted for 65 percent of the nearly $2 billion annual budget of Catholic Charities USA and 75 percent of the revenues of the Jewish Board of Family and Children's Services. These and similar studies provide evidence that—whatever the merits or flaws of current faith-based initiatives—it is simply inaccurate to suggest that government partnerships with religious providers are something new.[35]

Furthermore, in contrast to the frequent challenges to public religious displays and the persistent, vocal opposition to public funding for religious elementary and secondary schools, this long-standing allocation of public tax dollars to religious social services providers has gone virtually unchallenged. There are two major Supreme Court precedents: *Bradford v. Roberts,* an 1899 case permitting the flow of public dollars to religious hospitals, and *Bowen v. Kendrick,* decided in 1988. *Bowen* involved an Establishment Clause challenge to the Adolescent Family Life Act. The Family Life Act provided funding to a variety of local organizations, including religious organizations, to support counseling of teenagers about premarital sex and teenage pregnancy. The Court in *Bowen* acknowledged a danger that counseling services might be delivered by sectarian groups in a manner that violated the Establishment Clause but declined to find the act facially unconstitutional merely because that danger existed. According to the majority, a successful challenge would have to rest upon the particulars of a specific program; the mere inclusion of religious contractors in the program was held not to constitute a *per se* Establishment Clause violation.[36] In contrast, funding for religiously affiliated schools has generated a significant jurisprudence, and many efforts to direct public funds to such schools have been struck down.

Despite this seeming inconsistency between the cases involving social welfare services and those involving schools, the courts have actually been quite consistent—and virtually unanimous—in their insistence that, whatever else the Establishment Clause may mean, it absolutely forbids government funding of religion. What the case law in both areas has also recognized is that mere payment of tax dollars to a religious organization is not the same thing as funding religion. Historically, the relative lack of litigation over government support for religious social services can be explained, at least in part, by the fact that the secular nature of the services involved is so readily apparent. Hospitals and nursing homes are providing medical care; day care facilities are supervising children; job placement counselors, drug treatment facilities, and the like have secular counterparts engaged in providing similar, if not identical, programs. While economists remind us that dollars are fungible, so that support for one activity frees up funds that can then be used elsewhere, it is relatively simple to calculate the costs of nursing services or child care and reasonable to argue that, if payment of government dollars is only sufficient to cover those determinate costs, public money is subsidizing only the secular activity. (In the school context, where litigation of First Amendment issues has been copious, direct funding programs that have passed constitutional muster have generally been those involving an identifiably secular benefit available to all citizens—immunization, speech and hearing testing, transportation—where exclusion of children attending religious schools was deemed to burden the free exercise rights of parents opting for religious education.)

For many years, these legal and constitutional issues were salient primarily to large, sophisticated, religiously affiliated providers and their lawyers. Their current prominence is, in large measure, a result of the growth of American government during the past century and, more recently, the exponential growth of government contracting. Not only has the scope of government action increased at all levels, but the mechanisms through which government addresses public problems and delivers public services have also changed radically. The issues raised by this fundamental shift in the way government does business are central to the concerns over charitable choice and government partnerships with religious philanthropies; the shift has dramatically increased the visibility of such partnership arrangements.

As noted, government agencies in the United States have paid religious organizations to house, clothe, and counsel the poor since the earliest days of state involvement in social welfare programs, and the religious organizations providing those government-financed social services have ranged from 501(c)(3) affiliates of denominational entities, such as Catholic Charities and Lutheran Social Services, to "pervasively sectarian" organizations like the Salvation Army and individual congregations. In fact, many proponents of charitable choice legislation and faith-based initiatives describe those policies as simply an attempt to level a playing field that already includes significant numbers of religious players. They argue that fear of overzealous application of the First Amendment has kept some smaller religious providers from bidding on government contracts. They characterize the legislation as merely an effort to ensure that government officials do not inappropriately require participating "faith-based" contractors to diminish or eliminate religious components of their services. Whatever the merits of that claim, the fact is that public tax dollars are routinely used to purchase social services from sectarian providers—and have been so used for decades.

The passage of charitable choice laws thus built upon a substantial history of government cooperation with religious philanthropic organizations. But those laws also introduced a number of questions that—at least at this writing—remain unanswered. Some of those questions are overarching, philosophical ones: What are the dynamics—historical, ideological—of this debate? What does it tell us about the ongoing tensions of democratic governance and policy-making for a diverse citizenry? Other questions focus on more pragmatic and immediate concerns, many of which were raised by ambiguities in the legislation: What do these laws require of government managers? How will charitable choice and the faith-based initiative affect welfare clients and services? How do the First Amendment and other constitutional provisions affect program administration? The broad issues—and some of the specific questions raised by the legislation—can be categorized as follows:

Definitional issues. Government has contracted with religious organizations ever since it has provided social services. Furthermore, there are enormous variations among religious organizations. How are the faith organizations targeted by these measures different from Catholic Charities, Lutheran Social Services, the Salvation Army, and government's many other longtime religious partners? What are "faith-based" organizations, and how do they differ from other nonprofit organizations? What do we mean by "programmatic success" and "efficacy"?

Funding issues. The effort to recruit new faith partners was not accompanied by additional funding for social services. To the contrary, the amount of money budgeted for social services declined. With no new money, have charitable choice laws simply shifted funds from one set of religious providers to another—presumably, from government's traditional religious partners (who generally operate in accordance with applicable professional norms) to providers more focused upon the "personal transformation" of clients? (Thus far, these laws have had little impact on the identity of religiously affiliated contractors; whether that changes is an open question.) What will happen to small, grassroots, faith-based organizations if diminished public resources make funding streams unreliable? Will government funding affect the character or mission of small religious organizations new to the contracting regime? If so, how?

Constitutional issues. The First Amendment does not prevent government from doing business with faith organizations, but that does not mean that any program run by a religious provider will pass constitutional muster. There is a constitutionally significant distinction between programs that are offered by a religious provider, or in a religious setting, and programs in which religious observance or dogma are central to service delivery. What mechanisms are proposed to ensure that services are delivered in a constitutionally appropriate manner? What is the capacity of public managers to ensure constitutional accountability, and what resources are available to them for monitoring compliance? Can we avoid government favoritism for certain religious providers over others, or privileging of either religious or secular providers? How can we ensure constitutional accountability?

Evidence issues. John Dilulio, the first director of the White House Office of Faith-Based and Community Initiatives, readily admitted the absence of credible research supporting the assertion that religious providers are more effective, quoting the academic adage that "the plural of anecdote is not data." Dilulio expressed his hope that future studies would provide answers to such questions.[37] One can recognize that many faith-based and religious organizations do important, often exemplary, work without taking that indisputable fact as evidence that religious organizations as a category are more effective than secular ones. At the time the White House implemented its initiative, no evidence for such an assertion existed. (It is also worth noting that religious sociologists have criticized this emphasis on efficacy, suggesting that to focus on religion's "effectiveness" is to misunderstand profoundly the nature of religion—that such instrumental approaches to religion are self-defeating. As H. Richard Niebuhr reminded us, "The instrumental value of faith for society is dependent upon faith's conviction that it has more than instrumental value."[38])

Management issues. With the passage of charitable choice laws, the public officials whose job it is to manage faith-based contracts were faced with many ambiguities and unanswered questions. The question for them was not, for example, whether government should partner with religious organizations to provide social services—because it always has and undoubtedly always will. The question is, "Under what circumstances are such partnerships appropriate, and when they are, how should they be structured and monitored?" Similarly, the question is not whether, in the abstract, religious programs or secular approaches are preferable. The question for government program managers is, "What organizational characteristics are most likely to predict successful program delivery, and how can I determine which of the bidders for this contract possesses those characteristics?" "How will I define and measure accountability?" Complicating these management questions is the reality that, in a federalist system, different states approach implementation of charitable choice differently. Those differences will also pose management challenges. Finally, contracting with government presents nonprofit managers with challenges of their own: managing cash flow and absorbing transaction costs; responding to government monitoring and reporting requirements; and complying with constitutional restrictions and government program regulations. These management challenges can be particularly onerous for small organizations unaccustomed to a contracting environment.

Making a Decision to Participate

At some point, the small, grassroots religious charities and religious congregations that are the ostensible targets of charitable choice laws must decide whether entering into a partnership or contract with a government agency is right for them. A review of First Amendment philosophy and jurisprudence, an understanding of where they and others with whom they will be working fall on the spectrum of theological approaches to poverty, and a familiarity with the history of American social welfare partnerships will inform that question, but it will not answer it. The conceptual grounding is necessary but not sufficient to answer the numerous practical questions that should be identified and addressed before a final decision is made.

In the wake of President Bush's announcement of his particular faith-based initiative, I led a team of researchers in an exploration of that initiative and the charitable choice legislation on which it was based. One of the products of our research was a video for use by government agencies and congregations considering entry into a new faith-based partnership. In the video, entitled *Tempting Faith,* we identified questions that prospective partners should be prepared to answer in order to decide whether the proposed collaboration is likely to be mutually beneficial.[39] Those questions grew out of interviews with dozens of people in the religious community who have "been there"—agency directors, faith leaders, and constitutional experts who have managed and studied effective partnerships as well as those that have failed. Those interviews suggested three areas for careful consideration: capacity, commitment, and constitutionality. Questions in these areas are particularly important for congregations considering a first-time contract with a government agency.

By *capacity,* we meant an evaluation of the assets each partner brings to the collaboration: personnel, money, expertise, facilities. By *commitment,* we meant willingness based on a clear understanding of what such a partnership entails and the responsibilities the partners are assuming. By *constitutionality,* we meant affirmative answers to two important questions: Do both partners understand what the law requires? Are they prepared to abide by those requirements?

Capacity. Assessing capacity requires calculating how many people will be required to manage and staff the proposed program and whether those persons will be paid staff, volunteers, or a combination. Research suggests that congregations tend to be most successful with programs that are short term and finite. It is one thing to collect food for a food pantry, quite another to run a daily meals program. The average congregation is 75 people; the average annual congregational budget is $100,000.[40] If an average congregation is proposing to enter a contract to provide social services, it is likely that those services will depend heavily on volunteers. How dependable will those volunteers be during sustained program periods? Will they be diverted from other congregational tasks? If so, who will take over those jobs? Do the volunteers have the experience and background necessary to provide the services in question? If the congregation is counting heavily on a particular volunteer, does it have a plan for what would happen if she or he falls ill or moves or dies? Does it have a backup? The personnel challenge was summed up by the Reverend Odell Cleveland, who runs the very successful Welfare Reform Liaison Project in North Carolina:

> When you talk about replicating a program, you have to have compassion and expertise. Ninety-seven percent of my staff have degrees; some of them advanced degrees. It's more than sister so-and-so who's willing to help. People have to be trained. People have to be educated and trained and know what they're dealing with, because you can have all the good intentions in the world, but if you are not trained and qualified to handle these situations, if you're not careful, you can do more harm than good.[41]

Capacity also includes financial considerations. How will this program be funded? Will all the money come from the government? If so, what will happen if the contract is not renewed? What about cash flow? In many states, payment is only made when a desired outcome has occurred: when the client is placed in a job, or leaves welfare, or achieves whatever the program's goal may be. If services must be provided for several months before payment is received, can the congregation finance services during that time?

"Transaction costs" are an often overlooked capacity issue and can come as a real shock to small programs that previously did not have to cope with the accounting and paperwork demands of government agencies. These are not arbitrary or unwarranted requirements; if a government agency is committing tax dollars to a program, it has an obligation to ensure that the money is being properly spent. Such oversight, however, entails periodic audits, site visits, and paperwork that most congregations have not previously encountered. Does the congregation have the accountants, bookkeepers, and clerical support needed to comply? Have the costs of compliance been factored into the contract amount? Will resources have to be diverted from client services to compliance?

The final capacity question concerns program size. Will the contract require an expansion of services? If so, is the expansion feasible? Some social scientists have suggested that the virtue of many grassroots religious programs—the reason programs are successful—is their small scale and ability to engage clients personally. If the program must grow in order to comply with the government contract, will it lose the immediacy that made it work?

Commitment. The primary mission of a congregation is ministry. Before a congregation contracts to provide social services, it needs to consider whether the contract will divert attention and resources from that primary mission. A corollary question is whether contracting with government will mute the congregation's prophetic voice. As the Reverend John Buehrens of the Unitarian Universalist Association has warned, "If you're on the government dole, your independence as a servant of God who is called to comfort the afflicted, yes, but also to afflict the comfortable and also to speak the moral word to government, becomes diminished. That's a great danger. It's a spiritual danger."[42]

There are practical questions as well: If a preschool program is noisy and rambunctious, will members of the congregation be annoyed? If the meals program increases wear and tear on the church kitchen, will congregants balk at the expense of mainte-nance and repair? If the program serves people very different from those in the con-gregation—much poorer people, those from different racial and ethnic backgrounds, immigrants, ex-convicts—will the congregation still support the program?

Commitment can be evaluated by asking these questions: What is the congrega-tion's goal? Is it congruent with the government agency's goal? Is the congregation pre-pared for the inconvenience and disruption that may accompany the program? Perhaps most important, are the expectations on both sides of the partnership, governmental and congregational, clear?

Constitutionality. Questions of capacity and commitment apply to all proposed government contractors, secular or faith-based. But the First Amendment creates added issues for religious contractors—we have touched on only a few of those issues here. A congregation considering a government contract must be prepared to learn about and live within the constitutional rules, whether or not it agrees with them. As previously explained, the First Amendment prohibits the use of tax dollars to support religious organizations or for religious purposes. What constitutes support, however, or a reli-gious purpose, is often unclear. The Supreme Court has never ruled that government may not purchase secular goods or services from religious entities, and to take such a position would raise serious equal protection and free exercise concerns. Historically, however, the Court has refused to allow the flow of direct government aid (as opposed to vouchers) to organizations that are "pervasively sectarian." Congregations, by defini-tion, are pervasively sectarian. That makes it extremely important that the congregation be able to identify the secular service being provided and the means by which its secular nature will be ensured.

In an effort to determine whether congregational leaders are aware of the consti-tutional constraints applicable to faith-based partnerships, my research team surveyed congregations in South Bend, Indiana, a community large and diverse enough to be rep-resentative but small enough to be manageable. We constructed a simple, ten-question instrument, testing for very basic constitutional principles.

The results supported one clear conclusion: Large numbers of congregational lead-ers do not know what they need to know if they are to do business with government. Of 103 responses, seventy-five disagreed with the statement, "The First Amendment and other provisions of the Bill of Rights apply only to government action." Understanding that the Bill of Rights limits only government action is absolutely basic to understand-ing the operation of American constitutional principles, including—importantly—the Establishment Clause. Worse, seventy respondents disagreed with the statement, "If a congregation has a contract with government to provide services, the congregation may not include religious instruction or prayer as part of the services funded under the con-tract." Those were the most troubling responses, but forty-nine respondents (almost half) also disagreed with the statement, "The First Amendment's separation of church and state means that tax dollars cannot be used to fund religion or religious expression."

(In addition to a wrong response, several respondents wrote marginal notes to the effect that separation of church and state is not constitutionally required and that they would feel no compunction about using tax dollars to save souls. Two offered their opinion that "separation of church and state is an invention of the ACLU.")[43]

It bears emphasizing again that there is no constitutional reason that congregations cannot partner with government; the issue is how such partnerships are conducted. Existing law is very clear about some things: Government can buy food for the needy from a congregation, but the congregation cannot require recipients to pray before eating it. Government can rent beds in a faith-based homeless shelter, but use of those beds cannot be conditioned upon attendance at Bible study. Congregations need not take the crucifix off the wall or hide the Bibles, but they cannot use tax dollars to purchase those—or other—religious items. Failure to understand these rules (or unwillingness to abide by them) is a danger signal for any government partnership. Before a small religious charity or congregation signs on the dotted line, there should be full communication with the government agency proposing the partnership and with those in the organization or congregation who will become stakeholders in the project.

Conclusion

America's social welfare "safety net" is the least generous and most haphazard of any Western industrialized nation. There are reasons for that, some sound, many not. We can argue about the policy decisions from our respective spots on the theological spectrum, but, in the meantime, most of us will agree that we need to offer a helping hand to the millions of Americans who are struggling. Faith-based partnerships—done properly—are one way we can help.

Notes

1. Personal Responsibility and Work Opportunity Reconciliation Act of 1996, 110 STAT. 2105.

2. The term was undoubtedly intended to be inclusive of all religious charities; unfortunately, those responsible for coining it failed to recognize that equating faith with religion reflected a particularistic, Protestant conception of religion. Judaism and Buddhism are only two of the many religious traditions that are not "faith based."

3. Vincent Phillip Muñoz, "James Madison's Principle of Religious Liberty," *American Political Science Review* 97, no. 1 (2003): 17–32.

4. Everson v. Board of Education, 330 U.S. 1 (1946).

5. Ira C. Lupu and Robert W. Tuttle, *The State of the Law, 2003: Developments in the Law concerning Government Partnerships with Religious Organizations*, Roundtable on Religion and Social Welfare Policy (Albany, N.Y.: Rockefeller Institute of Government, 2003), 73.

6. U.S. Senate Judiciary Committee, *Faith-Based Solutions: What Are the Legal Issues? Hearing before the Committee on the Judiciary*, 107th Cong., 1st sess., June 6, 2001.

7. American Jewish Committee, *Report of Task Force on Sectarian Social Services and Public Funding* (New York: American Jewish Committee, 1990).

8. American Jewish Congress v. Bernick et al. (California, 2001).

9. See http://www.financeproject.org/index.cfm?page=24.

10. "Judge Halts Grants over Religion," *New York Times,* January 16, 2005; Freedom from Religion Foundation v. MORH, 2004.

11. U.S. Senate Judiciary Committee, *Faith-Based Solutions.*

12. Fredericka Kramer, Carol De Vita, and Kenneth Finegold, "Faith-Based Organizations, Federal Social Programs, and Local Services," in *Assessing the New Federalism: Eight Years Later,* ed. Olivia Golden (Washington, D.C.: Urban Institute Press, 2005).

13. Dana Milbank, "Bush Assails Faith-Based Critics," *Washington Post,* June 6, 2001.

14. Quoted from Sheila Suess Kennedy and Wolfgang Bielefeld, *Charitable Choice at Work: Evaluating Faith-Based Job Training in the States* (Washington, D.C.: Georgetown University Press, 2007), 159.

15. Jane Lampman, "Evangelicals Reach Out to Prison Population," *Christian Science Monitor,* June 15, 2000.

16. http://teenchallengeusa.com/docs/a_summary_of_teen_challenge_studies.pdf, 5, is the source of the first quote; the study by Bicknese is cited on 6 and 7 of ibid. (although both pages are mistakenly labeled as page 7). The second quotation is from Andrew Kenney, "Teen Challenge's Proven Answer to the Drug Problem: A Review of a Study by Dr. Aaron T. Bicknese, 'The Teen Challenge Drug Treatment Program in Comparative Perspective,'" http://www.acadc.citymax.com/f/NW_study.pdf.

17. Agostini v. Felton, 521 U.S. 203 (1997); Witters v. Washington Department of Services for the Blind, 474 U.S. 481 (1986); Zelman v. Simmons-Harris, 536 U.S. 639 (2002).

18. See Sheila S. Kennedy, "When Is Private Public? State Action in the Era of Privatization and Public–Private Partnerships," *George Mason University Civil Rights Law Journal* 11 (2001): 203–23; and Martha Minow, "Choice or Commonality: Welfare and Schooling after the End of Welfare as We Knew It," *Duke Law Journal* 49 (1999): 493–559.

19. Melissa Rogers has written an excellent history and explanation of the religious exemption offered under Title VII of the 1964 Civil Rights Act. See "Federal Funding and Religion-Based Employment Decisions," in *Sanctioning Religion? Politics, Law, and Faith-Based Social Services,* ed. David Ryden and Jeffrey Polet (Boulder, Colo.: Lynne Rienner, 2005), 105–28.

20. Carl H. Esbeck, Stanley W. Carlson-Theis, and Ronald Sider, *The Freedom of Faith-Based Organizations to Staff on a Religious Basis* (Washington, D.C.: Center for Public Justice, 2004).

21. Norwood v. Harrison, 413 U.S. 455 (1973): 465; Esbeck, Carlson-Theis, and Sider, *The Freedom of Faith-Based Organizations to Staff on a Religious Basis,* 38.

22. Rogers, "Federal Funding and Religion-Based Employment Decisions," 14; see also Dodge v. Salvation Army, 1989 WL 53857 (S.D. Miss., Jan. 9, 1989).

23. Lown v. Salvation Army, 393 F.Supp.2d 223 (2004).

24. Joel F. Handler Yeheskel Hasenfeld, *We the Poor People: Work, Poverty, and Welfare* (New Haven, Conn.: Yale University Press, 1997), 200.

25. Indiana Department of Public Welfare, *The Evolution of Indiana's Public Welfare System* (Indianapolis: Indiana Department of Public Welfare, 1985), 8.

26. Stephanie Coontz, *The Way We Never Were: American Families and the Nostalgia Trap* (New York: Basic Books, 1992), 69.

27. Ibid., 76.

28. Mary Jo Bane and Brent Coffin, "Introduction," in *Who Will Provide? The Changing Role of Religion in American Social Welfare,* ed. Mary Jo Bane, Brent Coffin, and Ronald Thiemann (Boulder, Colo.: Westview Press, 2000), 12.

29. Sheila S. Kennedy, *God and Country: America in Red and Blue* (Waco, Tex.: Baylor University Press, 2007), 129; though I quote this paragraph from my book, the content is based, in part, on Mary J. Oates, "Faith and Good Works: Catholic Giving and Taking," in *Charity, Philanthropy, and Civility in*

American History, ed. Lawrence J. Friedman and Mark D. McGarvie (New York: Cambridge University Press, 2003), 281–300.

30. Gordon Bieglow, "Let There Be Markets: The Evangelical Roots of Economics," *Harper Magazine* 310, May 1, 2005, available from http://mindfully.org/Industry/2005/Evangelical-Economics1may05. htm.

31. Spencer quoted in Andrew D. Walsh, *Religion, Economics, and Public Policy: Ironies, Tragedies, and Absurdities of the Contemporary Culture Wars* (Westport, Conn.: Praeger, 2000), 6; Sumner quoted in ibid., 7.

32. Bill J. Leonard, "The Modern Church and Social Action," *Review and Expositor* 85, no. 2 (Spring 1988): 243–53.

33. Susan Curtis, *A Consuming Faith: The Social Gospel and Modern American Culture* (Columbia: University of Missouri Press, 2001), 3, 5.

34. Theda Skocpol, "Religion, Civil Society, and Social Provision in the U.S.," in *Who Will Provide? The Changing Role of Religion in American Social Welfare,* 21–50.

35. B. J. Coughlin, *Church and State in Social Welfare* (New York: Columbia University Press, 1969); F. E. Netting, "Secular and Religious Funding of Church-Related Agencies," *Social Service Review* 56, no. 4 (1982): 586–604.

36. Bradford v. Roberts, 175 U.S. 291 (1899); Bowen v. Kendrick, 487 U.S. 589 (1988).

37. Quote from Kennedy and Bielefeld, *Charitable Choice at Work,* 27.

38. H. Richard Niebuhr as quoted in Robert P. Althauser, "Paradox in Popular Religion: The Limits of Instrumental Faith," *Social Forces* 69, no. 2 (December 1990): 585.

39. Nora McKinney Hiatt, *Tempting Faith* (Princeton, N.J.: Films for the Humanities and Sciences, 2003). This film was a part of the Charitable Choice Research Project funded by the Ford Foundation.

40. Mary Jo Bane, videotaped interview, in ibid.

41. Odell Cleveland, videotaped interview, in ibid.

42. John Buehrens, videotaped interview, in ibid.

43. Sheila Suess Kennedy and Leda Hall, "What Separation of Church and State? Constitutional Competence and the Bush Faith-Based Initiative," *Journal of Law in Society* 5, no. 2 (Winter 2004): 406–407.

8 Juggling the Religious and the Secular

World Visions

Susan McDonic

WORLD VISION INTERNATIONAL is a Christian multinational relief and development organization with operations in nearly one hundred countries. Their annual report for 2011 claims that they "served" 100 million people, directly benefited 4.1 million children through child sponsorship, and raised $2.79 billion in cash and goods.[1] As such, this organization of nearly unbelievable magnitude is growing at an exponential rate. For instance, the World Vision partnership's income has tripled in the last eight years. It has been called variously "the largest development organization aside from the United Nations,"[2] "the largest privately funded aid organization in the world,"[3] and the world's largest Christian development organization. World Vision is clearly a huge player in the international field of development, with representatives lobbying and consulting with governments and the United Nations and others working with international ecumenical groups such as the World Council of Churches and the Jubilee movement. Further, it acts as a media source monitoring on the ground the political, environmental, and economic state of the world, providing information and news stories to all the major news agencies. Beyond this, World Vision had, until recently, a publishing house in the form of its subsidiary, Mission Advanced Research and Communication Center (MARC) publications.[4] Additionally, each national office is involved in the production of numerous videos, magazines, and newsletters of its own. This is an organization with a massive global reach that circulates money, information, images, and material help transnationally, shaping and responding to global shifts of power, ideology, and economics.[5]

One of the things that makes World Vision so fascinating as an organization is its blend of Christian perspectives and development and its ability to translate these discourses across transnational space. Clearly, this is never an easy process, and a series of slippages is manifested as those discourses become rooted in far-flung and culturally varied places. For this reason, my research focuses on localized meaning and challenges analyses that often seem to assume homogeneous reception. World Vision is successful as a global organization, in large part, due to the fact that the various branches share idioms of Christianity and development. On one level, these discourses lend themselves to each other in ways that are both provocative and mutually reinforcing. They are both based upon an ethic of care and compassion, and they are both marked by an idealistic, if not utopian, dream for a more equitable and just world. On another level, however, the distinct idioms of development and Christianity strain and pull against each other in incompatible ways. Here the secular and the religious diverge because they have very different frameworks for explaining why the world is as it is.

The two branches of the organization considered here—Canada and Ghana—manage to minimize the tensions inherent in tacking between the secular and the religious by emphasizing and, indeed, instrumentalizing one over the other. World Vision Canada mutes its Christian message and foregrounds secular understandings of development practice and poverty alleviation, while World Vision Ghana foregrounds faith and conversion and reframes development as Christian mission. The various amplifications and emphases that each office enacts relate to the locus of power in these two locales. Each is able to attain local legitimacy and authority by speaking truths to power in the languages of the locally powerful. In addition, World Vision Canada needs and relies upon the excesses of the other in order to fulfill its full organizational mission, to give a religious inflection to a Wallersteinian model of the core/periphery.

The field of development itself has undergone dramatic transformations since its inception after World War II. To be sure, the prewar moment was also filled with colonial and missionary development schemes, but development as we know it today was built out of the rubble of World War II in 1945. As Arturo Escobar has cogently argued, the idea of an impoverished "Third World"—one that needed "development" and "modernization"—came into being as a global (world salvationist) ideology only in the 1950s and 1960s.[6] Early development philosophy from this time period, working within a modernization theory framework, imagined that incremental injections of aid money into impoverished areas of the Third World would lead to economic "takeoff." In this view, the newly independent states were to be the handmaidens of developmentalism, charged with building up infrastructure (roads, schools, hospitals), and setting up capital-intensive schemes like agribusiness. The failures of this 1960s and 1970s development moment are legion and include, among other things, its complicity in producing corrupt and overbloated states (what French political scientist Jean-François Bayart has referred to in the African context as the "politics of the belly"[7]) and an inattention to local realities.

The 1980s and 1990s saw a dramatic shift in development policy on the part of nongovernmental organizations (NGOs) away from the corrupt Cold War state (which was now everywhere being eclipsed in the neoliberal order) to a direct engagement with the local. Thus, development philosophy since the end of the Cold War has encouraged the direct participation of local communities themselves; it has shifted away from a language of paternalism to one of "partnership" and local participation. This shift led initially to broad calls for democracy and the end of dictatorships, what some might call the disastrous tying of aid dollars to democratic elections. The failures of this approach became obvious rather quickly, and development organizations responded with calls for a need to advance programs that would strengthen "civil

society." Since then, there has been an almost universal and rather uncritical glorifica-
tion of and focus on "the grassroots." It remains to be seen what the effect of this privileging of the local and small scale will be. At present, there is a clear trend away from
the state providing social services toward local organizations finding local solutions to
their social and structural problems.

Across all these periods (here simplified, of course, for the realities of the last sixty
years of development practice in Africa and beyond are far more complicated than any
brief schematization can provide), development has operated within a consistent and
hegemonic set of understandings about the causes of global poverty. Such poverty—
seen in terms that are familiar to academics—is rooted in histories of global expansion and even exploitation (including those of slavery and colonialism). This secularist
view of global underdevelopment and its causes, however, is only tangentially shared by
World Vision Ghana staff (and many within the Canadian office, as well).

The scholarly literature on development has, in some ways, mirrored these transformations in development practice (and, thus, also the transformations in post–World
War II geopolitics). Early work on development from within anthropology, much of
it from an "applied" perspective and often written by anthropologists working for the
development apparatus itself, was wedded to a modernization theory perspective and,
like the anthropology of the time, was deeply functionalist. More critical perspectives
on development began to emerge in the 1980s, triggered, of course, by the failures in
development practice but also informed by world systems and underdevelopment
theory. These critiques often emerged as well from within the development apparatus,
and, indeed, one of the interesting features of development policy all along has been its
self-reflexivity—a feature of World Vision International today. For all their relevance,
however, these world systems theory critiques remained functionalist and reified what
we would today see as a rather simple-minded view of the pristine local community
confronted by an exploitative global capitalist machine.

The 1990s scholarly literature took a very different turn, in large part due to two
important interventions: Jim Ferguson's *Anti-Politics Machine* (1994) and Arturo Escobar's *Encountering Development* (1995). These Foucauldian analyses focused on development as a largely self-contained and self-serving discursive apparatus, generating
"problems" and categories of analysis strictly from within the discourse itself, all the
while serving the interests of global power. The strength of the Foucauldian approach
was also its greatest weakness: a brilliant examination of discourses and yet an inattention to that which lay outside discourse. Thus, a series of important works—those
by Jonathan Crush (1995), John Rapley (1996), R. D. Grillo and R. I. Stirrat (1997), and
Akhil Gupta (1998)—emerged in the mid- to late 1990s and beyond. Often informed
by the practice theory perspective of Pierre Bourdieu (1977) and an emergent postcolonial theory, they examined on-the-ground realities of development practice in specific
locales and showed the ways in which development-as-power gets hybridized and refigured locally.[8]

World Vision International has, equally over time, modified its institutional structure and international programs to reflect and respond to these wider shifts in the development field. Initially, its institutional structure included support offices in the West that raised funds and field offices in the global South that utilized those funds. This dichotomous structure, it was ultimately decided, replicated core-periphery power dynamics and reflected a certain paternalistic perspective on the part of donor nations. The organization has, through internationalization, attempted to ameliorate these problems and create what it terms "a new federalism" in the global partnership that is marked by equality of status, position, and responsibility.[9] In order to achieve these ends, World Vision workers who used to live at a distance from the communities with which they were involved now live and work with the community members on a daily basis. Within this new model, power in the organization is more decentralized and, thus, more responsive (in theory) to the particular needs on the ground. More than this, responsibility for the full mission of the organization is now unilaterally shared. As a result, all offices are now responsible for both the raising of funds and the implementation of local development projects, regardless of locale. In the global South, practices have moved from simply providing funds for children in the program to supporting the wider communities through community development projects such as digging boreholes, building schools, providing immunizations, and, most recently, attempting to provide for whole districts through a combination of structural and personal interventions. These programs, which World Vision calls Area Development Projects (ADPs), make a minimum time commitment of fifteen years and have budgets that are usually in the millions of dollars. These projects attempt to be holistic and encompass everything from school building, immunizations, housing improvement, microcredit programs, capacity building, and community mobilization.

Obviously, Canada and Ghana are distinctly different cultures, different societies, and have different histories, but, as such, they provide very different conditions of possibility regarding the kinds of truths that can be told, which leads, at times, to competing, contradicting, and radically different understandings of history, development, and economics. These differing views, in turn, lead to very different terms of engagement, ones that are often at odds with one another. They are involved in not only creating cartographies of care and compassion (restructuring and focusing the hearts of the Canadian public in particular places and particular ways) but also mapping and remapping the globe into areas of relative wealth, poverty, violence, degradation, and disease.

Within the Canadian office, it is the Christian voice that is most muted. The organization clearly positions itself as Christian and is engaged in a plethora of outreach programs to local churches and ecumenical groups. This voice, however, often simply underlies the louder and more insistent secular voice that speaks for the silenced. As World Vision Canada minimally states on most of its productions, "World Vision is a Christian humanitarian organization reaching out to a hurting world." This muted tone of the Christian message within World Vision Canada has been the subject of some debate, particularly from those evangelicals who came into the organization from other, more fundamentalist structures and saw it as shifting away from its roots.[10]

In Canada, however, this emphasis on the secular voice of humanitarian compassion has been successful and has led to a broad base of Canadian donors. Second only to the Red Cross in terms of name recognition, World Vision Canada has found a credible voice in the development apparatus. It is clear from its own literature that World Vision believes that it has an uncommon insight into the problems plaguing the world and that it is well positioned to speak authoritatively about what the issues are and how best they should be addressed. According to World Vision Canada media, "World Vision Canada is a trusted source for information on emergencies, global events, and long-term development. We help journalists bring stories to Canadians."[11] As the World Vision International website puts it:

> World Vision invites its supporters and the Canadian public to address the root causes of global poverty. Rooted in our work with children and communities, we support and call for public policies and government practices that will help reduce poverty and injustice.
>
> In Canada, World Vision's advocacy work includes an Ottawa bureau that focuses on national policy makers. A larger team of policy experts provides field-based research and policy alternatives on global issues affecting children.[12]

In order to influence policy and act as a credible and effective advocate for the poor with governments, international bodies, and other NGOs, World Vision Canada adopts the language of the wider secular world, thus giving the impression that it shares the assumptions of this view regarding why the world is as it is.[13] The Christian message and worldview are always ever present, but here they are sublimated and subdued in order to access realms of authority and legitimacy that might be denied it otherwise.

In Ghana, however, the cultural milieu is very different. West Africa—and, indeed, the global South more generally—has, since the 1980s, undergone what some see as an explosion of interest in Pentecostal and charismatic branches of Christianity and a religious revival that has left no denomination unaffected. Harvey Cox argues that to call this a "movement" is to completely misrepresent it, and he sees the rise of Pentecostalism as being equivalent in force and import to the Protestant Reformation.[14] To give a sense of the scope of the popularity of Pentecostalism, Philip Jenkins states that it "now claims at least 350 million adherents worldwide."[15] These churches are most prominently known for their often conservative interpretations of Scripture—for their adherence to, and emphasis upon, spiritual gifts and belief in the inerrancy of the Bible. As Kim Lawton writes in *Christianity Today*, evangelicalism used to be considered a Western movement. However,

> it has become a global movement with startling new dimensions. Of the world's estimated 400 million evangelicals, 70 percent are non-Western, living in Africa, Asia,

Oceania, and Latin America. As the new millennium grows nearer, church leaders from around the world agree that such an enormous demographic has significant implications for theology, for missions, and for the future of evangelicalism.[16]

The balance of Christian power is shifting to the southern hemisphere. It is, therefore, important to understand how faith differs in these contexts as the global South is quite literally shaping the faith of the West in the contemporary context.

Upon my arrival in the Ashanti capital of Kumasi, I was immediately aware of the vibrancy and visibility of its churches; they seemed to be out every window. As a secular anthropologist, I was overwhelmed by the way in which Christianity was evident in the urban areas. Large billboards announced, "Christ is Coming!" and asked, "Are you ready?" A typical Christian Ghanaian's response to a salutation was "By God's grace, I am fine." Taxis (or *tro-tros* as the minibuses are called) bore slogans that announced that they are washed in the blood of Jesus, or exhorted the passersby to join the faith. So prevalent were these slogans that an American missionary friend commented, "There are so many vehicles that have been 'redeemed by the blood of Jesus'—I'm starting to think that there are more tro-tros in heaven than people!"

Further, the vast majority of Ghanaian films carried religious themes—a type of "secular" Pentecostalism that celebrates the life of the urban (and implicitly Christian) bourgeoisie and demonizes "tradition" and what are understood to be the Satan-infested villages.[17] Televangelists dominated the radio and television airwaves. Signs advertising Christian crusades draped all the major roads. Shops such as "Clap for Jesus Hair Saloon," "Jesus the Redeemer Autobody," and, my personal favorite, "Only Jesus Can Do It Mobile Phone Repair" were commonplace. My daughter and I were regularly awakened by staff members blaring Christian music or sermons on their radios at 4:30 AM. Additionally, a neighbor with a karaoke machine woke the entire Kentinkrono neighborhood with his high-volume reading of the Gospel. It seemed that the "louder one proclaims one's faith the better"—or, at least, the more *visibly* the better.

In a context such as the one I observed, the Christian message has significant local authority. Unlike in Canada, where the staff are of all different denominations, the vast majority of the Ghanaian staff are charismatic or neo-Pentecostal. Their brand of "transformational development" is one that mirrors the conservative and supernaturally based ideals and emphases of these churches. In Ghana, the reports, community assessment manuals, and evaluation materials follow the conventions of standardized reporting for NGOs, but development practice takes on a decidedly evangelical inflection. Here, the two discourses sit in tension with one another, held simultaneously but enacted differently. Project proposals largely follow the "scientific" models produced in the West but also include religious information as a way of framing the goals that the organization sets for the coming year. Thus, one report states:

> World Vision Ghana will follow Jesus Christ by promoting transformational development that seeks to address the issues of poverty, idolatry, nominal Christianity,

illiteracy, environmental degradation, injustice, gender discrimination, population, poor health and nutrition, food insecurity and emergency relief.[18]

The fact that the top three issues are poverty, idolatry, and nominal Christianity will gain salience as I argue that these priorities reflect the local Pentecostal understandings regarding poverty and its alleviation.

One of the most interesting events that I attended while doing fieldwork in Ghana was a pastors' conference, held by members of World Vision Ghana upper-level management. Drawing together forty pastors from the surrounding region, it was a good example of how the organization envisioned collaboration and networking in the village context. As it was organized by the Christian witness coordinator for the country, the views expressed by the conference could be understood to reflect the national office's approach to faith. These pastors' conferences are part of the institutional structure first initiated by the founder, Bob Pierce. They are held annually to foster connections between various churches and to help establish the Christian mission imperatives for the year. This particular pastors' conference was understood by the staff to be primarily a forum for training the local pastors and so had an expressed pedagogical element.

The theme for the conference was taken from a locally published book by Divine P. Kumah entitled *Is Ghana under a Curse?*[19] The conference was held in an empty church in the town nearest the ADP camp, where most of the staff live and work. It began with a general introduction and a discussion about the need to focus on the children in one's conversionary attempts. Then, suddenly, the conversation veered into the area of numerology. Drawing upon the events of September 11, 2001, which had happened just two months previously, the organizer began to outline what he saw as significant numerical similarities. He pointed out that the events took place on September 11 and noted that nine plus one plus one (the two ones of the eleven added together) equals eleven; that the name George W. Bush contains eleven letters; and that Afghanistan contains eleven letters. It was flight eleven that hit the south tower in New York. There were 254 passengers aboard the flight, and two plus five plus four equals eleven. He then pointed out that the two towers looked like the number eleven and that New York City has eleven letters. He asked us if we thought all of this was a coincidence; it was clear that he thought it was not. It took a while for him to make his point, but, eventually, we were made to understand that God has a specific interest in the affairs of nations. He additionally argued that this event had been preordained by God and was, thus, part of God's overall plan for humanity, although the purpose of September 11 was never fully explained.

Within this view, the present and future of nations can be understood to reflect their relation to and alignment with the will of God. As the conference summary sheet states, in bold text, "It is God Himself who decided on the boundaries of every nation!" This, the sheet claims, comes from Deuteronomy 32:28 (though, in fact, it is from Deuteronomy 32:8). As a secular academic educated to believe that nation-states are never more than historical constructs and "imagined communities,"[20] such a view was new to me.

The conference and the summary sheet around which it was organized got ever more interesting. We were told:

> God in His supreme wisdom, decided to give birth to a nation called the Gold Coast, now Ghana, through the British people. In spite of the atrocities against our fore-fathers, the British decided to make this nation a Christian Nation.
>
> Coming from a protestant country, the English allowed the missionary groups that were already operating in the country to continue. The graveyards at Abokobi, Greater Accra is a testimony to the dedication of the missionaries that came to this country. Some of the missionaries were willing to die not for silver or gold but to bring us the message about the love of God through Jesus Christ.[21]

The presenter said that missionaries would often ship their own coffins with them to Ghana, so great was their commitment. He then went on to outline each of the presidents of Ghana since independence and to delineate a few specific offenses each had committed against God and the nation. These ranged from mocking the Lord's Prayer (Nkrumah) and the deportation of foreigners under the Aliens Compliance Order of 1969 (Busia) to the withdrawal of the constitiution (Acheampong) and economic mismanagement (Akuffo). He held Rawlings accountable not only for the killings, beatings, and riots of the late 1970s and early 1980s but also for the introduction of "the many fetish and demonic national festivals like Panafest, Nafac, etc." Further, Rawlings's "deepening affiliation with Islamic nations, especially with the violent ones like Iran and Libya, associat[ion] with questionable characters like Louis Farrakhan, have not only worsened our spiritual state, but have brought religious polarization of the society."[22]

The conference speaker claimed that the categorization of Ghana as HIPC (heavily indebted poor country) by the Kufour government was further verification of the social decline of the country. His main point, however, was that Ghanaians individually had a responsibility to reweave issues of politics, social justice, and faith through an examination of and obedience to biblical commandments and edicts. The assembled group needed to understand that the political, social, and spiritual choices that they and their leaders were making were having a profound effect upon the positioning of the country. This, he argued, was because the Bible says that the iniquity of the fathers will be visited on the sons for four generations. In other words, the present state of Ghana was, in large part, due to the past sins of the fathers of the nation.

This biblical theme became ever more intimate as the speaker moved into the question of culture. He argued that the fall of the Ashanti empire was entirely due to their idolatrous practices. He spoke of particular atrocities committed by the Ashantis in "old times." Here, he talked of human sacrifices, cannibalism, witchcraft, and juju. Within moments, however, his reflections on the "evil" things that Ghanaians had done in the past to bring God's wrath upon the nation became conflated with the current religious practices of followers of _bosome_ (the Akan word for traditional faith practices). These idolaters, in his view, were continuing to "cause" the underdevelopment of the nation.

He urged personal responsibility because acts of individuals would have tangible effects on the relative level of development. The current downturn in the economy, within the logic of his argument, was due not to global economic forces but to the religious practices of groups staying in houses surrounding the building where the conference was being held. Ghana was, indeed, under a curse, and it was because of the actions of corrupt politicians and the idolatry of traditional culture.

The solution that World Vision and Divine P. Kumah's book offered was aggressive conversion and "spiritual warfare." The assembled crowd was told to "go back to God's word to show us how to correct the wrongs of the past. As a church we need to go back to prayer warfare and serious evangelism and missions, if we want to see Ghana on her feet again."[23] Because the problems in the country were framed as spiritual ones, we were asked to pray for repentance and for the destruction of the powers that were holding the country "hostage" and perpetuating its underdevelopment.

To many secular academics, such a rereading of history provides a distinct challenge to much of the rational logic that structures their understanding of the world. It is rather shocking to secular ears to hear slavery being recast as a positive event that enabled free access to the "true" faith. Perhaps it is even more jarring to hear a development professional explain away poverty and inequality as a spiritual problem. In framing the world this way, the World Vision Ghana staff engage in a dialectic that at once produces a link between idolatry and poverty and reduces the practice of development to a simple equation of conversion. Nonetheless, it is important to stress that real development interventions do take place. Indeed, World Vision Ghana has managed to decrease anemia by one-third in the country with its micronutrient programs, and water-borne diseases such as Guinea worm have been virtually eradicated in the Ashanti district through the drilling of more than 480 boreholes.[24] The organization also helps with microenterprise and financial training for women and sponsorship for orphans. While I was in Atebubu, World Vision Ghana was initiating a housing improvement project, building schools, starting up a mobile medical unit, and digging ventilated pit latrines. In the worldview articulated by the staff and the pastors' conference, however, such interventions are understood to be unsustainable without Christian conversion. Christianity is seen as the key element for ensuring that development will always be more than a bandage on a weeping wound. In fact, at a crusade paid for by World Vision, the manager of the project said in an introductory speech, "Tonight is about salvation and World Vision is about salvation. Part of salvation is improved water and sanitation, improved health care. But we are also concerned for your souls. Even if we give you everything, if we haven't cared for your soul, we have given you nothing." Certainly, such views have real-world effects in terms of how the staff of World Vision Ghana interacts with the local communities.

In Ghana, both the traditional faith and the emergent Pentecostal and charismatic churches deeply believe that the spiritual is simultaneously transcendent and material. In other words, what happens in the spiritual realm is understood to have immediate and tangible effects upon the material realm. In fact, as anthropologist Birgit Meyer and sociologist Paul Gifford have argued, the acknowledgment of and willingness to take seriously demons and spirits by the Pentecostal churches in Ghana largely explain their explosive growth over the last twenty years.[25] This is an environment where demons, devils, and witches are understood to lurk around every corner and where grace is said not to give thanks but rather to neutralize poisons that might have been placed in the food. Indeed, there is a certain amount of cultural capital to be gained by claiming that one is under the influence of Satan but has been or wants to be redeemed through Jesus Christ. For this reason, perhaps, there has been a simultaneous growth in witchcraft accusations and proliferation of "deliverance" camps and crusades. At these camps, the organizers say they can, through the laying on of hands, cast out demons and cleanse the people so possessed.[26]

The Ghana churches not only claim to perform healing miracles on a weekly basis, however, but also tout the miracle of giving wealth. The "prosperity doctrine" of many of these churches has been widely examined and critiqued because of its powerful resonance in the global South.[27] It holds that Jesus will not only reward the faithful for their devotion in the afterlife but will also give material rewards in this life. As Jean and John Comaroff state, "For them, and for their millions of members, the Second Coming evokes not a Jesus who saves, but one who pays dividends. Or, more accurately, one who promises a miraculous return on a limited spiritual investment."[28] In this view, personal suffering or impoverishment is an indication that something is not right in one's relationship with God. Only through devotion, faith, and a strict adherence to the Bible will one's prayers of advancement be granted. Philip Jenkins argues that the emergence and rise in popularity of deliverance camps could be a result of the failures of the prosperity doctrine; as the promises of the preachers do not come true, adherents begin to look for the reasons and explanations for the "blockages" in their lives. The answer most often found is witchcraft. They were doing everything right; Satan was just getting in the way.[29]

The rub of the prosperity doctrine is in the way it grounds the spiritual in the material. This makes one's faith and relationship to the spiritual realm a physically "readable" semiotic to outsiders. For Ghanaian Pentecostals then, one's relationship to God—or one's distance from God—can be read in a glance. As much as all difference is structured through systems of alterity, Christians in Ghana largely define and create themselves in opposition to what they understand to be furthest from themselves—the idolatrous other.[30] I was repeatedly told in Ghana—always by Christians—that one can tell the religion of a community by simply looking at it. They said a Christian community is the cleanest and most developed, a Muslim community is dirty, with houses in disrepair, and followers of *bosome,* the traditional faith, live in the most abject of circumstances.

This focus on the transparency of one's godliness places a fair amount of social pressure on Ghanaian Christians to model a form of spiritual progress, one that looks remarkably similar to the neoliberal subjectivity advocated by development agencies in their search for an emergent civil society. Putting a new spin on the Weberian Protestant ethic, some theorists argue that Christian development practices are successful precisely because they inculcate a kind of subjectivity that is exactly in line with what the neoliberal market needs. In Ghana today, one might say, religion is increasingly interwoven with class. This modeling of both development and faith, on the part of World Vision staff, means an intense focus on outward appearances. It is important to make one's faith visible, and staff seem to do this most obviously through their purchasing choices— what they purchase for their homes or to wear reflects their spiritual state as well as their taste. Clothing budgets are large because there is concern for looking good in church and in the communities where they work.

Overwhelmingly, the staff known as "Friends of the Family" in the Atebubu Family Sponsorship Project—who were the first staff members to live in the communities where they worked—see their primary responsibility as being a role model. They mean to model cleanliness, hard work, and frugality to the local communities. They take pride in World Vision having the latest model Land Cruisers and motorcycles, as these manifestations of physical wealth provide "encouragement" to the local communities. The staff believe that people are more likely to convert to Christianity if they can see the material benefits that God provides. The material benefits that World Vision staff members accrue through working for a large international NGO (such as relatively large salaries and all that those salaries provide) serve to validate their faith both to themselves and to others. They are godly, and the proof of their godliness is their wealth. Through their association with a Christian NGO, they model, and believe that they embody, a form of development that evades the pitfalls of Western progress, which is seen to be saturated with moral ambiguity.

In order not to replicate a long anthropological tradition of depicting the West as governed by scientific rationality and the African "other" as being deeply and essentially steeped in superstition and "irrationality," it is worth reiterating that both World Vision Canada and World Vision Ghana hold the two discourses in tension with each other. Pentecostal Christians, and this certainly includes many of the Canadian staff, think that secular understandings of development are equally irrational and that it is hubris to think that the world is as it is because of mere human industry. Through their eyes, God and the devil are everywhere, and the secular rationalism that was supposed to lift the veil of ignorance and bring objectivity has merely provided us with a new set of blinders. The argument that Africa is under a curse was first posited to me, in fact, by a staff member from the Canadian office after having spent a few months in West Africa.

The devil also makes periodic appearances in institutional World Vision documents. In the internal paper entitled "Global Context for Action: The Partnership Context Paper," the international office acknowledges, "History is going somewhere and it has a purpose." Tied to this history are the presence of Satan and the force of evil that Satan directs. "The Evil One is hard at work twisting those parts of the global context which have the potential to work for life and making them anti-life or life-denying. Rebellion is still the rule and the evidence, in the form of pain, suffering, injustice and idolatry is overwhelming."[31] What seems like a contradiction between the two branches of the organization is, in actuality, a productive way of fulfilling World Vision's mandate to "take the whole of their mission to the whole of the world." What seem to be the excesses of the Ghanaian offices can, in fact, be seen as a more honest working out of the organization's stated Christian mission, one that must necessarily be muted in the Canadian context. And, cynically perhaps, those same excesses in the global South serve to validate and further amplify North American access to the halls of power that speak in an excessively secular idiom.

In conclusion, organizations such as World Vision defy easy categorization; they push against the paradigms within which we, as academics, would like to analyze them. Clearly, this is not an easy case of discourses of development and faith being unproblematically transmitted across transnational space; we are therefore challenged to question critically those who might see this as a new form of imperialism. Nor is it, as some have argued, a simple case of Christian and developmental discourses mutually reinforcing each another in order to promote a globally uniform individualistic notion of capitalist personhood and progress. World Vision in Ghana provides us with the opportunity to look at the ways in which—in this one instance, at least—the discourses that emanate out of the West are being locally distilled, refigured, and put to use in very different ways than are intended at their perceived point of origin. In changing the meanings applied to development discourse—and, indeed, reframing Christianity itself—Ghanaian Pentecostal staff are involved in not only remaking local worlds both materially and spiritually but also exporting back to the West a decidedly more apocalyptic view of those locales. At a time when it has become clear that the power of the Christian church is in the process of shifting from the global North to the global South, it is imperative that we understand the South's views on faith, specific modes of performance, and the development process itself, as it may soon be the South that is defining these very terms.

Notes

1. World Vision International, *Annual Report 2011* (Monrovia, Calif.: World Vision International, 2011), 1–6.

2. This statistic was stated to me many times in Ghana by people who had heard it in workshops held by representatives from the U.S. office. When I enquired as to the veracity of this statement at the Canadian office upon my return, however, no one had heard it before.

3. World Vision UK, "World Vision at a Glance" (London, 2004).

4. The publishing house has upwards of fifty current titles at any given time and a library of more than two hundred titles. These titles are primarily books on missions and reference tools that missionaries can use while in the field. MARC has also produced many books on development from a Christian perspective. Because the current offerings are limited to World Vision promotional and informational materials, it seems that MARC has downsized and moved its publications in-house.

5. Through the production and dissemination of all of these materials and its high level of visibility, World Vision, at national and international levels, is very active in shaping how crises, development,

and poverty are conceptualized, problematized, and viewed, not only by sponsors but also by newsmakers, policy makers, and the general public.

6. Arturo Escobar, *Encountering Development: The Making and Unmaking of the Third World* (Princeton, N.J.: Princeton University Press, 1995).

7. Jean-François Bayart, *The State in Africa: The Politics of the Belly* (London: Longman Group, 1993).

8. James Ferguson, *The Anti-Politics Machine: "Development," Depoliticization, and Bureaucratic Power in Lesotho* (Minneapolis: University of Minnesota Press, 1994); Escobar, *Encountering Development*; Jonathan Crush, ed., *Power of Development* (London: Routledge, 1995); John Rapley, *Understanding Development: Theory and Practice in the Third World* (Boulder, Colo.: Lynne Rienner, 1996); R. D. Grillo and R. I. Stirrat, eds., *Discourses of Development: Anthropological Perspectives* (Oxford: Berg, 1997); Akhil Gupta, *Postcolonial Developments: Agriculture in the Making of Modern India* (Durham, N.C.: Duke University Press, 1998); Pierre Bourdieu, *Outline of a Theory of Practice* (Cambridge: Cambridge University Press, 1977).

9. World Vision International, "Global Context for Action: The Partnership Context Paper," 1997 (internal paper).

10. As Erica Bornstein points out, World Vision emerged in the United States in 1950 at a particular and rather specific moment in American religious and political life. Erica Bornstein, *The Spirit of Development: Protestant NGOs, Morality, and Economics in Zimbabwe* (Stanford, Calif.: Stanford University Press, 2005). Tied closely to the rise of the Cold War and its attendant anti-Communist fervor, the organization also reflected the rise and popularity of a new evangelicalism in American Christianity, one firmly tied to a belief in "the inerrancy of the Bible, active evangelism, human depravity and individual conversion, and the efficacy of atonement via the death of Christ" (19). She further argues that the organization was dedicated from the earliest days to integrating spirituality into all aspects of life, seeing it not just as a set of beliefs but also as a set of practices (esp. chap. 2). The Canadian branch of World Vision shares this history, and, indeed, many of its staff were and continue to be American. It is important to note, however, that it also has a slightly different trajectory, one that reflects the cultural and political temperament of Canada. Canadians, while clearly influenced by the United States, tend to have quite different relationships with church and the state. Canadians tend to be more muted in their faith expressions, and they tend to believe in the efficacy of state-run social programs. In 1996, the Angus Reid Group surveyed the Canadian public and found, among other things, that nationally only 23 percent of the population attends church weekly, yet nearly 81 percent believe that it is possible to be a good Christian without attending church (Angus Reid Group, *God and Society in North America*, Survey [Toronto: World Vision Canada Internal Report, 1996]). I argue that the muted nature of the Christian message disseminated by the Canadian office is something that reflects the wider Canadian culture.

11. World Vision Canada, "About Us," http://www.worldvision.ca/About-Us/Pages/AboutUs.aspx.

12. World Vision Canada, "International Programs," 2011, http://www.worldvision.ca/Programs-and-Projects/International-Programs/Pages/international-programs.aspx.

13. This is also a highly successful model, reflecting the culture as it does; as mentioned, it has enviable name recognition in Canada. World Vision U.S., in contrast, takes a decidedly more evangelical position in its promotional materials. In twelve years of teaching in the United States, I have come across only a handful of students who have ever heard of World Vision, and those students learned about World Vision almost entirely through their churches or through other religious events, such as Women of Faith conferences.

14. Harvey Cox, *Fire from Heaven: The Rise of Spirituality and the Reshaping of Religion in the Twenty-First Century* (Reading, Mass.: Addison-Wesley, 1995).

15. Philip Jenkins, *The New Faces of Christianity: Believing the Bible in the Global South* (New York: Oxford University Press, 2006), 12. This statistic omits the charismatic branches of the mainline

churches, noncharismatic denominations, and the more traditional mainline churches that have all also seen an upturn in attendance and conversions.

16. Kim Lawton, "Faith without Borders," *Christianity Today*, May 19, 1997, http://www.ctlibrary.com/ct/1997/may19/7t638a.html.

17. Birgit Meyer has done some wonderful work on the interplay between Pentecostalism and popular culture through Ghanaian film, most notably Birgit Meyer, "'Praise the Lord': Popular Cinema and Pentecostalite Style in Ghana's New Public Sphere," *American Ethnologist* 31, no. 1 (February 2004): 92–110; and Birgit Meyer, "Impossible Representations: Pentecostalism, Vision, and Video Technology in Ghana," in *Religion, Media, and the Public Sphere*, ed. Birgit Meyer and Annelies Moors (Bloomington: Indiana University Press, 2006), 290–312.

18. World Vision Ghana, "Program Background: Family Sponsorship Project Report," 5–6.

19. Divine P. Kumah, *Is Ghana under a Curse?* (Accra, Ghana: SonLife Books, 2000).

20. Benedict Anderson, *Imagined Communities: Reflections on the Origin and Spread of Nationalism* (London: Verso, 2003).

21. Kumah, *Is Ghana under a Curse?* emphasis in the original.

22. Ibid.

23. Ibid.

24. World Vision Canada, "International Programs," 2011.

25. Birgit Meyer, "'There Is a Spirit in That Image': Mass Produced Jesus Pictures and Protestant Pentecostal Animation in Ghana," *Comparative Studies in Society and History* 52, no. 1 (2010): 100–130; Birgit Meyer, *Translating the Devil: Religion and Modernity among the Ewe in Ghana* (Edinburgh: Edinburgh University Press for the International African Institute, 1999); Paul Gifford, "Ghana's Charismatic Churches," *Journal of Religion in Africa* 25 (1994): 241–65; Paul Gifford, *Ghana's New Christianity: Pentecostalism in a Globalising African Economy,* new ed. (Bloomington: Indiana University Press, 2004).

26. See Peter Geschiere, *The Modernity of Witchcraft: Politics and the Occult in Postcolonial Africa* (Charlottesville: University Press of Virginia, 1997), 206; Gifford, *Ghana's New Christianity,* 92.

27. See Jean Comaroff and John L. Comaroff, eds., *Millennial Capitalism and the Culture of Neoliberalism* (Durham, N.C.: Duke University Press, 2001); Rijk van Dijk, Ria Ries, and Marja Spierenburg, *The Quest for Fruition through Ngoma: Political Aspects of Healing in Southern Africa* (Cape Town, South Africa: David Philip, 2000); Meyer, *Translating the Devil;* Gifford, "Ghana's Charismatic Churches"; and Gifford, *Ghana's New Christianity.* The "prosperity doctrine" is often spoken of as an African invention, but it was actually first espoused and found its footing in the American South. Well-known evangelists (all Pentecostal or charismatic) such as Kenneth Copeland, Creflo Dollar, Kenneth Hagin, Jr., Benny Hinn, T. D. Jakes, Joyce Meyers, and Joel Osteen have all, at various times, adopted and been proponents of this position.

28. Jean Comaroff and John L. Comaroff, "Millennial Capitalism: First Thoughts on a Second Coming," in *Millennial Capitalism and the Culture of Neoliberalism,* 24.

29. Jenkins, *The New Faces of Christianity.*

30. Comaroff and Comaroff, eds., *Millennial Capitalism and the Culture of Neoliberalism.*

31. World Vision International, "Global Context for Action," 5.

9 Philanthropic Decisions of American Jews

The Influence of Religious Identity on Charitable Choices

Arnold Dashefsky and Bernard Lazerwitz

Introduction to the Problem and Its Empirical Investigation

A tourist to a foreign country entered the premier concert hall in the capital for a tour and inquired of the guide, "Is this hall named after the famous prize-winning author?" "No," replied the tour guide, "it is named after a local person." "So," inquired the tourist of the guide, "what great work did your local author write?" To which, the tour guide replied, "A check!" Gifts of charity are generally viewed as generous, selfless acts, but Marcel Mauss and other social scientists noted that there is a payoff of some sort to the giver, although it may be viewed by some as in this world (i.e., social recognition or psychic gratification) or by others as in the next world (i.e., eternal salvation or a heavenly abode).[1]

Despite these rewards, a specter is haunting American society and the European community. It is the specter of devolution—the devolution of the responsibility for the poor, the ill, and the infirm from the government to the citizenry. This essay examines the conditions under which charity may fill the gap. Charity and philanthropy are conceptualized as part of the literature on gift exchange in society. Such gifts have reached extraordinarily high levels in recent years in the United States: $260 billion in 2004, representing 2.1 percent of GDP, with about three-quarters of that sum (or $199 billion) coming from individuals.[2] The largest beneficiaries of those charitable gifts in 2004 were religious congregations and denominations, which received $93 billion or 36 percent of total contributions. That religion should receive the largest share of such contributions is not surprising since charity is a central tenet in the major religious traditions.

Substantial research in the behavioral sciences suggests that individuals may donate to a charity as a function of their consumer spending behavior (the economic explanation in the work of Barry Chiswick), situational constraints (the psychological approach, as in Peter Reingen), or self-interest (the sociological and anthropological perspectives of Joseph Galaskiewicz). Nevertheless, we suggest another possibility, a social-psychological conceptualization, as found in Leonard Berkowitz and William

H. Connor: Individuals give to a charity when they participate in a culture and network of social relations that stress mutual independence and responsibility, especially when that culture has socialized them to identify with it.[3] Thus, relying on a social-psychological perspective, the primary objective of this research is to understand and explain the motivations of individuals to make charitable gifts and to account for the incentives and barriers to such philanthropy.

A variety of factors accounts for the motivation to make charitable contributions. In this essay, the influence of religious identity on charitable choices is examined by focusing on one group—the American Jewish population. This group is generally viewed as generous, and abundant data exist for this population at both the national and local levels.[4] A set of three data sources and reports archived at the Jewish Data Bank website includes the National Jewish Population Surveys (NJPS) of 1971, 1990, and 2000–2001 (distributed in 1972, 1991, and 2003, respectively).[5] These data permit an examination of the factors that shape philanthropic giving. NJPS is a large, representative, nationwide sample that provides data on American Jewish contributions to the former United Jewish Appeal (UJA or local Jewish Federation) and other charities. In the current analysis (utilizing the NJPS carried out in 1990 and released in 1991 by North American Jewish Data Bank as the benchmark), there were 1,905 respondents representing a probability sample of American Jews. Reference to the first NJPS of 1970–1971 (n = 5,790), as well as to the most recent or third NJPS of 2000–2001 (n = 2,441), will be made subsequently, although a full comparison to the latter is not possible owing to a lack of comparability.

While about two decades have passed since the release of the second 1990 NJPS, it is most likely that the characteristics of its subgroups and individuals have remained stable. Since the major trends in American Jewish life are the result of social processes that have been at work over some time, the characteristics of those who make charitable contributions and those who do not have most likely remained fairly similar in the recent past, an assumption largely substantiated by interviews with professional fundraisers carried out in the past decade.[6] Hence, there is much to gain from a careful examination of the relationships among a variety of demographic, socioeconomic, and Jewish identification factors, including Federation/UJA involvement. (While the term UJA is used, it encompasses giving to the local Jewish federation, which represents the local affiliate of the relatively newly constituted Jewish Federations of North America [JFNA].)[7] Furthermore, the mid-range response rate of the 1990 NJPS makes it an especially valuable benchmark in moving both backward and forward in assessing trends in Jewish charitable giving.

Jewish Involvement in Charitable Giving

Table 9.1 gives the results of asking about respondent families' giving to their last local Federation/UJA drive. Overall, 45 percent claimed to have given. This is a high percentage of American Jewish adults and compares favorably with the 47 percent of Jewish adults who claimed a synagogue membership in the 1990 NJPS.

Table 9.1. Philanthropy of American Jews to various causes (NJPS 1990: "In 1989 did you and/or other members of your household together contribute or give gifts?")

A. To the Jewish Federation or UJA?

Yes	No	Don't Know/Refused
45%	52%	3%

B. To Jewish philanthropies, charities, causes or other organizations?

Yes	No	Don't Know/Refused
63%	35%	2%

C. To philanthropies, charities, organizations or causes that are not specifically Jewish?

Yes	No	Don't Know/Refused
72%	26%	2%

An even greater percentage of respondent families (63 percent) also claimed to have given to other local Jewish community fund drives. Finally, 72 percent of these families claimed to have given to non-Jewish charity drives, a figure not very different from the 70 percent of all Americans who contributed to religious causes, as reported by the American Association of Fund-Raising Counsel (AAFRC; now the Giving Institute).[8] A greater portion of American Jews gave to non-Jewish charity drives than to general Jewish causes or the UJA specifically, dispelling the notion that Jewish giving is only parochial. Nevertheless, Jews did not appear to give in greater proportions than other Americans—but they did appear to give in greater amounts.[9] Why this is so is an interesting question that few studies seem to address empirically. The assumption herein is that a normative religious and cultural obligation of charitable giving or *tzedakah* (literally, doing justice by giving charity) supports Jewish philanthropic generosity. In other words, a network of community ties, above-average income, and, possibly, a sense of greater political and social insecurity occasioned by the anti-Semitism of the Holocaust, or the present circumstances of Jewry in Europe and the Middle East, leads to charitable giving.

Fewer Jewish adults (24 percent) claimed to have done volunteer work in their local Jewish fund drives (see table 9.2). Furthermore, a still larger percentage of Jewish adults (41 percent) claimed to have worked for their local, general (not Jewish) charity fund drives. In table 9.3, one sees that 38 percent have given to both Jewish and non-Jewish fund drives. Seven percent gave to the Jewish but not to the general fund drive; 34 percent gave to the general but not Jewish fund drives; and 21 percent gave to neither.

Table 9.2. Volunteering of American Jews to Jewish and non-Jewish organizations (NJPS 1990: "During the past 12 months have you done volunteer work yourself or as part of a group?")

A. *For a Jewish organization?*

Yes	No	Don't Know/Refused
24%	76%	0%

B. *For a not specifically Jewish organization?*

Yes	No	Don't Know/Refused
41%	59%	0%

Table 9.3. Gave to UJA by giving to general charities

Gave to UJA	Yes	No	Total
Yes	38%	7%	45%
No	34%	21%	55%
			100%

A Model of Jewish Giving

One of the objectives of this essay is to understand better the factors that encourage as well as impede charitable giving by focusing on one group, American Jews, and the way they practice philanthropy. Obviously, they can give their financial resources to a wide variety of institutions. Within the Jewish community, the central fund-raising and dispensing organization has been the local Jewish federation. Hence, the first question of interest concerns giving to the local Jewish federation. This question obviously must be followed by one that asks about financial giving to other Jewish philanthropies, charities, causes, or other organizations. These two questions exhaust giving within the Jewish community. Consequently, these questions lead to inquiring about giving to non-Jewish philanthropies, charities, organizations, or causes. But it is possible to give of one's time in place of money. This requires questions that ask about volunteer work for Jewish organizations and about volunteer work for non-Jewish organizations. These combinations of financial giving or giving of oneself cover all aspects of the ways of giving to one's community.[10] Therefore, these questions form the dependent variables to be examined in the Jewish community: (1) gave to UJA, (2) gave to other Jewish charities, (3) volunteer work in Jewish voluntary associations, (4) gave to non-Jewish charities, and (5) volunteer work in general associations. A host of independent variables is examined to develop explanations for the variations in these dimensions of charitable giving.

Jack Wertheimer, in his excellent review of trends in American Jewish philanthropy and following up on Steven Cohen's earlier review, identified a number of key variables that affect giving, including demographic factors, socioeconomic status, and Jewish identification.[11] Here, we assesses the impact of a variety of such independent variables on giving to UJA, other Jewish charities, and volunteering for Jewish causes as well as giving to non-Jewish charities and volunteering for general causes. The statistical technique used in this section is multiple regression analysis, which enables a determination of the influence of one variable on another while holding statistically constant the influence of other variables. The first step in such an analysis is to specify the order in which the variables are to be entered into the statistical equations. Variables that appear early in the equation serve as controls. That is, their influence is held constant statistically when looking at the influence of the variable of central concern.

The resulting analyses provide two statistics of interest: the standardized coefficient of regression value (beta) and the squared multiple correlation coefficient (R^2). Beta indicates how much a dependent variable changes for each unit of change in one of its independent variables above and beyond the impact, or influence, of any other independent variable. R^2 indicates how much of the variation of a dependent variable is explained by the combined impact of all the independent variables of a regression equation.[12]

The independent variables that were used, in order of their appearance in the relevant equations, are:

1. *Demographic,* namely, gender, age, marital status together with the number of minor children in the household (called life cycle), and the number of generations that one's family has been in the United States;
2. *Socioeconomic,* such as the level of secular education, the occupation of the family head, and family income;
3. *Religious,* for example, the years of Jewish education in one's youth, current denominational preference, and synagogue membership.

These variables were selected due to the hypothesized influence they might have on charitable giving. For example, differences in generation or age might show younger people and more assimilated generations giving less. Likewise, socioeconomic status, particularly income, might be associated with higher levels of giving. Finally, religious variables might show that the more traditional and pious individuals are, the more likely they are to make charitable contributions.

By placing these three sets of variables first in the equation, the influence of demographic and socioeconomic factors as well as of Jewish education, denomination, and synagogue membership are statistically controlled. This statistical technique enables one to determine which variables relate to aspects of the respondents' Jewish and non-Jewish involvements above and beyond the influence of demographic characteristics, socioeconomic status, and these initial Jewish background factors. The particular aspects of the respondents' Jewish involvement are: attendance at religious services, religious practices at home, involvement with Jewish primary groups, activity in Jewish voluntary associations, and orientation toward Israel.

What do the components of the model tell us? First, in examining the demographic variables of gender, age, generations in the United States, and life cycle, table 9.4 shows that, for giving to the UJA or other Jewish charities, or activity in voluntary Jewish associations, women were slightly more involved than men. However, only for voluntary association activity did gender reach a moderate level of impact, with women being significantly more active than men. In regard to age and giving to the UJA or other Jewish charities, the older the respondent, the more the giving. The impact on the UJA was strong, while, for other Jewish charities, the impact was a bit lower. Age, however, had no effective impact on activity in Jewish voluntary associations. The other two demographic variables, generations in the United States and life cycle, had only weak impacts on giving and activity.

For the socioeconomic variables, education, occupation of family head, and family income provided an interesting picture. Neither education nor occupation had any meaningful impacts. Income had moderate impacts on the two giving variables, to no one's surprise, but income did not affect volunteer activity in Jewish associations.

In regard to the "Jewish variables," Jewish education had only a weak impact on giving to the UJA but moderate impacts on giving to other Jewish charities and voluntary association activity. Denomination had a moderate impact on giving to the UJA with adherents of the Conservative and Reform denominations most likely to give. Based on evidence from Bernard Lazerwitz and others, members of these denominations had higher incomes than the Orthodox and nonmembers.[13]

Synagogue members were quite likely to give and to be active. Those who attended synagogue more frequently were more likely to give to various Jewish charities and much more likely to have been active in Jewish voluntary associations. The performing of more home religious practices had a moderate impact only on giving to other Jewish charities. Those more involved in Jewish primary groups were more likely to give to the UJA and other Jewish charities. Finally, being Israel-oriented was associated with a moderate impact on giving to the UJA. There was a solid amount of overall variance explained for the two giving variables (R^2 =.31 for giving to UJA and .33 for giving to other Jewish charities) and somewhat less for volunteer work in Jewish associations (R^2 =.24 for volunteering in Jewish associations). (The value of R^2 refers to the proportion of variance, out of a maximum of 100 percent, that the independent variables explain of the dependent variables, with the qualification for cross-sectional data, that any given equation is unlikely to explain more than half the variance.) In summary, the findings of table 9.4 show that

Table 9.4. Betas and R^2 of the Jewish charity contributions model, NJPS 1990

Dependent Variables	Demographic Variables				Socioeconomic Variables		
	Gender	Age	U.S. Gener	Life Cycle	Educ	Head Occup	Family Income
a. Gave to UJA	−.05	.21	−.04	.04	.03	−.01	.11
b. Gave to other Jewish charities	−.05	.18	.07	.02	.01	.03	.14
c. Volunteer worker in Jewish vol. assoc.	−.10	.04	.06	.04	.01*	.04	.04

Dependent Variables	Jewish Variables							
	Jewish Education	Denom	Syn Memb	Syn Attend	Home Religious Practice	Jewish Primary Groups	Israel Orient	R^2
a. Gave to UJA	.08	.10	.16	.09	.06	.16	.14	.31
b. Gave to other Jewish charities	.10	.07	.11	.12	.13	.12	.09	.33
c. Volunteer worker in Jewish vol. assoc.	.12	.02	.15	.20	.03	.08	.08	.24

Notes: An asterisk means beta category values are not monotonic. A minus sign means (a) the smaller the independent values, the larger the dependent value; or, (b) for gender, men have smaller or less traditional values than women.

The values in this table may be interpreted as follows: Values less than .10 mean that the given independent variable has little or no influence on one of the three dependent variables. Values of .10–.19 have a moderate effect, and values of .20 and larger have a strong impact.

giving to the UJA or other Jewish charities was associated with age, income, Jewish education, denomination, synagogue membership, synagogue attendance, involvement with Jewish primary groups, home religious practice, and being oriented toward Israel. Being active in Jewish voluntary associations was associated with being a woman, Jewish education, synagogue membership, and frequent synagogue attendance.

Table 9.5 focuses on giving to non-Jewish charities and doing volunteer work for general (not Jewish) community voluntary associations. Generation in United States was the only demographic variable to have even a moderate impact. The more generations in the United States, the more likely to give to charities that were not Jewish, indicating a degree of greater assimilation. In addition, education had a moderate impact on giving and general volunteer work. Family income, as would be expected, had a moderate impact on giving to non-Jewish charities. Denomination had a moderate impact on volunteer activity in general associations. Those without a denominational preference were the most likely to be active followed by those who preferred the Conservative and Reform denominations. The Orthodox were the least likely to volunteer their efforts for general community voluntary associations.

Synagogue membership, synagogue attendance, or home religious practices all had weak impacts on both dependent variables. Jewish primary group involvement had a moderate impact on volunteer work in general community associations. The impact, however, was a negative one: the less involvement in Jewish primary groups, the more volunteer work for general community associations. Being active in Jewish organizations and giving to Jewish charities had moderate impacts on giving to non-Jewish charities, while actually doing volunteer work for Jewish organizations had a moderate impact on volunteer work in general community associations.

Regression equations (explaining giving to non-Jewish charities and volunteer work in general associations) accounted for the least variance of the full set of five regressions (see tables 9.4 and 9.5). The regression equation for giving to non-Jewish charities shows that activity in Jewish community associations and giving to Jewish charities both had moderate impacts upon giving to non-Jewish charities. For this regression equation, the variance explained increases to .18 from the .13 of the other regression equation, which accounts for volunteer work as an area of philanthropic activity.

Just how good are the predictors obtained by these regression equations? The regression equation calculations in the tables show how well they predict those who actually did contribute or did volunteer work and those who did not. In table 9.6a and table 9.6b, the predictions correspond quite well to reality. For giving to the UJA, table 9.6a shows correct predictions of actual giving at 73 percent and not giving at 75 percent. For giving to other Jewish charities, table 9.6b shows actual giving 87 percent of the time and the lower 62 percent for those who did not give. In table 9.6c, however, the ability to predict volunteering to work in Jewish organizations falls apart. It certainly shows very well predicting the failure to volunteer, but only 36 percent of those who did volunteer were predicted to have done this.

Tables 9.6d and 9.6e show predicted giving to non-Jewish charities or volunteering to work for non-Jewish associations. Actual giving is predicted exceedingly well with 94 percent who actually gave; but not giving is correctly predicted in just 29 percent of the cases (see table 9.6d). Table 9.6e shows the prediction of volunteering to work. The regression equation fails to predict actual volunteering half of the time; however, it does predict not volunteering in 78 percent of the cases.

Overall then, prediction is good for giving to the UJA and other Jewish charities. It is excellent for giving to non-Jewish charities but fails to do a good job of predicting not giving for this variable. The "volunteering to work" equations, however, do not work well. Only *not* volunteering for the non-Jewish associations is predicted with a high degree of accuracy.

Table 9.5. Betas and R² the non-Jewish charity contributions model, NJPS 1990

Dependent Variables	Demographic Variables				Socioeconomic Variables		
	Gender	Age	U.S. Gen	Life Cycle	Educ	Head Occup	Family Income
a. Gave to non-Jewish charities	-.05	.08	-.10	.06	.16	.06	.12
b. Volunteer work in general assoc.	0	.05*	.08	.02	.15	.03*	.01

Dependent Variables	Jewish Variables										
	Jewish Education	Denom	Syn Memb	Syn Attend	Home Religious Practice	Jewish Primary Groups	Israel Orient	Jewish Org Activity	Jewish Vol Work	Give Jewish Charity	R²
a. Gave to non-Jewish charities	.03	-.07	-.02	.06*	-.07	-.03	.03*	.17	—	.14	.18
b. Volunteer work in general assoc.	.02	-.12	.02	.06*	-.02	-.17	.04*	.02	.16	—	.13

Notes: An asterisk means beta category values are not monotonic. A minus sign means (a) the smaller the independent values, the larger the dependent value; or (b) for gender, men have smaller or less traditional values than women.

The value in this table may be interpreted as follows: Values less than .10 mean that the given independent variable has little or no influence on one of the two dependent variables. Values of .10–.19 have a moderate effect, and values of .20 and larger have a strong impact.

Table 9.6a. Predictability of giving to UJA

	Predicted Giving	Predicted Not Giving
Actually gave	73%	27%
Actually did not give	25%	75%

Table 9.6b. Predictability of giving to other Jewish charities

	Predicted Giving	Predicted Not Giving
Actually gave	87%	13%
Actually did not give	38%	62%

Table 9.6c. Predictability of volunteering in Jewish associations

	Predicted Volunteering	Predicted Not Volunteering
Actually volunteered	36%	64%
Actually did not volunteer	7%	93%

Table 9.6d. Predictability of giving to non-Jewish charities

	Predicted Giving	Predicted Not Giving
Actually gave	94%	6%
Actually did not give	71%	29%

Table 9.6e. Predictability of volunteering in non-Jewish associations

	Predicted Volunteering	Predicted Not Volunteering
Actually volunteered	51%	49%
Actually did not volunteer	22%	78%

In conclusion, it can be stated that the statistical patterns show that giving to Jewish causes was associated with aging and family income. Then, involvement in the life of the organized Jewish community combined with synagogue membership, synagogue attendance, home religious practices, involvement in Jewish primary groups, and an orientation toward Israel all reinforce giving to Jewish charities (including the UJA).

More than assimilation (as measured by U.S. generation—i.e., the more generations in the United States, the less giving), variables like aging and family income, along with Jewish communal involvement through formal and informal networks, sustained giving to the UJA and other Jewish charities. Nevertheless, as the tables show, fewer factors predicted volunteer activity in Jewish associations. Being a woman, having more Jewish education, and participation in the synagogue (in terms of denominational preference and membership) were the dominating factors. Note again that synagogue membership and attendance counted favorably. Activity in Jewish organizations and giving to Jewish charities were both associated with giving to non-Jewish charities. Also, the factors of more generations in the United States, more education, and more family income played important roles.

Volunteering for work in non-Jewish organizations was associated with more education. It was also connected with volunteering for work in Jewish associations as well as being marginal to the organized Jewish community. For example, those who had no denominational preference or synagogue membership were the most likely to volunteer in non-Jewish organizations; those who considered themselves Orthodox were the least likely to do this particular kind of volunteering. Finally, those who were least involved with Jewish primary groups were more inclined to do such volunteering. In short, activity in the Jewish sector is also associated with activity in the non-Jewish sector. However, those who were less involved with the organized Jewish community were more likely to be involved with the non-Jewish sector.

Jewish Charitable Giving in Retrospect

What additional insights as to the relationship between religio-ethnic involvement and charitable contributions can be gained by going back in time to the National Jewish Population Survey of 1971? In trying to answer this question, we analyze and then compare this earlier survey to the 1990 survey in order to understand better the direction of change across time.

The frequent problem in dealing with two or more surveys is the difference in the wording of the survey questions. This problem emerges as the wording about who gave a contribution is different. For example, the wording in the 1990 survey was: "In 1989 did you and/or other members of your household together contribute or give gifts to . . . ?" The wording in the 1971 survey was: (1) "In 1969 did family head contribute to the Jewish . . . ?" (2) "In 1969, I contributed to the Jewish. . . ." In other words, in the 1990 survey, the questions pertained to the entire household, be it the head or the randomly selected Jewish respondent, or anyone else living there. In the 1971 survey, the questions pertained to the head of the family or the randomly selected Jewish respondent, not the entire household. (In the 2000–2001 NJPS, the data again applied to the households.)

In the 1990 survey, the randomly selected adult respondents' characteristics are joined to household contributions. In the analysis of the data from the 1971 survey, the randomly selected adult respondents have their characteristics joined to their own contributions, together with a limited number of household questions, such as occupation of family head and total family income. Tables 9.7 and 9.8 give the percentages of household heads and randomly selected respondents in 1969 who claimed to have given to the UJA, their local Jewish federations, or their local general community fund drives. Table 9.9 gives the percentage of respondents who claimed to have been active as volunteers in these fund drives.

In 1971, 45 percent of heads of family and 64 percent of respondents claimed to have contributed to the UJA. Also, 57 percent of heads and 48 percent of respondents claimed to have contributed to their local Jewish charities apart from the UJA. Also in 1971, 70 percent of heads of family and 63 percent of respondents claimed to have contributed to their local general (not Jewish) charity fund drive. Finally, just 13 percent of respondents claimed to have been volunteers in their Jewish or general fund campaigns (see table 9.9).

Table 9.10 introduces the model for contributions to the UJA in the 1971 survey. For the most part, the beta values are weak. However, generation in the United States had a negative association with giving to the UJA. As the number of generations in the United States increased, the percentage giving decreased, especially after the first two generations in the United States. Life cycle had a strong association with giving to the UJA. The

Table 9.7. Philanthropy of American Jewish family heads to various causes (NJPS 1971: "In 1969 did family head contribute to . . . ?")

A. The United Jewish Appeal (UJA)?

Yes	No	Don't Know/Refused
45%	37%	18%

B. Other Jewish Campaigns?

Yes	No	Don't Know/Refused
57%	22%	21%

C. The General (not Jewish) Central Community Campaign?

Yes	No	Don't Know/Refused
70%	12%	18%

Table 9.8. Philanthropy of American Jews to various causes (NJPS 1971: "In 1969, I contributed to. . . .")

A. The United Jewish Appeal (UJA).

Yes	No	Don't Know/Refused
64%	38%	8%

B. Other Jewish Campaigns.

Yes	No	Don't Know/Refused
48%	41%	11%

C. The General (not Jewish) Central Community Campaign.

Yes	No	Don't Know/Refused
63%	29%	8%

Table 9.9. Volunteering of American Jews to Jewish and non-Jewish organizations (NJPS 1971: "In 1969, I was active as a volunteer in. . . .")

A. A Jewish Fundraising Campaign.

Yes	No	Don't Know/Refused
13%	82%	5%

B. A General (not Jewish) Fundraising Campaign.

Yes	No	Don't Know/Refused
13%	81%	6%

denomination variable had a moderate association with giving to the UJA, with a drop in percentage among those who preferred the Reform denomination or who had no denominational preference. The more home religious practices or the more involvement in Jewish primary groups, the more individuals gave to the UJA. Finally, synagogue attendance displayed an inconsistent relationship to giving to UJA.

Table 9.11 presents the findings of general (not Jewish) giving. Number of U.S. generations had barely a moderate impact on giving. The lowest contribution was for the first generation; then contributions peaked in the second generation. After this, there was a small drop and a leveling off. Age and life cycle had considerable impacts. The

Table 9.10. Betas and R^2 of the Jewish charity contributions model, NJPS 1971

Dependent Variables	Demographic Variables					Socioeconomic Variables		
	Gender	Age	U.S. Gener	Life Cycle		Educ	Head Occup	Family Income
a. Gave to UJA	.03	.06	−.12	.20		.03	.06	.08

Dependent Variables	Jewish Variables							
	Jewish Education	Denom	Syn Memb	Syn Attend	Home Religious Practice	Jewish Primary Groups	Israel Orient	R^2
a. Gave to UJA	.04	.10	.02	.10	.14	.11	.04	.28

Table 9.11. Betas and R^2 of the Non-Jewish Charity Contributions Model, NJPS 1971

Dependent Variables	Demographic Variables					Socioeconomic Variables		
	Gender	Age	U.S. Gener	Life Cycle		Educ	Head Occup	Family Income
a. Gave to non-Jewish charities	.04	.18	.10	.20		−.05	.06	.14

Dependent Variables	Jewish Variables							
	Jewish Education	Denom	Syn Memb	Syn Attend	Home Religious Practice	Jewish Primary Groups	World Jewry & Israel	J. Org. Activ.	R^2
a. Gave to non-Jewish charities	.12*	.08*	−.02	.07	−.03	.01	.08*	.16	.18

oldest age group was more likely to have given, followed by the middle-age group, and the youngest the least likely to have given. As would be expected, the more income individuals had at their disposal, the more likely they were to give.

As to Jewish characteristics, both Jewish education and denominational preference had inconsistent connections with giving. Apart from Jewish organizational activity, the other Jewish factors, including the World Jewry–Israel orientation variable, had little impact, being both weak and inconsistent. Nevertheless, activity in Jewish organizations had a moderate, positive impact on giving to non-Jewish charities. The more such

Table 9.12a. Predictability of giving to UJA in 1969

	Predicted Giving	Predicted Not Giving
Actually gave	93%	7%
Actually did not give	50%	50%

Table 9.12b. Predictability of giving to general charities in 1969

	Predicted Giving	Predicted Not Giving
Actually gave	91%	9%
Actually did not give	54%	46%

Jewish activity, the more likely respondents were to have given. This connection of prior activity in Jewish philanthropy and subsequent contributions to non-Jewish charities was clearly documented by Alan York in 1979.[14]

How good is the predictability of these two models? Let us examine tables 9.12a for giving to the UJA and table 9.12b for giving to general charities. Clearly, both tables are quite similar. Practically every respondent who, in the 1971 model, was predicted to have given actually gave to the UJA and general charities. However, it is much more difficult to assess those 1971 respondents who did not give. For both groups, there is about a fifty-fifty split on not giving.

Contrasting Two NJPS Models

The period from 1971 to 1990 saw a considerable change in the characteristics of the American Jewish population. American Jewry underwent moderate increases in synagogue attendance and religious practices performed at home in those two decades.[15] At the same time, there was a strong decrease in involvement in Jewish primary groups and moderate decreases in Jewish and general voluntary association activities.

The contrast of the two models for contributions to the UJA in each of the two survey years shows a number of important changes. Between 1971 and 1990, both U.S. generations and family life cycle variables changed from influential variables to weak ones. Age, however, went from being a weak variable in 1971 to having a strong impact by 1990. The older respondents were more likely to have someone in their household who gave to the UJA. Also, the impact of family income showed some increase between the two surveys. In addition, synagogue membership increased from a weak to a moderate impact variable. Home religious practices went from a moderate impact variable to a weak one. Jewish primary group involvement strengthened its impact.

In regard to contributions to general charities, from 1971 to 1990, age dropped from being a moderate to a weak impact variable. Life cycle went from being a strong impact variable to a weak one. By 1990, education emerged as a moderate impact variable from having been a weak one in 1971. By 1990, the dominant independent variables were socioeconomic status, education, and family income, together with activity in Jewish voluntary associations. However, for giving to the UJA, Jewish communal involvement variables dominated. Higher income, associated with being older, followed this dominant pattern.

NJPS 2000–2001

In the previous two National Jewish Population Surveys, different strategies were followed. In the design of each study, the slightly varied wording of questions and carefully constructed sampling frames produced successively lower response rates from1971 to 1990. For example, the response rate in 1971 was 79 percent; in 1990, it was 50 percent. The latter survey relied on telephone interviews based on random-digit dialing (RDD) and the former utilized face-to-face interviews in a "multistage, clustered, stratified sample design."[16]

The most recent NJPS of 2000–2001 also relied on RDD but, for a variety of reasons, produced an even lower response rate of 28 percent to the screening interviews and only a 40 percent cooperation rate. The challenge of gathering data on a representative sample of American Jews is that they are a very small percentage of the American population, equaling approximately 1.8 to 2 percent in 2000.[17] That is about half of the proportion they were in the 1930s. In sum, Jews are a "rare population," and gathering data on Jewish people in the United States (absent a census question on religion) poses great challenges of time and money.

As noted earlier, philanthropic giving among American Jews is relatively generous compared to other religious groups, but it is by no means uniform. In his study of Jewish philanthropy, Cohen found a demographic shift in Boston, which suggested the possibility that certain birth cohorts were less likely to contribute.[18] Based on an analysis of NJPS 2000–2001, Cohen then examined the question of who gives and how much. He reported the following results:

> Jews living in the West are less likely to give to Federations than Jews residing in other regions of the country.
> The association between Jewish institutional affiliations and contributions is stronger for Federation giving than for giving to other Jewish and non-Jewish causes.
> People with higher household incomes give more of their charitable dollars to Federations than those with lower incomes.
> Those born after 1950, who are today middle-aged or younger, display a more significant drop-off in Federation giving than in contributions to other causes.[19]

The age gap in giving, particularly to Federations, may be the result of individuals being in different stages of the life cycle or the result of the year in which they were born ("cohort effect"). As Cohen noted, "Those born after 1950 did not change their giving patterns to resemble those born before 1950; this is consistent with birth cohort rather than a life cycle explanation."[20]

In sum, NJPS 2000–2001 found that the variables having the most pronounced effect on greater Federation giving were age (born before 1950), income, institutional affiliations, and region (with westerners less likely to give). Despite the methodological variations among the three NJPS panels, the findings are rather similar. Nevertheless, the earlier two studies also found that home religious practices, involvement in Jewish primary groups, and a positive orientation to Israel also increased Jewish charitable giving.

Regional differences were found in the earlier 1971 and 1990 NJPS studies. Lazerwitz reported that, in the 1971 survey, residents of Los Angeles and other larger Jewish communities, including Boston, ranked lower on Jewish identification than the residents of other Jewish communities.[21] Similarly, NJPS 1990 revealed that the largest segment of secular Jews (with no religion) was in the West (somewhat greater than in the Northeast, nearly twice as great as in the South, and nearly three times as in the Midwest).

In contrasting the three survey years with regard to giving to federations (or UJA), the latest NJPS of 2000–2001 found only 30 percent of households had contributed,[22] down from 45 percent in 1971 and 1990. In addition, giving to other Jewish causes had decreased to about two-fifths of the population (41 percent), down from about three-fifths in the earlier surveys (57 percent in 1971 and 63 percent in 1990). Finally, donating to a non-Jewish cause was also down to 62 percent in 2000–2001 compared to 70 percent in 1971 and 72 percent in 1990. While differences in question wording might account for some variation, it seems as though the demographic and sociological changes producing more assimilation among American Jews lessened their propensity to contribute to both Jewish and general causes, a trend most noticeable in the period since 1990.

These patterns of the general decline in Jewish giving to Jewish causes are most dramatically seen among high-end givers. Gary Tobin summarizes the situation as follows:

> At the highest end of giving, donations of $10 million or more, Jews are disproportionately represented, making 23 percent of all such gifts. Only 6 percent of Jewish mega-gifts go to Jewish institutions. The lion's share goes to colleges and arts and culture. . . . Approximately $8–10 billion annually is directed into Jewish institutions including . . . synagogues.[23]

The most recent review of charitable giving in the United States for 2010 found that five of the top six spots on the annual list of philanthropists were Jewish, but gifts to Jewish causes represented only a minor share of their overall contributions.[24]

Summary and Implications for Social Policy

In a recent article, Mark Ottoni-Wilhelm inquired as to "why Jewish families give more to organizations that help people in need."[25] The findings reported here respond to that research request. The two NJPS surveys of 1971 and 1990 provided comparable, quality data on the variables associated with giving to and activities in charitable funding. Overall, age, family income, Jewish education, denominational preference, synagogue membership and attendance, involvement in Jewish primary groups, home religious practices, and a positive orientation toward Israel formed the normative factors that increased both giving to and activity in Jewish charitable fund-raising. For many Jews, activity in Jewish fund-raising, in its turn, led to activity in non-Jewish (general community) fund-raising.

The most recent NJPS of 2000–2001 supported the earlier findings of increased Jewish charitable giving linked to age, income, institutional affiliations, and region of the country. Some of the Jewish normative factors were also associated with giving to and activities in non-Jewish charities. Overall, more education, family income, activity in Jewish community voluntary associations, and contributions to Jewish charities had moderate impacts on contributions to non-Jewish (general community) charities. A small group of Jews, though not involved with their organized Jewish communities, were propelled by education and family income to make contributions to general community fund-raising. Finally, the model of giving to non-Jewish charities only accounted for about half of the overall model variance compared to that of giving to Jewish causes.

In summarizing the current state of American Jewish philanthropy, Wertheimer offered a balance sheet of trends, with which most would likely agree. On the plus side, Wertheimer observed that American Jews were noted for the following:

1. Great wealth and generosity;
2. Slow decline in annual federated campaign [which is] offset by gifts to endowments and other philanthropic foundations;
3. Resilient strength of overseas Jewish donations but with more contributions going directly to the charity and not through an umbrella organization; and
4. An impressive amount of religious giving to synagogues, day schools, and religious camps, among others.

On the negative side, Wertheimer observed:

1. The shrinking base of Jewish donors, leading [fewer] people to do more;
2. The changing demographics of American Jewry leading to [fewer] givers; and
3. The growing sense of individualism, pulling people away from communal norms of giving.

Nevertheless, Wertheimer concluded that, since so much of contemporary philanthropy is devoted to improving the civic life of all rather than lessening the poverty of some, "there is reason to believe that for the foreseeable future, enough Jews will heed the call to participate in and enhance the quality of Jewish life—for themselves and for all Jews."[26]

As Plotinsky observed, Jewish philanthropic tradition has been nurtured and transmitted through holiday observances, life cycle events, and everyday life, and one answer to Jewish philanthropic "continuity" may be found in religious tradition. It also leads to two general observations. The first is that it is possible for a philanthropic tradition to be transmitted deliberately and systematically from generation to generation. The second is that, even in a culture in which there is an extensive body of narrative literature, philanthropic behavior is learned by doing.[27]

By now, it is clear that fund-raising successes are achieved by building upon local community networks. People will give more generously when approached through such networks. The key is to discover the strands of such networks and to employ sophisticated, socially sensitive methods of approaching people for funds. The research presented here (including the model for giving developed from this research) considerably overlaps with the published research of Paul Schervish and John Havens, which is also about the relationship between social participation and giving. These two researchers examined data from a 1992 survey on the topics of giving money and volunteering conducted by the Gallup organization. They found that community participation variables were closely related to participation in institutions and organizations that maintain formal channels for receiving charitable contributions.[28]

As Schervish and Havens noted, "To understand giving behavior in the total population, it turns out one should focus on understanding the community of participation, with special emphasis on the role of religious participation."[29] Their conclusions echo the current research findings that participation in the organized Jewish community is the key to Jewish giving and support our assertion on the "norm of social cohesion": The more people feel integrated into and identify with a particular community or subcommunity, the more likely they are to aid their members or causes whom they perceive as in need. Together, the findings of Schervish and Havens and those reported herein can readily be applied to both the American Jewish community and the entire American population.

Therefore, in order to expand the ability of the private sector to augment the role of government in relieving social problems, it is necessary to improve the involvement of people in their local community networks. Furthermore, it is likely that government policies that ensure a progressive fairness are more likely to engender broader citizen support. With regard to the general community of fund-raising, the retreat of government from its traditional responsibilities toward the less fortunate only exacerbates the situation. The most likely effective policies for alleviating social problems can come from a partnership of an engaged public sector of government institutions supported by a generous private sector of charitable organizations. Can the community afford to do less?

Notes

This essay is based on a paper delivered at the symposium "Family, Friend, Foe? The Relationship of Religion and Philanthropy in Religious Philanthropic Organizations, October 2010, at Indiana University–Purdue University Indianapolis (IUPUI) and is also adapted from pages 37–56 and 137–39 from our book, *Charitable Choices: Philanthropic Decisions of Donors in the American Jewish Community* (Lanham, Md.: Lexington Books, 2009), with permission of the publisher. Thanks are due to Lorri

Lafontaine for her technical assistance and to Casey Daraz for her research assistance, both at the Berman Institute–North American Jewish Data Bank at the Center for Judaic Studies and Contemporary Jewish Life at the University of Connecticut.

1. Marcel Mauss, *The Gift* (1925; repr., Glencoe, Ill.: Free Press, 1954).

2. The most recent figures reported showed a similar three-quarters of all charitable contributions coming from individuals (or $227 billion in 2009). See Holly Hall, "Americans Didn't Pull Back on Their Giving Last Year, Report Finds," *Chronicle of Philanthropy,* June 8, 2010.

3. Barry R. Chiswick, "An Economic Analysis of Philanthropy," in *Contemporary Jewish Philanthropy in America,* ed. Barry A. Kosmin and Paul Ritterband (Savage, Md.: Rowman and Littlefield, 1991), 3–15; Peter H. Reingen, "Inducing Compliance with a Donation Request," *Journal of Social Psychology* 106, no. 2 (1978): 281–82; Joseph Galaskiewicz, *Social Organization of an Urban Grants Economy* (Orlando, Fla.: Academic Press, 1985); Leonard Berkowitz and William H. Connor, "Success, Failure and Social Responsibility," *Journal of Personality and Social Psychology* 4 (1996): 664–69.

4. See North American Jewish Data Bank, 2010, "Mandell L. Berman Institute North American Jewish Data Bank," http://www.jewishdatabank.org.

5. Alvin Chenkin and the Council on Jewish Federations and Welfare Funds, *Demographic Highlights: Facts for Planning. National Jewish Population Survey, 1971,* National Jewish Population Survey, 1971 (New York: Council on Jewish Federations and Welfare Funds [producer]; Storrs, Conn.: North American Jewish Data Bank [distributor], 1972); North American Jewish Data Bank, *Highlights of the CJF 1990 National Jewish Population Survey* (New York: Graduate School and University Center, City University of New York [producer]; Storrs, Conn.: North American Jewish Data Bank [distributor], 1991); United Jewish Communities, *National Jewish Population Survey, 2000–01: Strength, Challenge and Diversity in the American Jewish Population* (New York: United Jewish Communities [producer], Storrs, Conn.: North American Jewish Data Bank [distributor], 2003).

6. See Dashefsky and Lazerwitz, *Charitable Choices,* chap. 7.

7. JFNA is the umbrella organization for the Jewish Federations of North America (created in 2009 as a successor to the United Jewish Communities, founded in 1999). The latter was a merger of the United Jewish Appeal (founded in 1939 in the wake of Nazi attacks on Jews to help vulnerable co-religionists around the world) and the Council of Jewish Federations of North America (founded in 1932 to provide services to the local Jewish Federations of North America), along with the United Israel Appeal (founded in 1925 to distribute funds raised by local UJA/Federation campaigns) to support Jewish causes in mandatory Palestine and, beginning in 1948, in Israel. According to its website,

> The Jewish Federations of North America represents 157 Jewish Federations and over 300 Network communities, which raise and distribute more than $3 billion annually for social welfare, social services and educational needs. The Federation movement, collectively among the top 10 charities on the continent, protects and enhances the well-being of Jews worldwide through the values of tikkun olam (repairing the world), tzedakah (charity and social justice) and Torah (Jewish learning).

See http://www.jewishfederations.org/section.aspx?id=31.

8. AAFRC Trust for Philanthropy, *Giving USA 2002* (Indianapolis: Indiana University Center on Philanthropy, 2002).

9. As noted in Dashefsky and Lazerwitz, *Charitable Choices,* chap. 2.

10. For an analysis of giving and volunteering as alternative forms of "civic engagement," see Keely S. Jones, "Giving and Volunteering as Distinct Forms of Civic Engagement: The Role of Community Integration and Personal Resources in Formal Helping," *Nonprofit and Voluntary Sector Quarterly* 35, no. 2 (2006): 249–66.

11. Jack Wertheimer, "Current Trends in American Jewish Philanthropy," *American Jewish Year Book* 97 (New York: American Jewish Committee, 1997), 3–92; Steven M. Cohen, "Trends in Jewish Philanthropy," *American Jewish Year Book* 80 (New York: American Jewish Committee, 1980), 29–51.

12. For an elaboration of this statistical technique, see Frank Andrews, James Morgan, and John Sonquist, *Multiple Classification Analysis* (Ann Arbor: Institute for Social Research, University of Michigan, 1969); Hubert Blalock, *Theory Construction: From Verbal to Mathematical Formulation* (Englewood Cliffs, N.J.: Prentice-Hall, 1969); John Sonquist, Elizabeth Baker, and James Morgan, *Searching for Structure (Alias AID III)* (Ann Arbor: Institute for Social Research, University of Michigan, 1971); Frank Andrews and Robert Messenger, *Multivariate Nominal Scale Analysis* (Ann Arbor: Institute for Social Research, University of Michigan, 1973); Hubert Blaylock, *Social Statistics*, 2nd rev. ed. (New York: McGraw-Hill, 1979); and Frank Andrews, *Multivariate Nominal Scale Analysis* (Ann Arbor: Institute for Social Research, University of Michigan, 1986).

13. Bernard J. Lazerwitz, Alan Winter, Arnold Dashefsky, and Ephraim Tabory, *Jewish Choices* (Albany, N.Y.: SUNY Press, 1998).

14. Alan York, "Voluntary Associations and Communal Leadership among the Jews of the United States" (PhD diss., Bar-Ilan University, Ramat-Gan, Israel, 1979).

15. As reported by Lazerwitz et al., *Jewish Choices*, 72, Table 4–3.

16. Ibid., 178.

17. See Ira Sheskin and Arnold Dashefsky, "Jewish Population in the United States, 2010," *Current Jewish Population Reports*, no. 1, http://www.jewishdatabank.org.

18. Cohen, "Trends in Jewish Philanthropy."

19. Steven M. Cohen, *Philanthropic Giving among American Jews: Contributions to Federations Jewish and Non-Jewish Causes*, Report 4 (New York: United Jewish Communities, 2004), 1.

20. Ibid., 8.

21. Bernard Lazerwitz, "The Community Variable in Jewish Identification," *Journal for the Scientific Study of Religion* 16 (December 1977): 361–69.

22. United Jewish Communities, *National Jewish Population Survey, 2000–01*, 13.

23. Gary A. Tobin, "Jewish or Non-Jewish Philanthropy: How about Both?" *United Synagogue Review* 57, no. 1 (2004): 31; see also Gary A. Tobin, Jeffrey R. Solomon, and Alexander C. Karp, *Mega-Gifts in American Philanthropy: General and Jewish Giving Patterns between 1995–2000* (San Francisco: Institute for Jewish and Community Research, 2003).

24. Jacob Berkman, "Jews Take 5 of Top 6 Spots in Annual List of Top U.S. Givers," http://jta.org/news/article/2011/02/08/2742903/jews-show-well-on-annual-list-of-top-givers.

25. Mark Ottoni-Wilhelm, "Giving to Organizations that Help People in Need: Differences across Denominational Identities," *Journal for the Scientific Study of Religion* 49, no. 3 (2010): 389–412.

26. Wertheimer, "Current Trends in American Jewish Philanthropy," 81, 81–82, 83.

27. Anita H. Plotinsky, "From Generation to Generation: Transmitting the Jewish Philanthropic Tradition," *New Directions for Philanthropic Fundraising*, 7 (Spring 1995): 129.

28. Paul G. Schervish and John J. Havens, "Social Participation and Charitable Giving: A Multivariate Analysis," *Voluntas* 8, no. 3 (1997): 252.

29. Ibid., 256.

10 Myth vs. Reality

Muslim American Philanthropy since 9/11

Shariq A. Siddiqui

T HERE ARE DEFINING moments in our lives. I remember my parents describing the moment they first heard that John F. Kennedy was assassinated and when my professors talked about the moment Martin Luther King, Jr., or Robert Kennedy was killed. I was amazed by their memory and used to be thankful that such an event had not occurred in my generation's lifetime. That changed on September 11, 2001.

As I watched the horrific images on television, praying that the perpetrators were not Muslims, I knew that this moment was significant, but I did not realize that it would be a defining moment for Muslim Americans. The lives of Muslim Americans were changed in profound ways on that day. Many have argued that the events that followed due to the tragedy of 9/11 have had a negative effect on Muslim Americans and especially their philanthropic activity. In order to understand the impact on Muslim American philanthropy after September 11, 2001, it is important first to understand Islamic philanthropy, learn about Muslim American history, and explore who Muslim Americans are before looking into their philanthropic activities.

Overview of Islam and Philanthropy

There are two primary sources of Islamic law—the Quran and the Sunnah. The Quran is the holy book of Islam that Muslims believe is the direct word of God revealed to the Prophet Muhammad through the Angel Gabriel. The Sunnah is known as the traditions of the Prophet Muhammad. The Sunnah is preserved through narrations of the companions of Muhammad through very strict guidelines. Philanthropy is a central feature of the Islamic faith and is considered one of the five pillars of Islam. Both primary sources of Islam prominently feature examples that promote philanthropy.

There are three forms of Islamic philanthropy: *zakat, sadaqah,* and *waqf.* Some scholars question whether *zakat* is a philanthropic instrument because they understand philanthropy to be a voluntary action for the public good, as Robert Payton defines it.[1] Indeed, as one of the five pillars of Islam, *zakat* is not voluntary for Muslims, who are required to pay 2.5 percent of their surplus income and assets toward specific causes. *Zakat* can be used to assist the poor and needy, to support employees of *zakat* administration, to spread Islam, to free slaves, to free people of debt, and to help travelers. Historically, the state has collected and distributed these funds. The nonpayment of *zakat* has sometimes been considered a crime against the state. The "Apostates War" during the time of Caliph Abu Bakr al-Siddiq was not motivated by the rebels' conversion away from Islam but by their refusal to pay *zakat*. Therefore, *zakat* would seem to be closer to taxation than philanthropy. *Zakat* may not fall within the definition of philanthropy as stated above, but Muslim scholars and others do consider it to be the primary tool of charity.[2] While in the past Muslims may have been held accountable for their nonpayment of *zakat*, scholars note that most Muslims today do not pay *zakat* through the government and, in fact, use it to further their charitable interests.[3]

The second form of philanthropy in Islam is *sadaqah*, which is understood to be voluntary charitable giving as compared to the obligatory *zakat*. Muslims do not consider failing to give *sadaqah* a sin, but they are promised divine rewards if they engage in this voluntary practice. There are no limitations on *sadaqah*, and it is presumed that most non-*zakat* charity by Muslims falls within this category.

The third institutionalized form of philanthropy is the *waqf* or endowment. The *waqf* originates from a *haddith* about Umar ibn al-Khattab, who acquired a property and asked the Prophet whether he should donate it to charity. The Prophet replied, "Encumber the thing itself and devote its fruits to pious purposes."[4] Umar instructed that the property could not be sold and its income was to be donated for specific charitable purposes. Thus, a *waqf* is a form of charity that is designed to give long after the initial act of donation takes place.

Philanthropy is encouraged in Islam as an important part of living. Promoting the benefits of charity is illustrated in the Sunnah of the Prophet. A man sought to give charity. The first day, he accidentally gave charity to a man who was a thief. When he found out that he had given charity to a thief, he decided to give charity again to get the blessings of God. This time, he accidentally gave charity to a prostitute. When he found out that the woman was a prostitute, he was devastated and sought to correct the deed by giving charity again. This time, he accidentally gave charity to a rich undeserving man. When he discovered his mistake, he went to the Prophet in despair. He was told that his charity was still important as the charity he gave to the thief might prevent him from stealing and the prostitute from selling her body, while teaching the rich man to give charity himself.

The following injunctions in the Quran also stress the importance of charity. "Allah tells us that 'Those who spend in charity their properties by night and by day, in secret and in public, have their reward with their Lord; on them shall be no fear, nor shall they grieve'" (Quran 2:274). "And spend in the way of Allah and cast not yourselves to destruction, with your own hands, but do good; for Allah surely loveth those who do good" (Quran 2:195). "The parable of those who spend their funds in the way of Allah is that of a grain: it groweth seven ears and each ear hath a hundred grains" (Quran 2:261). "Behold, ye are those invited to spend in the way of Allah: but amongst you are some that are niggardly. But any who are niggardly are so at the expense of their own souls" (Quran 47:38). The blessings from philanthropy do not end but in fact have a multiplying effect if done with the right motivation.

Islam prefers the generous over the miserly. "The generous is close to God, close to paradise, close to people and far from hell; and the miserly is far from God, far from paradise, far from people and close to hell. Indeed, an ignorant but generous [person] is dearer to God than a scholar who is miserly" (Sunnah). Islam repeatedly talks about giving away surplus wealth. "And they ask thee what to spend; say: the surplus (that you can spare). Thus doth Allah make clear to you His signs, in order that ye may reflect" (Quran 2:219). Thus, Islam promotes neither the extreme of stinginess nor giving in such extravagance that it becomes excessive. The Prophet says, "The upper hand in charity is better than the lower hand: begin with your dependents; the best of charity is that which is given after one is satisfied." Islam suggests that the best form of giving is the kind that is given at the right time for the right reason for the right cause. The Prophet echoes this when he states, "There is no envy except in two things: a person whom Allah has given wealth and he spends it, all, in the proper way, and a person whom Allah has given wisdom and he uses it in judgment and teaches it" (Sunnah).

Islam has specific suggestions on how one can give charity to obtain approval from God. "If ye disclose acts of charity it is well but if ye hide them and give them to the poor that is best for you, and will remove from you some of your stains of evil. And Allah is well acquainted with what ye do" (Quran 2:271). God knows our intent and gives us credit for good intent. If the motivation behind giving is glory or material gain, it defeats the spiritual purpose of the gift. Furthermore, while it is permissible to give publicly, it is preferable to give anonymously. What is vital is the motivation behind the gift. A gift certainly benefits the cause receiving the charity, but it is better to make gifts with the motivation to please God. "O ye who believe! Cancel not your charity by reminders of your generosity or by injury like those who spend their funds to be seen by people but believe neither in Allah nor in the last day. They are in Parable like a hard barren rock on which is a little soil; on it falls heavy rain which leaves it just a bare stone. They will be able to do nothing with what they have earned. And Allah guideth not those who reject faith" (Quran 2:264).

While one's charity may benefit another if given for the wrong reason, it will not benefit the giver. This is not to discourage giving but to help develop a charitable human being. To love God truly requires understanding God's message and instilling virtues like selfless giving. The reward one should seek from one's giving is not the advantages that may result in this world but what one may attain in the hereafter. This does not mean that if one benefits from one's charity in this world it is not considered by God. God simply requires that the motivation to give not be the rewards that one receives in this world.

Another example of charity is in a story narrated by the Prophet. A man walking on a deserted road felt very thirsty. On his way he found a well and climbed down and quenched his thirst. When he climbed back up he found a dog that was breathing hard due to thirst. The man climbed down and brought the dog some water for its thirst. The Prophet states that even this is considered philanthropic in the eyes of

God. Philanthropy in Islam is about making the world a better place. This can be done through giving or generous deeds.

The perception of philanthropy today is very different from its historic roots. Philanthropy is understood now in terms of money and volunteerism. Classical Islamic definitions of philanthropy, however, are more expansive than the modern definition. "But forgive them, and overlook their misdeeds: for Allah loveth those who are kind" (Quran 5:13). To forgive others for their misdeeds is considered a charitable or philanthropic act in Islam. God does not limit one's charity to the amount one can give. This would limit the spiritual benefits of philanthropy to those who could afford to give.

The Prophet states, "Every Muslim has to give for charity. They asked, O Prophet of Allah, How about one who has nothing to give? He said, He should work with his hands and benefit himself and also give in charity. They said: If one cannot do even that? He replied: He should help one who is eager to have help. They said: And if he couldn't do that? He answered: Then he should do good action and abstain from evil, this is a charity for him" (Sunnah). Thus, all Muslims can participate in the benefits of philanthropy. Those who can afford can give of their wealth; those who have nothing and those who can give nothing can give charity by refraining from doing evil deeds.

Philanthropy in Islam is not just about the benefits that society gets from charity but the development of a compassionate, caring, engaged human being. Just as important as the giving is the effect that giving has on the donor. While theologically even voluntary inaction may be deemed as an act of charity, Muslims today see charity in terms of donations and volunteerism. It is important that we look next at the nature of philanthropy among Muslim Americans.

Muslims in America

There are an estimated 2 to 6 million Muslim Americans in the United States according to major Muslim American organizations and various academic studies. The number of Muslim Americans has been a focus of many academic studies but has been very difficult to determine as the U.S. Census does not collect information about religious affiliation and because of Muslims' ethnic diversity. The Pew Research Center estimated in 2007 that there were 2.35 million Muslims in the United States.[5] It is estimated that more than 65 percent are immigrants. The largest ethnic group of Muslim Americans is African American. Of the 65 percent foreign born, nearly a third are from the Arab world, a third from South Asia, and the remainder from across the Muslim world. Of the 35 percent native-born Muslims in the United States, nearly 60 percent are African American while the remainder is a mix of other ethnicities. Only 21 percent of Muslims in the United States have converted to Islam. The study shows that, while Muslims are new to the United States, they are highly assimilated and try to adapt and become a part of their new country. Nearly 53 percent of Muslim American's believe that it has become more difficult to be a Muslim since September 11, 2001. The study suggests that most Muslim Americans believe that the government has "singled out" Muslim Americans for increased surveillance and monitoring.[6] The study also shows that 73 percent of Muslim Americans state that they have never faced discrimination. Finally, only 13 percent of African American Muslims feel satisfied with national conditions compared to 45 percent of immigrants.

While the number of Muslim Americans has been in dispute, most studies state that there are more than 1,200 mosques and 200 full-time Islamic schools in the United States.[7] This has become the standard number quoted by most scholars, yet it should be noted that, in 1998, the *Tablighi Jamaat,* after going from city to city, released a directory of more than 3,000 mosques that they had visited.[8] It is very possible that, as the project took a few years, mosque addresses changed and what they were really identifying were prayer areas rather than full-fledged mosques or Islamic centers. Furthermore, the number of full-time Islamic schools is generally considered to be larger. The encyclopedia *Philanthropy in America* puts the number at 300.[9] The Islamic Schools League of America conducted a survey that found 235 full-time Islamic schools in America.[10]

The Pew Research Center reported in 2007 that 54 percent of Muslims in America were male while 46 percent were female; 56 percent were between the ages of 18 and 39, while only 13 percent were 55 or older. Among Muslim Americans, 42 percent reported that their financial situation was excellent, and 41 percent reported that they were homeowners; 16 percent reported incomes more than $100,000, 10 percent between $75,000 and $99,999, 15 percent reported between $50,000 and $74,999, and 24 percent reported between $30,000 and $49,999. Among them, 24 percent reported that they were self-employed or small business owners. Regarding Muslim households, 84 percent had multiple people living in them, and 59 percent had children living in them.[11] According a Zogby poll, 58 percent of the Muslims in America were college graduates, and an additional 24 percent had some college. Seventy-nine percent reported that their faith was very important while 17 percent reported that it was somewhat important; 31 percent reported that they attended mosque more than once a week, 24 percent attended the weekly congregational Friday (*jumaah*) prayers, 10 percent attended mosque once or twice a month, and 14 percent attended a few times a year, especially for Eid prayers.[12]

American Muslim Philanthropy since 9/11/2001

These studies include the kinds of philanthropic activities that Muslims in America have been involved in since September 11, 2001. The American Muslim Poll by the Zogby organization asked if Muslims were involved in various kinds of civic engagement. The poll defined "involved" as having donated time or money or having served as an officer of an organization. In the poll, 77 percent reported being involved with an organization to help the poor, sick, elderly, or homeless; 71 percent with a mosque or religious organization; 69 percent with a school or youth program; 46 percent in a professional organization; 45 percent with a neighborhood, civic, or community group; 42 percent in an arts or cultural group; 36 percent with an ethnic group; 33 percent with a Muslim political or public affairs committee; 24 percent with a veteran or military service organization; and 17 percent with a trade or labor union.[13]

Surprisingly, at a time when Muslim Americans had an increased fear of hate crimes, discrimination concerns about civil liberties, and being "singled out" as Muslim, the highest philanthropic priority was the poor, sick, elderly, and homeless. One would have assumed that civil rights, political, and advocacy organizations would have been at the top of the list. These organizations, however, fell toward the bottom of Muslim American priorities. The same Zogby survey showed that 96 percent believed that they should donate to non-Muslim social service organizations; 96 percent believed that they should be involved with American civic and community development organizations; 93 percent believed that they should be involved in the American political process; and 88 percent believed that they should support interfaith activities.[14] Despite feeling under pressure and being "singled out" since 9/11, Muslim Americans have heightened their participation in mainstream civic institutions.

In the 2007 Pew Study, 76 percent of Muslim Americans reported that giving charity or *zakat* was very important, while 14 percent stated that it was somewhat important, and only 8 percent stated that it was not too important or not at all important. When ranking the five major religious practices, *zakat* was second only to fasting and came ahead of a pilgrimage to Mecca, reading the Quran daily, and daily prayer. It was ranked first when answers of "very important" and "somewhat important" are combined.[15]

Mosques are also important parts of philanthropy among American Muslims. Eighty-four percent of mosques were reported in 2001 to give cash assistance to families or individuals; 74 percent provided counseling services; 60 percent had prison or jail programs; 55 percent had a food pantry or soup kitchen or collected food for the poor; 53 percent had a thrift store or collected clothes for the poor; 28 percent had a tutoring or literacy program; 18 percent had an antidrug or anticrime program; 16 percent had a day care or preschool program; and 12 percent had a substance abuse program.[16]

An analysis of mosques in America also provides us with an important aspect of immigrant Muslim American giving.[17] The Mosque Study Project (2001) looked at funding levels of mosques in America. The study reported that 16 percent of mosques reported incomes of less than $10,000; 15 percent between $10,000 and $19,999; 18 percent between $20,000 and $39,999; 11 percent between $40,000 and $59,999; 11 percent between $60,000 and $99,999; 24 percent more than $100,000; and only 5 percent reported incomes of $0. This suggests that, while Islamic centers have some funding, they are not the central conduit of Muslim American philanthropy. Most Islamic centers do not have a budget large enough to sustain paid staff and clergy and, therefore, are largely volunteer driven.

When we couple these numbers with the location of the mosques, however, we find some interesting results. Generally, immigrant Muslim American mosques were situated in the suburbs while indigenous Muslim American mosques were located in the city. Of mosques with budgets of more than $100,000, only 20 percent were inner-city mosques while 43 percent were identified as suburban mosques. Inner-city mosque incomes generally represented larger proportions of the mosques reporting under $39,999, and suburban mosques represented larger proportions of the $100,000 or more category. Muslim American philanthropy, while motivated through faith, is not delivered through its faith-based institutions.

Effects of Government Raids after 9/11 on Muslim American Philanthropy

Government raids on Muslim American organizations in the aftermath of 9/11 has created controversy within the Muslim American community. The narrative promoted within the Muslim American community and by civil rights advocacy groups is that these raids have had a chilling effect on Muslim American philanthropy. The government seizure of charitable funds creates two concerns among donors. First, there is a fear of guilt by association—donors are concerned about being investigated or scrutinized by the government if their names are found in the database of a suspected charity. Second, the philanthropic purpose of the gift will not be achieved because funds will either be seized by the government or (as in the case of the Holyland Foundation money) depleted in the legal defense of the officeholders of the organization. In fact, a common question of Muslim Americans is whether their *zakat* obligation is fulfilled if the funds they donated never reach the recipient due to government action.

Many Muslim Americans are concerned that their donation to a charity will "come back to haunt them."[18] A report in the *Los Angeles Daily News* (October 30, 2004) stated that Muslims are afraid and confused and shying away from philanthropy.[19] People simply do not want to give money only to find out later that it was misused for financing terrorism. *News Hour with Jim Lehrer* (September 12, 2004) reported that Muslim Americans are afraid of giving checks because they do not want to come under government scrutiny. Concern is such that, beginning in 2003, assistant secretary of treasury Juan Zarate started meeting with Islamic charities through the auspices of the Islamic Society of North America. In 2008, at the World Congress of Muslim Philanthropists, as U.S. State Department and USAID officials listened, the executive director of the Council on American Islamic Relations stated that the civil liberty violations and scrutiny of Muslim Americans had had a chilling effect on Muslim American philanthropy.

Lack of research makes it difficult to argue for or against the narrative stated above. While no comprehensive data exist, there is sufficient partial data to help us examine this claim. An analysis of fourteen of the largest Muslim American relief agencies' 990 tax forms shows that charitable giving to these organizations rose from a little more than $29 million in 2002 to more than $96 million in 2008.[20] Similar analyses of organizations like the Islamic Society of North America, Council of American Islamic Relations, Muslim Public Affairs Council, along with other national and regional organizations suggest an increased level of funding. The relief agency numbers are particularly important as the organizations that have been under government scrutiny (Holyland Foundation,

Global Relief, Islamic American Relief Agency, and Al-Haramain Islamic Foundation) are all relief organizations. Therefore, one would expect that the organizations that would be affected the most would be relief organizations. As we have seen from the Form 990 analysis, however, the opposite is true. Relief organizations have increased their revenue through donations by 230 percent over a six-year period.[21] Furthermore, when factoring in the in-kind donations of the largest Muslim American charity, Islamic Relief (USA), donations actually went up more than 600 percent.[22]

Similarly, a 2006 study of Pakistani Americans by Adil Najam shows that philanthropy and civic engagement increased after September 11, 2001.[23] In fact, most anecdotal self-analysis of Muslim Americans is that "the community has awakened and become active after 9/11." It is clear, however, that the fear of government reprisals and misuse of funds is a concern to them. Najam found, through focus groups, that the perception about the decline in philanthropy existed among Pakistani Americans. Yet, when he interviewed participants, he found that their own giving levels had actually increased since 9/11.[24] Therefore, the perception about a decline in Muslim American philanthropy prevailed even among Muslim Americans who themselves had increased their giving levels.

Najam found that people became vigilant after 9/11 about charities, but they did not reduce their giving. Muslim American charities have responded to government scrutiny and donor concern by taking steps to create greater transparency and stronger financial controls. Examples of this are the increase in Muslim American charities seeking four-star Charity Navigator status and accredited charity status with the Better Business Bureau. Founded in 2001, Charity Navigator has become the nation's largest and most-utilized evaluator of charities. To help donors, their team of professional analysts has examined tens of thousands of nonprofit financial documents. As a result, they know much about the true fiscal operations of charities and use this knowledge to develop an unbiased, objective, numbers-based rating system to assess the financial health of more than five thousand of America's best-known charities.

Specifically, Charity Navigator's rating system examines two broad areas of a charity's financial health—how responsibly it functions day to day as well as how well positioned it is to sustain its programs over time. Each charity is then awarded an overall rating, ranging from zero to four stars. To help donors avoid becoming victims of mailing-list appeals, each charity's commitment to keeping donors' personal information confidential is assessed. The site is easily navigable by charity name, location, or type of activity and also features opinion pieces by Charity Navigator experts, donation tips, and top-ten and bottom-ten lists that rank efficient and inefficient organizations in a number of categories. Charity Navigator accepts no funding from the charities that it evaluates. Furthermore, it does not charge users for its data to help America's philanthropists of all levels make informed giving decisions. Charity Navigator is a nonprofit 501(c)(3) organization that depends on support from individuals, corporations, and foundations.

Muslim American charitable organizations proudly display their Charity Navigator status to encourage charitable giving. Furthermore, these charities seek external sources to reaffirm their good stewardship. For example, Islamic Relief USA includes its Charity Navigator status as well as its income and expense breakdown on the homepage of its website. Its homepage includes a press release entitled "Islamic Relief USA Ranks in Philanthropy 400 List." Also included in its website and annual report is a statement from Charity Navigator. "Only 2 percent of the charities we rate have received at least seven consecutive 4-star evaluations," Charity Navigator's president, Ken Berger, wrote in a 2010 letter. "This 'exceptional' designation from Charity Navigator differentiates Islamic Relief USA from its peers and demonstrates to the public it is worthy of their trust."

Muslim American charities realize that, in order to continue their work, they must employ more sophisticated methods of reassuring their donor base. Most Muslim American relief organizations and a growing number of Muslim American nonprofits are having their financial statements audited by an independent accounting firm. In fact, many more would like to achieve this goal but are impeded by inadequate funding.

The emergence of groups like the Muslim Advocates is another result of the national state of fear related to Muslim American charities. The Muslim Advocates is a 501(c)(3) organization established in 2005 by the National Association of Muslim Lawyers. The Muslim Advocates focus on civil rights, donor advising, and charity accreditation. The organization has specifically launched the Muslim Charities Accreditation Program in partnership with the Better Business Bureau's Wise Giving Alliance.[25] The Muslim Advocates provide technical legal assistance to Muslim American charities that then move on to receive accreditation through the Wise Giving Alliance. Since 2008, only three Muslim American charities have sought this certification. None of the three charities is a relief agency, the type most subjected to government and donor scrutiny. The Muslim Advocates' donor advising program provides literature and technical assistance in making strong philanthropic choices. Their assistance includes best practices, a guide to international giving, and other informational tools.

Another step taken by many Muslim American nonprofits after 9/11 was voluntarily to submit 990 forms to the IRS. An analysis of GuideStar shows a sudden increase of Muslim American nonprofits that have 990 data available after 2001.[26] What is striking is the growing number of charities that are exempt by the IRS from submitting 990s but continue to do so.

Our analysis of major Muslim American charities suggests that the Muslim American nonprofit sector did not see a decline in funds after September 11, 2001. Further, the number of Muslim American charities has actually increased since then. Muslim Americans realized it was vital to become more involved in American society and that they needed to be ambassadors of their faith. Muslim Americans established a diverse number of nonprofits dealing with different issues, and the focus of these new nonprofits is both international and domestic.

There is evidence that the method of payment for Muslim American philanthropy has changed. For example, at meetings of the Islamic Society of North America in 2003 and 2004 in Chicago, Muslim American charities reported that the number of people not wanting receipts for their donations or not wanting to pay by check to prevent their identification as a donor had increased. In a town hall meeting with members of the Indiana branch of the FBI, organized by the Muslim Alliance of Indiana (MAI) in 2005, individual donors expressed fear of being targeted by virtue of giving to Muslim American charities. While these donors remain a very small number among the larger Muslim American donor population, it is significant to note that there is still a growing number of Muslim Americans who are willing to forego the benefits of tax deduction, gaining credit card points, and recognition by making donations in the form of cash. The fear of being on the donor list of another seized charity continues to concern Muslim American donors, and a small but growing minority goes to the extreme of forgoing the "tangible" benefits of their philanthropy.

It is unfortunate that the national narrative among Muslim American advocates since 9/11 has focused on the decline of the Muslim American nonprofit sector. While this narrative has resulted in stronger and more transparent charities and in donors becoming more vigilant, it has also created a state of fear. It is also unfortunate that the narrative focused on formal philanthropy. It is clear that Muslim Americans were concerned about terrorism and government scrutiny of Islamic charities. Advocacy organizations echoed that concern to both the government and the Muslim community. The result was greater effort by the U.S. government to alleviate the concerns of the Muslim community through increased dialogue and the establishment by Islamic charities of best practices that earned them accolades from the Charity Navigator. While there was benefit to voicing concern, it distracted attention from the private remittances of the majority of Muslim Americans who have an immigrant background. The government raids after September 11, 2001, primarily affected Muslim American relief nonprofits that had international programs.

Analysis of different studies of immigrant communities in the United States suggests that immigrant giving can be divided into the following: development of national nonprofit organizations focused on the immigrant group, development of local nonprofit organizations that focus on the immigrant group, assistance of nonprofit organizations that focus on assistance to the countries from which the immigrant comes, and, finally, private remittances back to the country of origin.[27] While we have been able to develop formalized information about the first three, there is very little immigrant group-specific information about private remittances.

Government scrutiny of *hawala* money transfers (an informal system for transferring funds from one location to another through service providers) during its search for terrorist networks was also a concern for Muslim Americans who used such networks to send money to family and friends in their countries of origin. Private remittances never became part of the broader charitable debate because most people do not view those remittances as a charitable gift. The money is generally sent back to the home country to help relatives or members of their village. Scholars of diaspora giving, the World Bank, and foreign aid have increasingly, however, seen these private remittances as a form of philanthropy.

In fact, private remittances are seen as a vital aspect of foreign aid to the developing world. Studies by the World Bank and UN suggest that they are important elements of poverty reduction and community development, and have an important economic growth element due to the spending power it provides the local community. In order to fully understand Muslim American philanthropy since 9/11, a study of such remittances is needed to help form a complete picture of the philanthropic activity among Muslim Americans.

Notes

1. Robert L. Payton, *Philanthropy: Voluntary Action for the Public Good* (New York: American Council on Education/Macmillan, 1988).

2. Ilyas Ba-Yunus and Kassim Kone, *Muslims in the United States* (Westport, Conn.: Greenwood Press, 2006), 15.

3. Robert D. McChesney, *Charity and Philanthropy in Islam: Institutionalizing the Call to Do Good* (Indianapolis: Indiana University Center on Philanthropy, 1995), 7.

4. Quote in ibid., 8.

5. Pew Research Center, *Muslim Americans: Middle Class and Mostly Mainstream* (Washington, D.C.: Pew Research Center, 2007).

6. Ibid.

7. Ihsan Bagby, Paul M. Perl, and Bryan T. Froehle, *The Mosque in America: A National Portrait,* report from the Mosque Study Project (Washington, D.C.: Council on American-Islamic Relations, 2001).

8. Interview with Dr. Sayyid M. Syeed, director of the Islamic Society of North America (ISNA) National Office, Washington, D.C.

9. Dwight Burlingame, *Philanthropy in America: A Comprehensive Historical Encyclopedia* (Santa Barbara, Calif.: ABC-CLIO, 2004).

10. Karen Keyworth, "Fast Facts about Full Time Islamic Schools in the United States," http://www.theisla.org/filemgmt_data/admin_files/Fast%20Facts%20About%20Islamic%20Schools%20in%20the%20US.pdf.

11. Pew Research Center, *Muslim Americans.*

12. *American Muslim Poll* (Zogby, 2001, 2004).

13. Ibid.

14. Ibid.

15. Pew Research Center, *Muslim Americans.*

16. Bagby, Perl, and Froehle, *The Mosque in America.*

17. Ibid.

18. Adil Najam, *Portrait of a Giving Community: Philanthropy by the Pakistani-American Diaspora* (Cambridge: Harvard University Press, 2006), 13.

19. Ibid., 14.

20. All four of the Muslim American charities closed by the U.S. government for alleged terrorism links were relief agencies.

21. Comparison of revenue pre- and post-9/11 based on IRS Form 990.

Table 10.1. Revenue of Select Muslim American Charities before and after 9/11/2001

Organization	Form 990 before 2001 Revenue	Year	Form 990 after 2001 Revenue	Year
Global Relief	$1,710,060	1998	0	Shutdown
Holyland Foundation for Relief and Development	$12,892,866	2000	0	Shutdown
Islamic American Relief Agency–US	$1,891,542	2001	0	Shutdown
Islamic Relief USA	$5,708,019	2001	$75,879,207	2008
Islamic American Zakat Foundation	$69,115	2001	$148,450	2008
Al-Harmain Islamic Foundation	$102,084	2001	0	Shutdown
Zakat Foundation of North America	$239,787	2002	$2,052,307	2008
ICNA Relief	0	formed 2005	$1,760,439	2008
Indian Muslim Relief and Charities	$1,739,792	2003	$3,623,716	2008
Ummah Relief	$68,875	2001	$190,717	2008
Hidaya Foundation	$320,048	2001	$3,032,146	2008
Helping Hand	0	formed 2005	$4,488,951	2008
Mercy International	$4,004,237	2001	$4,897,467	2008
Afghanistan Relief	$469,897	2001	$204,970	2008
TOTAL	$29,216,322		$96,278,370	

22. According to National Fund Director of Islamic Relief (USA).

23. Najam, *Portrait of a Giving Community,* 13.

24. Ibid., 169.

25. The Wise Giving Alliance is the charity-accrediting arm of the Better Business Bureau and is a voluntary program for nonprofits seeking accreditation. The charities must go through a series of steps to fulfill the terms of the program before being accredited.

26. See www.guidestar.com. GuideStar is a nonprofit organization that collects information about nonprofit organizations and publishes this information on its website. The website provides an easy-to-use search engine to gather data. GuideStar is a good resource for copies of the Form 990 that nonprofit organizations are required to submit to the IRS. The website is a resource of management and other information about the many charities included in the database.

27. See Jacqueline Copeland-Carson, "Kenyan Diaspora Philanthropy: Key Practices, Trends and Issues," study prepared for the Philanthropic Initiative and the Global Equity Initiative, Harvard University, March 2007.

Contributors

ALLAN W. AUSTIN is Professor of History at Misericordia University in Dallas, Pennsylvania. He is the author of a number of books, including *From Concentration Camp to Campus: Japanese American Students and World War II* (University of Illinois Press, 2004) and *Quaker Brotherhood: Interracial Activism and the American Friends Service Committee, 1917–1950* (University of Illinois Press, 2012).

ARNOLD DASHEFSKY is Professor of Sociology and the Konover Chair of Judaic Studies at the University of Connecticut, Director of the Center for Judaic Studies and Contemporary Jewish Life, and Director of the Berman Institute—North American Jewish Data Bank. Among his several books are *Charitable Choices: Philanthropic Decisions of Donors in the American Jewish Community* (Lexington Books, 2009, with B. Lazerwitz) and *Jewish Choices: American Jewish Denominationalism* (SUNY Press, 1998, with B. Lazerwitz, J. A. Winter, and E. Tabory).

THOMAS J. DAVIS is Professor of Religious Studies, Professor of Philanthropic Studies, and Managing Editor of *Religion and American Culture: A Journal of Interpretation* at Indiana University–Purdue University Indianapolis (IUPUI). His most recent work includes *John Calvin's American Legacy* (Oxford University Press, 2010, editor), and "Philanthropy," in *Encyclopedia of Religion in America,* 4 vols., ed. Charles Lippy and Peter Williams (CQ Press, 2010).

ELIZABETH G. FERRIS is Senior Fellow in Foreign Policy and Co-Director of the Brookings–LSE Project on Internal Displacement at the Brookings Institution in Washington, D.C. She served for six years as the Director of the Refugee Program at Church World Service, and, for thirteen years, she worked with the World Council of Churches, directing humanitarian response and long-term development. She is the author of *The Politics of Protection: The Limits of Humanitarian Action* (Brookings Institution Press, 2011).

FRED KAMMER, S.J., is Executive Director of the Jesuit Social Research Institute at Loyola University New Orleans. He was President of Catholic Charities USA from 1992 to 2001, and, from 1990 to 1992, he was policy advisor for health and welfare issues at the United States Conference of Catholic Bishops. His books include *Doing Faithjustice: An Introduction to Catholic Social Thought* (Paulist Press, 1991; rev. ed., 2004) and *Faith. Works. Wonders.—An Insider's Guide to Catholic Charities* (Wipf and Stock, 2009).

SHAUL KELNER is Associate Professor of Sociology and Jewish studies at Vanderbilt University and is Director of Vanderbilt's Program in Jewish Studies. He is the author of *Tours That Bind: Diaspora, Pilgrimage and Israeli Birthright Tourism* (New York University Press, 2010), which received the Association for Jewish Studies' 2010 Jordan Schnitzer Book Award in the category of Social Sciences, Anthropology and Folklore.

SHEILA S. KENNEDY is Professor of Law and Public Policy at the IUPUI School of Public and Environmental Affairs. From 1992 until 1998, she was the executive director of the Indiana Civil Liberties Union. Among her books are *American Public Service: Constitutional and Ethical Foundations* (Jones and Bartlett, 2010, with David Schultz) and *Charitable Choice at Work: Faith-Based Job Programs in the States* (Georgetown University Press, 2006, with Wolfgang Bielefeld).

DAVID P. KING is Assistant Professor of Church History at Memphis Theological Seminary in Tennessee. In 2011, he was awarded the Lake Doctoral Dissertation Fellowship. His dissertation project, "Seeking a Global Vision: The Evolution of World Vision, Evangelical Missions, and American Evangelicalism," also received funding from the Louisville Institute. In 2010, he won the Sidney E. Mead Prize from the American Society of Church History for the best article stemming directly from dissertation research.

BERNARD LAZERWITZ is Professor Emeritus of Sociology at Bar Ilan University, Ramat Gan, Israel. Among his books are *Charitable Choices: Philanthropic Decisions of Donors in the American Jewish Community* (Lexington Books, 2009, with A. Dashefsky) and *Jewish Choices: American Jewish Denominationalism* (SUNY Press, 1998, with A. Dashefsky, J. A. Winter, and E. Tabory).

SUSAN McDONIC is Assistant Professor of Sociology at American University in Washington, D.C. Her research interests include contemporary religious movements, international development, and Africa and globalization. Specifically, she studies one of the world's largest development organizations, World Vision. Her book, *Material Faith: Contending with Development, Belief, and Truth in World Vision International,* is forthcoming from the University of Chicago Press.

SHARIQ A. SIDDIQUI is a PhD candidate in Philanthropic Studies at IUPUI. He is an attorney and former Executive Director of the Muslim Alliance of Indiana. His publications include "Islamic Society of North America," in *Encyclopedia of Muslim-American History,* ed. Edward E. Curtis IV (Columbia University Press, 2010), and "Giving in the Way of God: Muslim Philanthropy in the U.S.," in *Religious Giving: For Love of God,* ed. David H. Smith (Indiana University Press, 2010).

DIANE WINSTON holds the Knight Chair in Media and Religion at the Annenberg School for Communication and Journalism at the University of Southern California. Between 1983 and 1995, she covered religion at a number of newspapers, including the

Baltimore Sun. She has won numerous press association awards and was nominated for a Pulitzer Prize. Among her books are *Red Hot and Righteous: The Urban Religion of the Salvation Army* (Harvard University Press, 1999), *Small Screen, Big Picture: Lived Religion and Television* (Baylor University Press, 2009), and *The Oxford Handbook of Religion and the American News Media* (Oxford University Press, 2012, editor).

Index